The New York Young Lords
and the Struggle for Liberation

Darrel Wanzer-Serrano

The New York Young Lords
and the Struggle for Liberation

TEMPLE UNIVERSITY PRESS
Philadelphia • *Rome* • *Tokyo*

TEMPLE UNIVERSITY PRESS
Philadelphia, Pennsylvania 19122
www.temple.edu/tempress

Library of Congress Cataloging-in-Publication Data

Wanzer-Serrano, Darrel, 1977–
    The New York Young Lords and the struggle for liberation / Darrel
Wanzer-Serrano.
        pages   cm
    Includes bibliographical references and index.
    ISBN 978-1-4399-1202-7 (hardback : alkaline paper) — ISBN
978-1-4399-1203-4 (paper : alkaline paper) — ISBN 978-1-4399-1204-1
(e-book)   1. Young Lords (Organization)—History.   2. Puerto Ricans—
New York (State)—New York—Politics and government—20th century.
3. Community activists—New York (State)—New York—History—20th
century   4. Puerto Ricans—Civil rights—New York (State)—New York—
History—20th century.   5. Civil rights movements—New York (State)—
New York—History—20th century   6. Puerto Ricans—New York (State)—
New York—Social conditions—20th century.   7. New York (N.Y.)—Ethnic
relations—History—20th century.   8. New York (N.Y.)—Social conditions—
20th century.   I. Title.
    F128.9.P85W36 2015
    323.1168'7295097471—dc23

                                                            2014044766

∞ The paper used in this publication meets the requirements of the
American National Standard for Information Sciences—Permanence
of Paper for Printed Library Materials,
ANSI Z39.48-1992

Printed in the United States of America

9 8 7 6 5 4

In memory of the New York Young Lords

Contents

Acknowledgments

Without new visions we don't know what to build, only what to knock
down. We not only end up confused, rudderless, and cynical, but we
forget that making a revolution is not a series of clever maneuvers and
tactics but a process that can and must transform us.
—Robin D. G. Kelley, *Freedom Dreams*

I t is perhaps cliché but no less true to note that this book would not have been
possible without the help, guidance, and friendship of countless people.
While any errors in this book are no one's fault but my own, it owes its
strengths to the personal and professional relationships on which my life and
career have been anchored. I want to begin by thanking two incredibly important women in my life. My mother, Elba Iris (Arocho Rosa) Petersen, has always
been my role model. Perhaps because of her limited education in colonial
Puerto Rico, she always prioritized my education and underscored the
importance of a college degree. She always wanted more for my brother and
me than she had for herself, and she worked long hours at multiple jobs to
make that dream a reality. I have only a fraction of her work ethic, persistence,
and perseverance; yet I am certain that I owe everything I have accomplished
and any good qualities I have (along with my stubbornness) to her. I love you,
Mom. Thank you for all that you have done and continue to do to make my life
better; for reading along with me about Puerto Rican history, politics, and culture; and for being such a strong advocate for me over all of these years.

Nicole, my spouse, is my true love. We met when I volunteered for a tournament she was hosting as executive director of the Dallas Urban Debate Alliance; but we almost met at my last college debate tournament in 1999. We
hadn't been dating long when I was offered my position at The University of
Iowa; and although I moved away for the job, we grew closer and closer as the
months passed. Across the 860 miles between Iowa City and Dallas, Nicole
was a sounding board for my frustrations, an inspiration for my writing, a
beacon of understanding, and a constant source of encouragement. She has
grounded me in this world and helps me daily to become a better person who

is more committed to family, friends, and community. As I began penning these acknowledgments, she uprooted herself to move to Iowa—ending the difficulty of our long-distance life but also leaving her beloved job, where she made a world of difference for countless kids by introducing them to competitive debate. As she settles into her new position at the National Speech and Debate Association and we begin a new chapter of our lives together, I am eternally grateful for her sacrifices, for her love, and for her companionship. I love you, Nicole, and look forward to every day to come in our future together.

I wish I had the space to thank all my friends and teachers from middle school and high school—especially those from the world of interscholastic debate. Debate, ultimately, is what gave me an "in" at a private liberal arts college that cost more money per year than our family made in income. In college at the University of Puget Sound, I continued debating and learning under the guidance of Glenn Kuper and with a host of friends and teammates. At Puget Sound, I had too many great professors to count. In addition to being my coach, Glenn was my first professor and helped teach me how to be a good college student (advice I probably too often ignored). Sue Owen had a profound impact on my education; I still use the books she assigned as resources for my own students. I took most of my rhetoric classes from Gabrielle King and owe much of my relatively smooth transition into graduate education to her (especially the two-student seminar on the public sphere I had the joy of taking with her). Finally, Jim Jasinski pushed (and continues to push) me to become a better rhetorical critic and theorist.

At Indiana University, I had the pleasure to work with some outstanding faculty and graduate students. The Department of Communication and Culture, which will be disbanded in July 2015 as part of a university-led initiative to reorganize communication disciplines, was a special place to do my MA and PhD work because of the ways the program questioned disciplinary boundaries and encouraged work across the represented areas of rhetoric and public culture, film and media studies, and performance and ethnography. Bob Ivie, whose general encouragement and commitment to "mucking things up" in the academy I welcomed greatly, advised me during my MA work and served on my committees through the PhD. When I transitioned into the PhD, I began working more closely with John Louis Lucaites. As my advisor, John always challenged me to be a better writer and scholar. Years later, after I had all but given up on this project, John took me aside and called me to task. In more ways than one, this book would not be a reality without him. I took more classes from Robert Terrill than any other professor. Robert was always a model teacher and scholar, and he was one of my most trusted mentors as a graduate student. Yeidy Rivero was the first Puerto Rican professor I ever met. She played a key role, through the feedback she gave me as a graduate student, in the development of some of the arguments in this book. With historian Arlene Díaz I got my start studying Puerto Rican history. Many other professors at Indiana University had an immeasurable impact on my education: James Andrews, Patricia Andrews, Richard Bauman, Carolyn Calloway-Thomas, Nicola Evans, Jane Goodman, Russell Hanson, Joan Hawkins, Jeffrey Isaacs, Roopali Mukherjee, John Nieto-Phillips, Phaedra Pezzullo, and Ted Striphas, to name a few.

One of the most important things contributing to my success and sanity through the process of completing my PhD was the friendship, support, playfulness, and solidarity of my friends in school: Courtney Bailey, Cara Buckley, Jeff Bennett, Nathan Carroll, Chris Dumas, Tonia Edwards, Suzanne Enck, Claire Sisco King, Matt King, Scott Makstenieks, Irwin Mallin, David Moscowitz, Leigh Moscowitz, Jeff Motter, Dave Naze, Kate Newcomer, Kate Hess Pace, Bob Rehak, Dan Showalter, Jamie Skerski, Margie Thorpe, Isaac West, Dave Worthington, and many others I am shamefully leaving off.

I also owe a great deal of gratitude to the colleagues I have had since graduating from Indiana. Kelly Happe at the University of Georgia remains a dear friend and one of my closest confidants. Arlene Torres (now at Hunter College, City University of New York), Ricky Rodriguez, Jonathan Inda, Julie Dowling, and everyone else in the Department of Latina/Latino Studies at the University of Illinois at Urbana-Champaign (where I competed a one-year postdoc) helped me strengthen my roots in Latin@ studies and complete my edited book, *The Young Lords: A Reader*. My wonderful colleagues at the University of North Texas (Jay Allison, Karen Anderson-Lain, Suzanne Enck, Cindy Gordon, Brian Lain, Louie Petit, Brian Richardson, Shaun Treat, Justin Trudeau, Rebecca Walker, and Zuoming Wang), my graduate student advisees (Rachelle Avery, Gazi Ayyad, Brett Farmer, Tiffany Jones, and Lauren Sabino), and my Latin@ colleagues around the university (Marianne Bueno, who provided invaluable feedback on a draft of this book; Robert Figueroa; Valerie Martinez-Ebers; Mariela Nuñez-Janes; Priscilla Ybarra; and others)—all of these people helped guide me through some wonderful years in my career, and many I still count as close friends.

Since 2012, my colleagues at The University of Iowa have created a welcoming, intellectually vibrant, supportive, and fun environment in which to finish this project. My colleagues in rhetoric and public advocacy—Jeff Bennett, Natalie Fixmer-Oraiz, David Hingstman, Jiyeon Kang, and Isaac West—are truly a wonderful, diverse, and immensely bright group of scholars who push me day in and day out to do good work. They are thoroughly enjoyable and unimaginably compassionate colleagues and friends. I am particularly grateful for the feedback Isaac and Jeff offered on drafts of chapters, which helped me reach levels of clarity that otherwise would have been absent. I'm also grateful for Jiyeon and Natalie welcoming me into their Friday writing group and being sounding boards for difficult passages I was working through. I'm thankful for all of my junior colleagues in the department—Natalie, Jiyeon, Andy High, Mary High, Rachel McLaren, David Supp-Montgomerie, Jenna Supp-Montgomerie, and Rita Zajacz—for their support and wisdom as we all traverse the sometimes-weird world of the professoriate. I'm also thankful for senior colleagues, like Kembrew McLeod (who helped when I was beginning to shop the book proposal), Tim Havens (my office neighbor who has been a welcomed and welcoming colleague since I arrived at Iowa), and all of the others who make the Department of Communication Studies at Iowa so fantastic: Tammy Afifi, Walid Afifi, Leslie Baxter, Shelly Campo, Steve Duck, Joy Hayes, Kristine Muñoz, and John Peters. I also want to thank our office staff—Jeff Donoghue, Troy Fitzpatrick, Andrea Krekel, Sarah Moeller, Wanda Osborn, and Jenny Ritchie—for all of the hard work that they do on a daily basis to make this kind of work possible and hold the department together.

Other folks in The University of Iowa community have been essential to my transition from the exceedingly diverse (and Latin@) north Texas region to the comparatively white Iowa City. I offer heartfelt thanks to my *camaradas* in Latin@ studies across the university, especially Tlaloc Rivas, Omar Valerio-Jiménez, and Claire Fox. Tlaloc and I entered Iowa together as two of the few Latin@ tenure-track assistant professors at the university. His friendship as someone situated similarly at the university has meant so much over the last few years. Omar and Claire offered feedback on early drafts of Chapters 1 and 2, respectively—feedback that helped me hone my interdisciplinary voice. Furthermore, Omar and Claire have played a central role in crafting spaces for Latin@ studies at the university (including a new Latin@ studies minor) and have made me feel truly welcome here. Deborah Whaley and the Comparative Ethic Studies working group (sponsored by the Obermann Center) have also provided a great community for the kind of work that interests me most. I owe her and the working group much gratitude for their help in refining my book proposal. Finally, Susan Stanfield did a fantastic job assembling the book's index.

Beyond Iowa, I will forever be grateful for the leadership, friendship, and mentorship of a host of Latin@ communication scholars around the country. Fernando Delgado was the first to encourage me to think about Latin@ issues in rhetorical studies. Nathaniel "Nacho" Córdova, may he rest in peace, was my Boricua brother and is sorely missed. Bernadette Marie Calafell has been a strong supporter, loving critic, and honest friend over the years. Lisa Flores has always found ways to simultaneously hold me to task and make me blush from her praise. Richard Pineda consistently reminds me to "keep it brown" while practicing acts and attitudes of generosity. Roberto Avant-Mier, Karma Chávez, J. David Cisneros, Teresita Garza, Alberto González, Michelle Holling, Isabel Molina-Guzmán, Kathleen de Onís, Frank Pérez, Stacy Sowards, Angharad Valdivia, and many others—all of these bright people form a community of scholars without whom my earlier work and this book would not be possible. We still need more Latin@s in communication studies, and we will achieve that only by continuing to cultivate the sense of community and kinship that we already have.

The research for this project would not have been possible without the financial and research support of various organizations. Funding for some aspects of my research was provided by the Indiana University Graduate and Professional Student Association and the Department of Communication and Culture; the University of Georgia Department of Speech Communication; the University of Illinois Department of Latina/Latino Studies; the University of North Texas Department of Communication Studies and Office of Research and Economic Development; and The University of Iowa Department of Communication Studies, College of Liberal Arts and Sciences, and Office of the Vice President for Research and Economic Development. The archives at Hunter College's Center for Puerto Rican Studies (especially via former research librarian Jorge Matos, who is now a close friend), New York University's Tamiment Library and Robert F. Wagner Labor Archives, and the New York Public Library (in the Schwartzman Building and the Schomburg Center for Research in Black Culture) were quite helpful.

Some chapters evolved from previously published materials. Small portions of the Introduction and Conclusion come from my essay "Delinking Rhetoric, or Revisiting McGee's Fragmentation Thesis through Decoloniality," published in *Rhetoric and Public Affairs* 15 (2012): 647–57. Portions of Chapter 3 appeared in Michelle A. Holling and Bernadette Marie Calafell's edited book *Latina/o Discourse in Vernacular Spaces: Somos De Un(a) Voz?* as a chapter entitled "Gender Politics, Democratic Demand and Anti-Essentialism in the New York Young Lords"; I am thankful to Lexington Books for permission to use that material here. Chapter 4 is partially derived from my essay "Trashing the System: Social Movement, Intersectional Rhetoric, and Collective Agency in the Young Lords Organization's Garbage Offensive," which was originally published in the *Quarterly Journal of Speech* 92 (2006): 174–201. Finally, Chapter 5 is derived from "Decolonizing Imaginaries: Rethinking 'the People' in the Young Lords' Church Offensive," which appeared in the *Quarterly Journal of Speech* 98 (2012): 1–23. In the conclusion, a stanza from Sandra María Esteves's poem "Here" is reprinted from *Yerba Buena* (Greenfield Center, NY: Greenfield Review; 1980) with permission from the author.

I am also grateful for all of the support and professionalism from the staff at Temple University Press for making this book possible. My editor, Micah Kleit, expressed interest in the project nearly from the moment he got his hands on it (to be fair, I think it took twenty-four hours). His excitement has made me confident I chose the right press and proud to have the book included in Temple's excellent Puerto Rican studies list. I am eternally thankful for the thorough feedback from two reviewers: Aimee Carrillo Rowe (who revealed her identity in order to offer extended feedback beyond the written review) and a second reviewer who remains anonymous to me. Sara Jo Cohen, the rights and contracts manager, has been an amazingly responsive point of contact at Temple, as has Gary Kramer, the press's publicity manager. The rest of the production team with whom I've interacted—Kate Nichols (art manager), Bruce Gore (cover designer), Joan Vidal (production editor), Ann-Marie Anderson (marketing director), Irene Imperio-Kull (advertising and promotions manager), and Stephen Barichko (production editor at Westchester Publishing Services)—have been a joy to work with in seeing the book to its conclusion in print.

Last but not least, I want to thank all of the former Young Lords who met with me over the years. Given that there is still so little scholarship on the Young Lords and archival materials remain scattered, I could not have gained my understanding of the organization without the access folks have given me to their personal collections and stories. I am particularly thankful to three women from the organization, Denise Oliver-Velez, Iris Morales, and Olguie Robles, who met with me many times and welcomed me into their homes; and two male cadre, David "Pelú" Jacobs and Carlos "Carlito" Rovira, who helped me understand so many crucial aspects of the day-to-day activities of members. It is to them and to all of the New York Young Lords that this book is dedicated. A portion of the proceeds from book sales will be donated to grassroots organizations in New York City that empower Latin@ and black youths to change the world, as the Young Lords so aptly did.

The New York Young Lords
and the Struggle for Liberation

INTRODUCTION

The Young Lords and the Rhetoric of Decoloniality

I am where I do and think. . . . What that means is not that you "think where you are," which is common sense, but that you constitute yourself ("I am") in the place you think. And that place is not, in my argument, a room or office at the library, but the "place" that has been configured by the colonial matrix of power.

—WALTER D. MIGNOLO, *The Darker Side of Western Modernity*

Don't push me too far. Don't force me to tell you what you ought to know, sir. If YOU do not reclaim the man who is before you, how can I assume that you reclaim the man that is in you? If YOU do not want the man who is before you, how can I believe the man that is perhaps in you? If YOU do not demand the man, if YOU do not sacrifice the man that is in you so that the man who is on this earth shall be more than a body . . . by what conjurer's trick will I have to acquire the certainty that you, too, are worthy of my love?

—FRANTZ FANON, "The 'North African Syndrome' "

In the summer of 1969, a group of young Puerto Ricans in New York City, angered and fed up with what they perceived as oppressive approaches to the health, educational, and political needs of the Puerto Rican community, took matters into their own hands. The group, calling themselves the Young Lords, was a multiethnic, though primarily Nuyorican, liberation organization that formed in El Barrio (a.k.a. East Harlem or Spanish Harlem) in July of that year.[1] The Young Lords' activism was enacted in conjunction with symbolic resources that articulated revolution as essential to "the people" and vice versa. This revolutionary tradition was first set in motion in the sixteenth century, after the conquest led by Christopher Columbus, and peaked in moments like the 1868 independence revolt known as El Grito de Lares (The Cry of Lares) in Puerto Rico and through Puerto Rican Nationalist Party armed activism on the island and in the mainland United States in the 1950s. Meg Starr observes that, influenced by Latin American revolutionaries, U.S. American revolutionaries, the Black Power struggle, and others, "the Young Lords centered their work on a combination of community-based empowerment and national liberation."[2] The Young Lords simultaneously operated through coalitional politics with other self-described Third World radical organizations (the Black Panthers, the Brown Berets, the Young Patriots, I Wor Kuen, etc.) and advanced a "revolutionary nationalist" agenda, which sought to address the material, political, and psychological needs of the community. In so doing, they struggled to discern the most appropriate tactical maneuvers for negotiating systemic constraints and overcoming the stacked deck out of which their hand had been dealt.

After initiating the process of articulating a space for revolutionary activism in El Barrio through their garbage offensive—a protest organized around increased trash pickups, which realized a short-lived victory at the conclusion of the summer of 1969—the Young Lords turned their attention to expanding activities in the community and concretizing what they envisioned in their "13 Point Program and Platform" by terms such as "community control," "self-determination," and "liberation." Faced with a long history of outsiders controlling nearly all aspects of community members' daily lives, the Young Lords instituted practical programs to challenge the exercise of power by the state and outsider-run institutions—an exercise of power that had profound effects on both their material and mental conditions. Such programs generated community service and activism surrounding health care, food, clothing, education, and more.

One of the first points of programmatic expansion revolved around the issue of health (see Figure I.1). Lead poisoning was reaching near epidemic proportions in New York City, and the Young Lords resolved to take a leadership role in addressing the problem. Reporting in the *Village Voice* in late 1969, Jack Newfield noted that "Medical authorities estimate there are 30,000 undiagnosed cases of lead poisoning each year in the city. The victims are usually children between the ages of one and three, who eat flaking or peeling paint from tenement walls."[3] In response to this health disaster and the city's unwillingness or inability to address it, the Young Lords struck a deal with the Health Department to administer detection tests. Using the same kind of Saul Alinsky–style grassroots community organizing they had employed in the peaceful phase of the garbage offensive (when the Young Lords organized community members to clean East Harlem), the activists leafleted El Barrio with flyers that read: "We are operating our own lead poisoning detection program with students from New York Medical College. . . . The Young Lords and medical personnel will knock on your door Tuesday and ask to test your children for lead poison. Do not turn them away. Help save your children."[4] Having learned lessons from their interaction with the Sanitation Department during the garbage offensive, the Young Lords later staged a sit-in to acquire the tests the Health Department had originally offered; thus, the organization sparked community awareness of both the health problems associated with lead paint and the community's ambivalent reliance on the city's social services.

Figure I.1   Back cover of *Palante* 2, no. 6 (July 3, 1970).

Although an important program in its own right,[5] lead poisoning testing was symbolic of one of the most important points in the Young Lords' platform, which read:

> WE WANT COMMUNITY CONTROL OF OUR INSTITUTIONS AND LAND
> We want control of our communities by our people and programs to guarantee that all institutions serve the needs of our people. People's control of police, health services, churches, schools, housing, transportation and welfare are needed. We want an end to attacks on our land by urban renewal, highway destruction, universities and corporations. LAND BELONGS TO ALL THE PEOPLE![6]

As a gesture toward community control of health care, the lead poisoning testing program was among the earliest of many subsequent attempts to assert the peoples' liberation and reduce reliance on an oppressive, ultimately racist, classist, and colonialist system.

Such a demand for community control, however, was not made out of whole cloth. Quite the contrary, the history of Puerto Ricans in the United States and on the island is marked by colonial state control of land and institutions to the detriment of the people. Once a self-sustainable country, conditions changed in the late fifteenth century when Spain colonized Borikén and renamed the island nation for its rich ports, thus "Puerto Rico." As its economy began to shift to accommodate greater export production of goods, domestic agricultural production declined. Spanish control and influence grew over the years, and Puerto Rico became more reliant on others for basic necessities like food.[7] When the United States took control of Puerto Rico in 1898, this trend toward an export economy accelerated, and its impact was amplified by colonial policies that made the cost of basic foods 8–14 percent higher than in New York City (in spite of the fact that wages in Puerto Rico averaged less than $1 a day compared with $4–$10 a day in New York).[8] With greater reliance on U.S. food imports came further intrusion in areas like education, which was designed to inculcate the locals in "American values"[9] and extend colonization into the mind.[10]

The inability of Puerto Ricans to take control of their economy, education, and other local institutions on the island because of U.S. colonial policies continued in new urban centers once they migrated. In New York City, the primary migration target from the 1920s through the 1970s, Puerto Ricans were often only marginally better off than they were on the island. While wages were higher and food was cheaper, Puerto Ricans in New York still fared worse than any other racial or ethnic group.[11] President Johnson's "Great Society" social programs were eventually enacted with the intent of alleviating some of the financial pressures felt by African Americans, Latin@s,[12] and others; but for

Puerto Ricans (and many others), the programs were horribly inefficient and failed to elevate them out of an embedded position in the underclass. Tenements were run by landlords with questionable ethics (read: slumlords); social service organizations were ruled by "poverty pimps";[13] hospitals in poor neighborhoods were understaffed, underfunded, and, in the case of Lincoln Hospital, operated despite having been condemned by the city.[14] Politically, the community was disparaged as "docile," and professionals, so-called experts, and elites monopolized the role of political activism.[15] By most accounts, life for the working class Puerto Rican in El Barrio left much to be desired. Community members basically had two choices: move out or put up with it; and given deep structures of poverty and a colonized mentality, this was a false choice.[16]

During their brief tenure (1969–1976), the New York Young Lords were a revolutionary nationalist, antiracist, antisexist group who advanced a complex political program featuring support for the liberation of all Puerto Ricans (on the island and in the United States), the broader liberation of all Third World people, equality for women, U.S. demilitarization, leftist political education, redistributive justice, and other programs as these fit into their ecumenical ideology. Their activism took many forms. They gave speeches, held rallies, taught political education courses out of their community offices, and produced a newspaper and radio program (both called *Palante*) that articulated their vision of democratic egalitarianism, anticolonialism, and socialist redistribution. They started numerous community initiatives such as the lead poisoning and tuberculosis testing programs, childcare for working mothers, and meal programs for poor children. They also engaged in acts of civil disobedience such as the garbage offensive, two separate takeovers of an East Harlem church (which they renamed the "People's Church" each time), sit-ins and disruptions at a local hospital that the city had condemned, and support of acts of civil unrest sponsored by other groups (e.g., Black Panther Party and student groups). In all, they engaged in what they believed were strategically and tactically sound actions to advance their cause and transform their people. Operating in a colonial borderland that was mapped onto their spaces, bodies, and minds, the Young Lords advanced decolonial sensibilities in El Barrio and beyond.

Despite being the first post-McCarthy era radical Nuyorican organization[17] and having a street named after them in El Barrio in the summer of 2014, the discourse and activism of the Young Lords remains drastically understudied to this day. Unfortunately, such historical omissions are not unusual where Puerto Ricans are concerned. Writing broadly about scholarly inattention to Puerto Rican movements of that era, Andrés Torres laments that "the historical record on this experience is almost nonexistent. Even within the 'social movements' and 'diversity' literature, we find barely a mention of the Puerto

Rican contribution to the insurgency that changed the United States."[18] In their edited volume titled *The Puerto Rican Movement*, Torres and José E. Velázquez start filling the intellectual gaps and addressing the ways in which mainland Puerto Ricans began generating consciousness and organizational structures to mount resistance against lived oppression that had long-standing historical, political, socioeconomic, and cultural roots. The "*'Nuevo Despertar'* [New Awareness] of Puerto Rican radicalism"[19] that took place across U.S. communities in the 1960s had roots in a complex mixture of (a) contemporary black, Chicano, Asian, and other Third World and student activist influences; (b) a renewed sense of a history of struggle against the colonial domination of Puerto Ricans; and (c) an emergent vocabulary to engage critically the intersections of race, class, gender, and nation. Central to this Nuevo Despertar in New York City was the Young Lords. Notwithstanding their centrality, no scholarly monograph to date has focused sustained attention on what Marta Moreno calls "this group of young men and women of color who made [a] significant impact on history."[20] At one level, then, *The New York Young Lords and the Struggle for Liberation* makes such a contribution.

Through careful archival research and theoretically informed critical perspectives in the pages that follow, I contextualize and craft an account of the Young Lords that rescues them from historical obscurity and recovers stories of resistance that remain useful and significant today, especially for Puerto Ricans and other Latin@s who continue to be politically disenfranchised and systematically marginalized. As Emma Pérez reminds us, though, "There is no pure, authentic, original history. There are only stories—many stories."[21] With Pérez's exhortation in mind, this book is an exercise in *historia*: one engaging the past through interpretation but also productive of a particular story of that past and its meanings.[22] This story—a meaningful/meaning-full account of change over time—is one that is, necessarily, indivisible from my encounter with an archive of materials and a repertoire of embodied and lived memories that emerge from former Young Lords and their places of activism.[23] Indeed, it is a story inseparable from my own personal transformation through which I came to see myself as located within the Global South.[24] As such, my goal is to offer one partial, perspectival, and contingent critical-interpretive engagement of the Young Lords that grapples with the geographic and body-political situatedness of their discourse and activism as well as my own position as a diasporic Puerto Rican academic who is thinking and writing from within the Global South, rather than dominant Euro/American-centric modalities.

Beyond the historical point, then, this book engages the Young Lords as a critical touchstone that can enrich and inform contemporary discussions about Latin@s specifically and decolonial politics more broadly. Approaching the Young Lords from theoretical and critical perspectives informed by Latin@ studies, rhetorical and communication theory, American studies, and history, my goal is to augment contemporary scholarly discussions of colo-niality, nationalism, and vernacular discourse by mobilizing the Young Lords' discourse and activism. While Nelson Maldonado-Torres argues that "the social movements of the late 60s and early 70s . . . provide[d] the intellectual and political project of decolonization with more substance and theoretical precision,"[25] he and his peers writing on coloniality often focus less on those movements themselves and more on the theoretical perspectives that emerged from and were enabled by those movements at later dates (general-ly beginning in the 1980s and 1990s). By turning attention directly to these movements, in my case the New York Young Lords, I believe we can cultivate a better sense of how these ideas can work on the ground and enrich our understandings of what things such as decoloniality, epistemic disobedience, and delinking might actually look like. Furthermore, by focusing on those discourses in their contexts, we can avoid overgeneralizing and making uni-versal claims of our own about how modernity/coloniality functions in the world. In this book, I make the case that the New York Young Lords' enactment of differential consciousness pushes the boundaries of decolonial theory.[26] Through critical performances of border thinking, epistemic disobedience, and delinking, the Young Lords crafted a decolonial praxis that resisted ideological oversimplification and generated new possibilities and spaces for activism in their immediate contexts and beyond. Engaging such complexity in the Young Lords' decolonial praxis, however, requires critical/theoretical perspectives that can be attentive to the uniqueness of their epistemic and ontological chal-lenges, which is a point I return to in a moment.

All of that said, I should be clear about two related limitations of this book. First, I am not attempting to write the complete and definitive history of the New York Young Lords. Although the organization existed for only a short period of time, the scope of their activism was too expansive to be covered with sufficient depth in a critical-interpretive project such as this. Much of the work I am doing *is* historical, however, and I will address the Young Lords' scope in Chapter 1 and elsewhere; but my attention is focused most on key components of their complex, ecumenical, sometimes contradictory ideology and early instances of their activism—especially in their first phase as the Young Lords Organization. Left out, also, is an extended engagement of the Chicago-based Young Lords Organization. While the New York group got its start as a chapter that answered to the Chicago leadership, the Chicago chap-ter had their own political and rhetorical style that warrants somewhat sepa-rate attention.[27] It is my deepest hope that someone else takes up that charge with a study on the original Chicago chapter. Second, while I am interested greatly in advancing theoretical perspectives as they relate to the techniques for delinking from modernity/coloniality, I do not intend this book to be a philo-sophical project on decoloniality. I seek, instead, to enrich our understandings of *how* activists perform epistemic disobedience and enact delinking though a critical engagement of the Young Lords' grassroots rhetoric and political action. In this way, my hope is that this book acts as a conversation and a bridge between historians, rhetoricians, and decolonial theorists alike—a bridge that moves us into a space where we can appreciate better the connections between theory and practice and envision the lived potentials of decoloniality. Learning from the example of the Young Lords and from decolonial scholarship, and doing my best to escape what Chela Sandoval calls the "apartheid of theoretical domains,"[28] I aim to enact some decolonial sensibilities of my own over the course of the chapters that follow.

On Coming to the Young Lords

My journey to the Young Lords and this project began in graduate school, long after I thought I knew who I was as a scholar and had finally settled into the epistemic zeitgeist of critical communication studies. Sometime late in my master's degree coursework I had become enamored with radical democratic theory and psychoanalysis and convinced my mentors and myself that a dissertation on election ballots as the "sublime object" of democracy would be a good idea. But as I went through my coursework, my department made some new hires that helped shift my perspectives and began leading me down another path. First, we hired Yeidy Rivero, an amazing media scholar and the first Puerto Rican professor I had ever met. Although I never had the chance to take a course with her, she and I began informally discussing Puerto Rican history, politics, culture, and so on; and she provided me with some reading list suggestions to start me on the path of ascertaining a bit more about my own ethno-racial background. Discovering more about Puerto Rico's colonial history led me to also talk with another professor in my department, Roopali Mukherjee, about postcolonial theory and the politics of race/racialization. These conversations with Rivero and Mukherjee remained in the background—side work that I investigated half-heartedly for my own personal edification rather than scholarly pursuits. Second, we hired Phaedra Pezzullo, an abundantly smart and savvy feminist and environmental rhetorician, who offered her first graduate course on "feminist rhetoric" during what was supposed to be my last semester of coursework in the spring term of 2003.

Pezzullo's class became a key moment in my personal and intellectual development. About a third of the way through the semester, we met to discuss final project ideas. We had been reading some feminist scholarship on autoethnography and performative writing,[29] and knowing that I wanted to tackle the ideas I first broached with Rivero, Pezzullo offered the idea of letting me do a kind of autoethnographic piece related to my Puerto Rican heritage. Never before had a teacher or professor ever encouraged me to research something so intimately tied to who I was. Knowing virtually nothing and unsure where to begin, I started by turning to Roberto Santiago's edited collection *Boricuas: Influential Puerto Rican Writings—An Anthology.*[30] Eagerly opening the pages of the book, I experienced multiple revelations. First, reading Sandra María Esteves's "Here," I *got* poetry for the first time . . . and I wept. Her words spoke (and continue to speak) to me on a level that I struggle to verbalize. Second, I ran across a small piece by Felipe Luciano, excerpted from the Young Lords' book *Palante: Young Lords Party,* and was entranced. Identifying with his experiences surrounding a lack of access to language (i.e., not being fluent in Spanish), culture, history, and more, I became excited and hurriedly began researching the New York Young Lords as best as I could from Bloomington, Indiana. The experience was transformative both on an intellectual level and on a personal one, as I *became* Boricua (Rivero would affectionately refer to me as a "born-again Boricua") through my research and writing. While I was born a Puerto Rican in Washington State, it took three professors (all of whom are women, two of whom are women of color) to jump-start the process of getting me to think *from* a position rooted in Puerto Ricanness and *latinidad.*

I turn to this fragment of my own origin story, the kind of thing usually relegated to a book's preface, because I think it is central to how I approach the Young Lords and to the place from which I write as a scholar committed to decoloniality. Without these encounters and subsequent enduring relationships formed with other Latin@s in communication studies and Latin@ studies, I would probably continue to locate myself firmly within the epistemic terrain of "the West." One of the hallmarks of decolonial thinking is a challenge to what Walter D. Mignolo calls "zero point epistemology," under which the "geopolitical and bio-graphic politics . . . of knowledge" gets occluded or hidden in a "grounding without grounding" that is best (but not exclusively) captured by Descartes's famous dictum "I think, therefore I am."[31] Mignolo's reversal, detailed in the first epigraph of this chapter and in U.S. Third World feminist writings that also influence my work, recovers the centrality of *location* and *embodiment* to knowledge production and "sets the stage for epistemic affirmations that have been disavowed."[32] Such affirmations were central to the New York Young Lords' own challenges to the coloniality of knowledge and being—challenges seen within and beyond that excerpt from Luciano that I read more than a decade ago—which have pushed me to rethink again and again *how* best to engage critically this group of young Latin@s who escape oversimplified categorization.

In addition to extending my coursework to complement a research project on the Young Lords, I immersed myself in primary materials—embarking on my own process of recovery and discovery tied intimately to the research archive. I began by acquiring copies of the Young Lords' writings that were available through interlibrary loan: their book, *Palante: Young Lords Party*; issues of their *Palante* newspaper available on microfilm; mass media news coverage of the group; published *testimonios* of leaders; and documentary films. There was little scholarship on the Young Lords at the time, but I gathered the handful of book chapters and journal articles that were available. Quickly, I realized the need to travel to New York City to conduct research and made arrangements to spend some time in the archives and collections of the Center for Puerto Rican Studies at Hunter College. Surrounding that trip, I tracked down former Young Lords (leaders and cadre) whom I could interview. As word spread that I was not yet another person looking to merely capitalize off the legacy of the Young Lords, more doors were opened.[33] Over the course of about three years, from 2004 to 2006, I conducted about two dozen oral histories of former members and allies. Across multiple visits, I collected materials from additional archives—New York University's Tamiment Library, the New York Public Library, the Schomburg Center for Research in Black Culture, private collections—including images, ephemera (e.g., flyers and buttons), and recordings of their radio program and other radio and television appearances. Some of this textual and imagistic material made it into an earlier collection of primary sources titled *The Young Lords: A Reader.* Other materials, however, have sat in my archive only to be reencountered as I was preparing the manuscript for this book.

My experience assembling an archive of materials was anything but disinterested. Former Young Lords opened their homes, hearts, and mouths in a manner that often transcended the researcher-subject divide. I have felt welcomed, not just as a guest but as kin, into many people's lives. I do not know whether they shared the same feelings of kinship; I suspect that some did and others did not. But the affective dimension of the research project was (and still is) significant to me—and a big part of the reason why I sought to publish the edited collection of primary texts first. Despite such feelings of kinship and love, time I spent in El Barrio doing fieldwork for research and to simply hang out with friends taught me that I *am* an outsider, that I am not *of* El Barrio. Once, while photographing murals and gardens for a tangential research project, I was even accused by a passerby of being a "pig"—an epithet shouted to sonically mark the neighborhood space as unsafe due to my very presence. Yet on other occasions, I have been harassed by police for merely standing on a corner and chatting with friends. Such tensions between belonging and unbelonging haunt my thoughts and sometimes engulf my body with teeming emotions. Such tensions also underscore the importance of *thinking from* the literal and figural locations from which the Young Lords discourse emerged. This book is an attempt to do justice to their living memory.

On Coloniality with a Rhetorical Inflection

I can barely begin to imagine the countless number of ways the story of the Young Lords could be encountered and told.[34] I suspect that historians, sociologists, anthropologists, comparative literature scholars, American studies

scholars, Latin@ studies scholars, critical race theorists, communication critics, and human geographers, among others (and the myriad different subper-
spectives within each of those), would all have unique and interesting things
to say about the Young Lords. Although I am guided by many questions related to history, sociology, communication, and social theory, I remain most
interested in a set of questions about the ways in which the Young Lords
engaged their lived experiences of coloniality: How did the Young Lords craft
a history of colonialism on the island? Relatedly, how did they craft a history
of resistance to colonialism on the island and throughout the Global South?
How did they develop a critical, theoretical perspective of "internal colonialism" and turn attention to both the psychic and otherwise material dimensions of colonialism within the geographical boundaries of the continental
United States generally and diasporic Puerto Rican communities specifically?
In what ways did they explore the linkages between racism, classism, sexism,
and heterosexism within a context defined by coloniality? How did they generate practices designed to resist coloniality as they experienced it in New
York? What are some of the formal qualities of the Young Lords' decolonial
sensibilities? Alternatively, how can we learn from the *kinds of things they did*
in order to challenge decoloniality outside of the Young Lords' specific social/
cultural/economic conjuncture? Addressing these questions requires a background in the theoretical perspective I identify as coloniality/decoloniality
(or, for brevity's sake, *de/coloniality*).

Coloniality, according to Maldonado-Torres, "refers to long-standing patterns of power that emerged as a result of colonialism, but that define culture,
labor, intersubjective relations, and knowledge production well beyond the
strict limits of colonial administrations."[35] At one level, scholars of coloniality are interested in those contexts for which colonialism is a defining feature
even (perhaps especially) when *de jure* colonialism is absent. Theories of coloniality, in this sense, share a commonality with postcolonial theory as both
often turn attention to formerly colonial contexts. For purposes of conceptual
distinction, however, the similarities stop there. Where postcolonial theory
has roots largely in British and French colonial contexts, coloniality and decoloniality hail from Latin American, U.S. Latin@, and American indigenous
history, politics, culture, and theory, which makes them particularly well suited
for studies in the U.S. context. Furthermore, the scholars I cite throughout
this book have a mixed relationship to postcolonial theory—arguing off and
on that it is undergirded by a modernist rationality, tied too strongly to postmodernism and, ironically, Eurocentrism.[36] Decolonial theorists distinguish
themselves, then, in two ways. First, decoloniality is framed as an attempt to
delink from modernity/coloniality in theory and practice, embarking in what
Mignolo calls forms of "epistemic disobedience" that are attentive to geographic and body-political modes of theorizing and acting in the world.
Second, while certainly interested in contexts marked by an explicit history of

direct colonialism, decolonial theorists broaden the focus to all of modernity, which makes the perspective an alternative to modernism, poststructuralism, and postmodernism, in addition to postcolonialism. While postcolonial and decolonial scholars will oftentimes end up on the same side of any given issue, each is guided by a different critical vocabulary and conceptual genealogy.

Indeed, this issue of genealogy is an important one for understanding this book and where I see my arguments fitting into the larger literature on de/coloniality. As Mignolo argues, "Decolonial thinking needs to build its own genealogy of thought; otherwise it would fall prey to genealogies of thought already established and would, in the process, disregard and devalue all other possibilities. Decolonization of knowledge and of being requires one to engage in rebuilding what was destroyed and to build what doesn't yet exist."[37] Mignolo's call, here, is quite programmatic and future oriented—demanding that we begin considering modes of knowing and being, and sources for that knowledge, that do not fit neatly into the rhetorics of modernity and, I would add, the academy. Doing so helps to ensure that we do not merely reproduce dominant ways of thinking and acting in the world; his is a call, in other words, to think and act *otherwise*, to chart an epistemic terrain *from* and *of* the Global South. One might reasonably inquire, here, that even when one writes against the grain of an epistemology, or writes to avoid an epistemology, is that epistemology not still *there* in some odd way? Perhaps; but the question is more appropriately one of epistemic *privilege* rather than mere *existence*.

In the context of this book on the Young Lords, I think the questions of genealogy and theoretical influences are uniquely significant. Although I could read the Young Lords from perspectives guided principally by Foucault, Deleuze, Marx, Lacan, Laclau, Mouffe, some other poststructuralist, or whoever the hottest European theorist happens to be at the moment, why should I? There are political stakes in crafting an alternative genealogy that can help us understand our world in ways that deny the epistemic privilege of those dominant theoretical perspectives, even if those perspectives make guest appearances from time to time throughout the book. Furthermore, there is no easy way to say "*this* is when it is okay to reappropriate and cite from the West, and *that* is when it is not okay to do so"; such distinctions would replicate an arhetorical and acontextual logic that would weaken the decolonial perspective I advance. As a question of orientation, however, I think it is possible and desirable to be guided chiefly by decoloniality and perspectives that emerge from the Global South. In the context of this book, I think there is a case to be made that perspectives emergent from and speaking principally to the West are ill suited to an engagement of a group like the Young Lords, whose locus of enunciation was not within the West. Rather, even while addressing audiences inside the metropole, the Young Lords spoke *from* and *to* the Global South by crafting their epistemic location, social space, and inventive discourses as "Third World" in origin, intent, and direction. I am particularly persuaded by

Mignolo's assessment that "modernity has its own critics . . . but in the Third World the problems are not the same as in the First, and therefore to transplant both the problems and methods from the First to the Third World is no less a colonial operation than transplanting armies or factories to satisfy the needs of the First World."[38] To guard against reproducing colonial violence in scholarship, Bernadette Marie Calafell echoes, "we must meet [marginalized discourses] on their own terms methodologically."[39]

Critical-interpretive scholarship is always "both served and confined by theory and method."[40] Calafell's demand to take up rhetorics on their own terms and the complementary need to craft genealogies of thought from the margins of modernity/coloniality compel me to actively ignore a host of theoretical perspectives and methodologies. By turning to decoloniality, I am making a political and methodological choice to prioritize the Global South, to heed the calls of the dispossessed and work from within this particular epistemic location. My adherence to these theoretical and practical commitments underscores my general belief that this is the best way to approach the Young Lords' discourse and activism. Taking some other approach (e.g., radical democratic theory or identity performativity) and grafting it onto the Young Lords would be historically disingenuous, risk an unreflexive presentism, and do a kind of epistemic violence to their words and deeds by forcing them into modern/colonial forms of legibility.

In the chapters that follow, I turn my attention to specific examples of the Young Lords' discourse and activism to craft a richer story of what they accomplished, elucidate some specific ways in which decolonial delinking can function "on the ground," and model a scholarly praxis that takes discourses up on their own terms. For example, in Chapter 1, I offer an overview of the historical conditions enabling and informing the emergence of the New York Young Lords in July 1969. Tracing those conditions of emergence, as the Young Lords did, to Puerto Rico's colonization in the late fifteenth century, my story is guided by those things that seemed most important and significant to the Young Lords: direct colonial rule by Spain and the United States, indigenous Taíno culture and political resistance, nineteenth-century liberation movements (including slave revolts), and the development of Nationalist Party politics and the independence movement in the twentieth century. In crafting that story, I am guided partly by the Young Lords' own engagement of this history in their biweekly newspaper *Palante*; therefore, I explore some of the ways the Young Lords crafted a useable history highlighting colonization, nationhood, resistance, racism, and sexism. I also direct attention to the immediate context of 1960s radicalism in the United States (especially black freedom struggles) and decolonization struggles worldwide, both of which functioned as important enabling conditions for the Young Lords' emergence. Built from that historical backdrop, I offer an extended engagement of the Young Lords' origins and organizational transformations—from the Young

Lords Organization (1969), to the Young Lords Party (1970), to the Puerto Rican Revolutionary Workers Organization (1972)—to help situate the critical engagements in subsequent chapters. Just as the Young Lords imagined and produced ways to challenge coloniality within their contexts, so too should a scholarly engagement of their history and memory adopt a position committed to decoloniality.

That said, such a decolonial turn does not require a wholesale rejection of everything that happens to come from the West. Rather, Maldonado-Torres suggests, decoloniality "highlights the epistemic relevance of the enslaved and colonized search for humanity. It seeks to open up the sources for thinking and to break up the apartheid of theoretical domains through renewed forms of critique and epistemic creolization."[41] Creolization operates outside of an either/or logic that would require some kind of Third World fundamentalism. It is a kind of border thinking that initiates a *preference* for those voices that have been historically and politically silenced or marginalized but does not seek a complete supplication. Mignolo concurs, describing this decolonial move as "a double movement: unveiling the regional foundations of universal claims to truth as well as the categories of thought and the logic that sustains all branches of Western knowledge."[42] In other words, *decoloniality seeks to challenge the privilege and universalism of various forms of knowledge.* Such a normative stance requires that we better situate knowledge in its geographic and embodied specificity and *resist attempts to universalize any particular episteme.* It does not require, however, that we reject "European modernity," just that we reject the West's claim to epistemic privilege.[43] That is, indeed, a fine line to walk.

In my reading of contemporary decolonial scholarship, people seem to risk slipping into one of a couple of related problems in negotiating such a fine line. On the one hand, you have scholars like Maldonado-Torres and Enrique Dussel who resist an overreaction to coloniality in theory by drawing from and recovering ideas located within Western philosophy in order to support rethinking our epistemological commitments and decentering the West.[44] In doing so, however, these scholars direct less attention to actual, geographically located and embodied grassroots discourses and actions. They philosophically justify doing so (which is their goal, after all) but provide readers with a limited sense for what decoloniality looks like in geographically specific and sociohistorically contingent contexts. On the other hand, you have scholars like Mignolo who disengage from Western philosophical discourses nearly altogether but in the process risk propagating a kind of determinism of perspective.[45] While I do not think this is his intention, Mignolo can come across to some readers as offering a totalizing discourse that minimizes room for resistance. While concepts like "border thinking" seem designed to remedy this, there are ways in which Mignolo's position is so damning of modernity/coloniality— for instance, his critique of "the logic that sustains all branches of Western knowledge" cited in the last paragraph—that there seems to be little chance for those inside that system to challenge it.[46] When he does turn to examples (e.g., the Zapatistas in Mexico or the emergence of a concept of "the communal" in South America), they seem exemplary of a wholesale rejection of modernity/coloniality: a *stepping outside* that, despite the way Mignolo explicitly qualifies his argument, implies that (a) resistance is generally futile, (b) the only practical solution is wholesale rejection, and/or (c) the scholar's only option is demystification/debunking.

Often stuck making bigger theoretical arguments justifying their shifts in perspective, decolonial theorists can lack a level of rhetorical specificity that, ironically, makes it harder to explore the geographic and embodied discourses they see as paramount. There are some exceptions, but in general, the disconnect between theory and practice is pronounced.[47] And there is nothing wrong with that, so long as others can extend such theoretical innovation through more grounded forms of scholarship and activism. As a corrective, I submit that de/colonial scholarship can benefit from a more rhetorical orientation that is highly attentive to practices of radical contextualization, sociohistorical contingency, and the situatedness of public discourses and activism. In making a turn to rhetorical perspectives and attitudes, I am not interested in engaging in some kind of parochial elucidation of rhetoric from within the disciplinary terrain of U.S. communication studies. Such an exercise is neither necessary to understand the arguments in this book, nor would it be particularly fruitful given the differences of perspectives on rhetoric within the discipline as a whole. That said, I think it is important to set out a basic understanding of what I mean by "rhetoric" throughout the chapters that follow and how that understanding undergirds the core methodological orientation of this project. Rhetoric is not reducible to empty verbiage, deceitful speech, or a form of inaction.[48] Instead, I see rhetoric as both an object of inquiry and a perspective for engaging that object. Rhetoric as a discipline is, itself, highly problematic in the ways in which it perpetuates modern/colonial commitments; it is, for example, tied strongly to a master narrative fully imbricated with the story of "Western civilization."[49] In other forums, I have started to challenge some of those biases;[50] but for the purposes of my argument here, I think some core commitments can be productive. At the most basic level, I feel comfortable defining rhetoric as (the study of) situated public discourse. Each term in that brief definition is open to contestation and elaboration, and I want to explore a little more fully my own orienting proclivities about each and how they relate to de/coloniality.

Situated

To be attentive to the situatedness of discourse means that one must adopt a perspective committed to radical contextualization.[51] Lawrence Grossberg, for example, underscores the importance of contextualization for cultural studies when he highlights its need to produce political histories of the present in "a radically contextualist way, in order to avoid reproducing the very sorts of universalisms (and essentialisms) that all too often characterize the dominant practices of knowledge production, and that have contributed (perhaps unintentionally) to making the very relations of domination, inequality and suffering."[52] This warrants, perhaps, a challenge to decolonial theory insofar as some scholars carry a risk of replacing one universalism, modernity/coloniality, with another rooted in its total rejection. I think that risk can be slim to none, however, *if* we (a) resist an either/or formulation of decoloniality that stakes out agency in border spaces operating through differential modes and (b) do a better job of engaging in practices of theorizing that are rooted in highly contextual analyses. In other words, decoloniality might be unproductive if it operates principally as a "no"—as an absolute rejection of the rhetoric of modernity and the logic of coloniality. Instead, it needs to be crafted as a "yes"—an affirmation of critical, interpretive, rhetorical, and political practices that inventively negotiate the problematic power relations of modernity/coloniality to stake out ways of acting within *and* against. Being more attentive to context, then, helps to strengthen the theoretical, critical, and practical goals of decoloniality.

Discourse never occurs in a vacuum; rather, any specific discursive act emerges out of a complex context (historically, socially, economically, politically, discursively, etc.) and participates in its own acts of recontextualization. Jennifer Daryl Slack similarly posits that "identities, practices, and effects generally, constitute the very context within which they are the practices, identities, and effects."[53] Hence, context is recursive. Practically and methodologically speaking, then, situatedness means at least two things. First, one cannot separate out discourse from its imbricated contexts. A Young Lords speech to college students in Hawaii, for example, should not be examined as if it were a hermetically sealed or whole/complete text. Speeches like that (and other rhetorics) emerge as responses, engagements, and fragments of broader discourses and institutional relations that exceed any specific utterances.[54] In that sense, one must look at clusters of speeches, images, embodied discourses, and so forth—at the full intersectionality of rhetorical forms and their relationships to contexts.[55] Second, rhetoric should be understood as the contingent product of particular sociohistorical contexts. Such an appreciation of situatedness demands, at a certain level, the abandonment of abstract universals and ahistorical theorizing in preference for grounded theorizing that is attentive to the spatiotemporal and, I would add, embodied emergence of particular discourses in a "multiplicity of overlapping contexts."[56]

Along these lines, I argue in Chapter 2 that an examination of the New York Young Lords' articulation of "revolutionary nationalism" in its sociohistorical situatedness challenges commonsense understanding of nationalism. The Young Lords were guided by a Nuyorican translation of Puerto Rican nationalist political commitments, which were coupled with a decolonial stance. Their ideas were further augmented by a Third World critical race feminist critique, which was enriched through coalitional politics with the Black Panthers, Young Patriots, and others. The Young Lords therefore eschewed mainstream political participation in preference for an inventive Latin@ vernacular discourse[57] that labeled itself "nationalist." Their cultural, political, and ideological intervention ultimately challenges how we read nationalism as inherently exclusive or reactionary. Failing to engage their context productively enough, however, existent scholarship on the Young Lords' nationalism misreads the organization's *particular* enunciation of "revolutionary nationalism." As such, I argue that the New York Young Lords' rhetoric of revolutionary nationalism advanced a decolonial critique that delinked their political program from modernity/coloniality. Rather than centering a modern/colonial construction of the nation, the Young Lords' rhetorical "nationalism" functioned differentially as a "symbolic agency"—a signifying *means*—through which the group decolonized their imaginary, reformulated political subjectivity and opened the space for radical possibility. This figural nationalism complicates decolonial scholarship's rejection of nationalism as a productive politics[58] and underscores the importance of a more nuanced engagement of situated public discourse.

Public

Since the claim that rhetoric is inherently public will probably be seen as the most conservative move in my definition, I first want to address what I do *not* mean. My understanding of rhetoric's publicity has nothing to do with a Habermasian (or any other specific) normative conception of the public sphere; nor is "public" meant to imply anything singular. I do not even mean, here, to reinforce a sharp division between public and private, the boundaries between which I believe are often porous and contingent. While there probably remains much productive work to be done in publics/counterpublics theory, it is not an intervention I seek to make in this book. Whatever "public" may mean, the important element for my working definition of rhetoric is that it implies a dimension of *relationality* and *address* that exceeds something strictly interpersonal. In other words, situated discourses are addressed to some kind of real and/or imagined audience.

By audience, I am not referring to a collection of warm bodies immediately present, though sometimes audiences may include that. Instead, audiences are always imagined and discursively constituted—they are the complex and contingent product of sociohistorical contexts and are disclosed through rhetoric. According to Ronald Walter Greene, "A constitutive model of rhetorical effectivity focuses on the role of public discourse in the process of world disclosure. A constitutive model concerns itself with how, for example, subjects, personas, situations, and problems emerge as the effects of rhetorical practices."[59] Audiences have a recursive relationship to rhetoric insofar as they are both preconditions for rhetoric and themselves rhetorical products. "The people of El Barrio," for example, is an audience for much of the Young Lords' discourse, but it is also (a) part of a chain of signification (e.g., "the people") rooted in a powerful fiction that authorizes their discourse in the first place and (b) itself the contingent product of myriad discourses of identification, including prior Young Lords' utterances and contemporaneous articulations. One might object that my conception of publicity would exclude oral histories, personal correspondence, journals/diaries, and so on, but I do not mean it to be exclusive in that manner. Instead, I think such materials are quite significant because they shed light on how more evidently public discourses emerge from and in relation to complex contexts. Discourses that seem, prima facie, to be private help to radically contextualize public discourses in relation to different people, institutions, ideologies, and yet other discourses. In the end, however, the primary focus of my interpretive and critical activities are those discourses and activist practices that are addressed and that serve an important constitutive function.

The Young Lords' own transformation on the issue of gender is an excellent example of the relevance of rhetoric's addressed dimension. Following Chapter 2's focus on nation and agency in multivalent contexts, Chapter 3 examines the broader texture of the Young Lords' revolutionary nationalism as it is manifest in feminist and antiracist demands attentive to the interrelationships between sexism, racism, and capitalism. When the Young Lords formed, they were guided by masculinist ideologies and sought a radicalization of machismo for their imagined (male) audience.[60] Women and young male cadre in the organization challenged this perspective and advanced an enlargement of the audiences addressed and constituted by their rhetoric and activism. Informed by U.S. Third World feminist theory, interviews with former members, archival and textual material from the organization, and the perspectives of critical decolonial scholars,[61] I unpack the Young Lords' "revolution within the revolution" and show why it is a mistake to separate out claims to gender, race, or class justice. Through multiple sites of struggle, the Young Lords became attentive to the way manifold and complex oppressions intersected and multiplied as they encountered one another. This intersectional perspective was central, I argue, to a kind of decolonial critical politics that eschewed a focus on rights in preference for attentiveness to and claims for liberation. In this framework, which is also advanced by most scholars of de/coloniality, liberation is an alternative to emancipation—the latter of which relies on claims to recognition that fortify the legitimacy of the modern/colonial system. Liberation, then, seeks a liberty delinked from classical liberalism, mindful of affiliations and fraternal connections, and guided by an ethic of decolonial love, even as colonial wounds can never fully heal.

Discourse

I understand "discourse" to encapsulate all the forms of constitutive symbolic action, including the linguistic and nonlinguistic, that makes reality out of mere existence.[62] Rejected in this study is what Ernesto Laclau and Chantal Mouffe call "the distinction between discursive and nondiscursive practices," and with them I "affirm the *material* character of discourse." Discourse is "the entire material density of the multifarious institutions, rituals and practices through which a discursive formation is structured."[63] As such, "discourse" should not restrict our critical optics to the verbal domain; rather, a host of material practices beyond the word can and should be interrogated as discursive and (when situated and public) rhetorical acts. It is worth underscoring, here, that this perspective does not deny that things have a material existence beyond discourse; but how we come to *understand* those things, how they take on a *reality* for us, is the product of their articulation to geographic and embodied networks of discursive praxis.[64] Practically speaking, this means that I understand speeches, newspaper articles, artwork, embodied performances, theatricality, photography, and more to constitute the material discursive practices of the Young Lords; and when those discourses are engaged in their situated public contexts, we are in the realm of rhetoric.

On Delinking: The Rhetoric of Decoloniality

As I have been trying to show in this introduction and will continue demonstrating throughout the book, I believe that decolonial scholarship can benefit from more robust rhetorical sensibilities. While the larger critiques of modernity/coloniality are helpful for orienting a critic within a set of philosophical principles to guide her or his orientation, rhetorical perspectives that are attentive to studying situated public discourses can serve as a valuable check against theoretical abstraction and, at the end of the day, better ensure the normative and ethical commitments of decoloniality. It is one thing to say "we must be resolved to highlight the located and embodied emergence of knowledge production," and it is another thing to actually do that in a way that maintains fidelity with those philosophical objectives. Delinking is an excellent case in point. Beyond the telos of decoloniality established well by most authors writing on the subject, Mignolo identifies delinking as a key technique for resisting modernity/coloniality. At the most basic level, delinking is about disengaging from (though not operating completely outside of) the logic and rhetoric of modernity.[65] In an essay on contemporary antisystemic movements, Ronald Walter Greene and Kevin Douglas Kuswa turn to Samir Amin's formulation of delinking,[66] which "refers to an exodus from the rules of the global regime that enforces the laws of market value as the price for integrating national economies into the world capitalist system."[67] Although not tied to an explicitly socialist analysis, decolonial critics advocate a similar exodus from modernity/coloniality—one that requires challenging modern, Western, colonial epistemic privilege through diverse sets of embodied discursive practices.

Mignolo does well to describe delinking's necessity, critical thrust, and directionality; but he gives his readers little by way of identifying and cultivating specific techniques through which to delink. Claiming that it "runs parallel" to Amin's delinking and "leads to de-colonial epistemic shift and brings to the foreground other epistemologies, other principles of knowledge and understanding and, consequently, other economy, other politics, other ethics,"[68] Mignolo's version of delinking is positioned against modernity/coloniality while also claiming that Amin's version aspires only to "radical emancipation within the rhetoric of modernity and the logic of coloniality."[69] Delinking is necessary, Mignolo argues further, "because there is no way out of the coloniality of power from within Western (Greek and Latin) categories of thought."[70] Without some kind of delinking and its attendant forms and habits of epistemic disobedience, we remain stuck within the colonial matrix—constantly seeking alternatives along the same arc of history that has damned us since the sixteenth century.

But if there is "no way out," then what is the point? How could we begin to talk about border thinking or other differential alternatives that operate simultaneously within and without modernity/coloniality? How could there be any room for innovation from the Global South, which, by the agreement of all of these scholars, operates under the heavy weight of "the darker side of modernity"? Related to a criticism I mentioned above, I think Mignolo's formulation of delinking sometimes risks leaving a critic with few alternatives but debunking and demystification. In what remains of this introduction, then, I provide an alterative conceptualization of delinking that supplies a greater degree of specificity while helping to delineate how it can function both as a descriptor of certain decolonial activist practices by the Young Lords and as an orienting term to guide scholarly critical-interpretive practices. In the chapters that follow, I focus on some specific rhetorical techniques, which we might read as related technologies of Sandoval's "methodology of the oppressed," that help tease out particular ways in which the Young Lords delink from coloniality. To frame it all, however, I draw attention to the rhetorical functionality of *accents* and their relationship to delinking.

Accent and tone have long had a place in rhetorical and cultural theory, but that place remains understudied. Offering perhaps the clearest explanations of the concept, both Mikhail Bakhtin and Valentin Vološinov write about the accentuality of words. For Bakhtin, like many who write about meaning, words have a history of usage that makes them sedimented, layered with meaning by others' utterances.[71] When we speak, we appropriate, recontextualize, and otherwise make discourse our "own" by populating it with a particular accent, "adapting it to [our] own semantic and expressive intention."[72] Similarly, Vološinov explores the ways that words (and other signs) *live* through their multiaccentuality—through the multiple, intersecting accents that make signs contested ideological terrains. "By and large," he writes, "it is thanks to this intersecting of accents that a sign maintains its vitality and dynamism and the capacity for further development." It is, he underscores, "precisely a word's multiaccentuality that makes it a living thing."[73]

More recently, critical communication scholars have turned attention to accents to explore the politics of place/space in two different contexts. In my own work on contemporary Nuyorican cultural production in East Harlem, for example, I draw from Frances R. Aparicio and Susana Chávez-Silverman to argue that particular practices of fugitive communication enact "a kind of tropicalization—a troping that imbues a rhetorical scene with an indelibly Latina/o ethos—that accents everyday material forms in East Harlem and demonstrates a productive form of cultural citizenship."[74] In a related fashion, Greene and Kuswa put accent at the center of their critical regionalism. For Greene and Kuswa, "Regions express an unstable geography of place because they can encompass sub-national, transnational, continental, and intercontinental configurations of people, territory, and practices." Analogically, they argue that "the multiaccentuality of a region is what makes it a rhetorical thing" and that "regional accents are rhetorically responsible for moving and removing regions into and out of maps of power."[75] Greene and Kuswa's case is particularly interesting for me because they explore the manners in which neoliberal capital accents regions in specific ways and, more important, how such regional accents can be challenged through a "socialist accent of regionalism" found in the practice of delinking.[76]

As I already mentioned, I mean something different by "delinking" than Greene and Kuswa. While for them (and Amin), delinking is rooted in a socialist political and rhetorical accent, such is not the case for myself and others writing on de/coloniality. That said, I think Greene and Kuswa's formulation is helpful because we both deal with the ways in which competing discursive, epistemic, economic, and political frameworks intersect to *accent* and *re-accent* literal and metaphorical *places*. Decolonial scholars, for example, are incredibly interested in the ways in which knowledge emerges from particular places and circulates. The problem, however, is that under coloniality, regional specificity often gets lost in the universalizing gesture of the zero point, an aspatial paradigm that denies knowledge's locatedness as well as its connections to located bodies. Decolonial critical regionalism becomes a corrective, not a descriptor, to wrench lose modernity/coloniality's epistemic stranglehold—one possible form of delinking that generates short circuits in the colonial matrix of power. Accent, here, takes on added significance. One way to understand coloniality is to see it as a multifarious articulation of modern/colonial discourses and logics that totalize the social in a manner exclusive of the Global South even as it is constituted by the Global South. Knowledge and being are accented by coloniality. *Decoloniality is an alternative accent*—one marked by pluriversal commitments, geo-historical attentiveness, and bio-graphical configurations.

In the Young Lords' first instance of direct-action politics, which I explore in Chapter 4, we see explicitly the emergence of such an alternative accent. In that chapter, I demonstrate the ways in which the Young Lords set out to *trope* (to symbolically inflect) El Barrio. I place the scholarship on de/coloniality into conversation with Aparicio and Chávez-Silverman's work on *tropicalization* to explain how the Young Lords crafted a decolonial collective agency altering the space in which they engaged social and political work.[77] Their tropicalization of El Barrio, a place that Arlene Dávila argues is a complicated and dynamic site of latinidad,[78] accented the space in a manner that activated political subjectivities and practices delinked from procedural democratic politics, transcending both liberal individualism and narrow identity politics. Importantly, the garbage offensive is also an ideal case study in the practices of delinking in three additional and distinct ways. First, exhibiting the ability and desire to *listen* to the residents of El Barrio and tackle the problem of garbage, the Young Lords enacted the quintessential practice of decolonial love, which I discuss in more detail below. Second, the Young Lords mobilized the very materiality of garbage as a rhetoric of presence that accented the community and its residents as colonized, thus crafting such a colonial accent as an exigence to address. Finally, by drawing attention to the residents' own complicity in the production of trash through the practices of a decadent consumer capitalism, the Young Lords performed among themselves and generated in their audience a critical self-reflexivity that is central to delinking from coloniality.

But what *is* delinking? This remains a tough question because it can be many things, and over the course of this book, I will tease out some of the specific ways the Young Lords engaged in practices of delinking through retrofitted memories, symbolic agencies, intersectional liberation politics, spatial accents, reformulations of political grammar, and so forth. Rather than try to codify a single operational definition of delinking, a better question might be: *How* can one go about delinking? Approaching it from a perspective of contextualized practice—as something that is in flux and contingent, based on the particularities of any given situation—delinking should be understood as a technique for challenging coloniality, which bears a resemblance to three concepts that are commonplace within communication and critical/cultural studies: dis/articulation, exnomination, and disidentification. When tied to a genealogy "structured in the planetary space of colonial/imperial expansion,"[79] these terms can help fill out what delinking can become in myriad contexts.

To begin, articulation is a common concept that speaks to the ways in which disparate cultural elements are linked together, form a "unity," and become naturalized. "The 'unity' which matters," argues Stuart Hall, "is a linkage between that articulated discourse and the social forces with which it can, under certain historical conditions, but need not necessarily, be connected."[80] As such, articulation is always contingent and temporary—the continuous product of ever-shifting cultural and discursive formations, political and economic structures, ideological investments, and specific rhetorics. Without much effort, for example, we can imagine the ways in which a term like "Latino" gets filled with different social, political, economic, and ideological commitments in different contexts (e.g., within grassroots activist contexts in El Barrio versus by anti-immigrant politicians in Washington, DC). Similarly, a term like "Latino" can become divested of those interests through processes of disarticulation and rearticulation (e.g., the symbolic shift from "Latino" to "Latin@" used to signify a rejection of hegemonic masculinity and bigender normativity). Delinking functions sometimes as a form of disarticulation/rearticulation, as a praxis that "signals the moment of fracture and breakage, a moment of opening" into other ways of thinking;[81] but delinking does not always have to disarticulate, especially if doing so would simultaneously deny the ability to practice forms of epistemic disobedience. For example, sometimes the best way to delink may be through a reinvestment, even if only temporary, in the ideology of liberal reformism. Furthermore, if decoloniality always seeks to delink with a decolonial tone, then articulation theory on its own is insufficient as a critical heuristic because, for Hall and others, there is no necessary connection between articulations.[82]

Exnomination is a concept from Roland Barthes's work on mythology that can have two meanings.[83] On the one hand, it can (and usually does) function conservatively to depoliticize speech and solidify the naturalization of myth. Exnomination removes the name from an ideological position (Barthes refers to the bourgeoisie), securing its mythic work. On the other hand, exnomination can function in a protorevolutionary manner, as what Sandoval calls "another resistant language that functions both within and against ideology."[84] Understood in this second way, Sandoval reads exnomination as a key technology of the methodology of the oppressed, which she renames "meta-ideologizing." "This challenge to dominant cultural forms best occurs," Sandoval argues, channeling Barthes, "not by speaking *outside* their terms . . . nor through manifestly setting new terms linked to the real, as in 'revolutionary speech,' but through the *ideologization of ideology* itself."[85] Fueled by the enactment of differential consciousness, "poetry, silence, and all other technologies of resistance can be viewed as ideological weaponry"[86] that can break down oppression from a subject that is *both* and *neither* inside and outside of dominant ideologies. Exnomination, especially as extended by Sandoval, can play a central role in delinking and assist in avoiding the risk of binary logics that simply reject all things Western; but like disarticulation, I think it names only one possible technique and fails to capture the other possibilities offered by delinking (e.g., refusing to engage the dominant ideology and drawing from alternative discourses, spaces of knowledge production, and traditions). In other words, delinking *might* engage in disarticulations or meta-ideologizing, but it is not *required* to do so.

Like meta-ideologizing, disidentification seeks a third alternative to either unquestioning obedience to and identification with a dominant ideology or complete rejection and division from an ideology. Drawing from Michel Pêcheau, José Esteban Muñoz argues that disidentification "neither opts to assimilate within such a structure nor strictly opposes it; rather, disidentification is a strategy that works on and against dominant ideology." Muñoz continues that "this 'working on and against' is a strategy that tries to transform a cultural logic from within, always laboring to enact permanent structural change while at the same time valuing the importance of local or everyday struggles of resistance."[87] Disidentification, like meta-ideologizing, represents a crucial component of epistemic disobedience insofar as it challenges the presumption of an either/or choice and provides another way of explaining the kinds of "border thinking" that Mignolo, Maldonado-Torres, U.S. Third World feminists, and others value.[88]

Chapter 5 represents a good example of how disarticulation, exnomination, and disidentification alone are insufficient. In that chapter, I attempt to come to terms with the Young Lords' populist liberation rhetoric spawned during the church offensive. Building from Michael Calvin McGee's observation that " 'the people' are more *process* than *phenomenon*," I explore the ways the Young Lords craft "the people's repertory of convictions"[89] from diverse rhetorical resources in their verbal, visual, and embodied discourse surrounding the church offensive, which was their second major direct political action. Specifically, I read the Young Lords' rhetoric of "the people" as a radical, decolonial challenge to what Charles Taylor calls the modern social imaginary.[90] While Maldonado-Torres argues that "the people" is fundamentally exclusionary in relation to "the condemned of the earth,"[91] who most readily feel the effects of coloniality, I argue that the Young Lords' rearticulation of "the people" as a plural-universal collective, demanding material and epistemic liberation, delinks and denaturalizes constructions of a homogenous liberal/Western "people." As such, I show how delinking does not require a complete rejection of the grammar of modern/Western politics so much as it denies the epistemic privilege that often undergirds the articulation of such grammars. While there are ways in which the Young Lords' reappropriation of "the people" can be read as disarticulation, exnomination, and disidentification, those terms are better understood as instrumental rather than conclusive in exploring the texture of how the Young Lords divest from modernity/coloniality and invent conceptions of peoplehood that remain in contact with, yet not epistemically subordinate to, coloniality.

Drawing from these terms (dis/articulation, exnomination/meta-ideologizing, and disidentification), I believe that *delinking can be any practice, discursive or otherwise, that facilitates a divestment from modernity/coloniality and invents openings through which decolonial epistemic shifts can emerge.* "Delinking doesn't mean," argues Mignolo, "to abandon, but instead to *invent* decolonial visions and horizons, concepts and discourses."[92] Delinking requires changes in both content and form. In content, one cannot simply continue to reproduce dominant logics and rhetorics that maintain "the hubris of the zero point" and lock people into imperial ways of knowing and being. It requires being oriented toward shifts in our genealogies of thought, including drawing authority from colonized spaces/voices and resisting latent imperialisms—even when such resistance may not be exclusively oppositional. In form, delinking generates hybridizations that otherwise would not seem possible: nationless nationalisms, noncapitalistic economies, nonliberal democratics. There is no single way to delink, but *delinking will always re-accent with a decolonial tone*—and that goes for how one practices scholarship as well.

Delinking compels us to be attentive to the ways in which scholars, activists, and others communicate *from* embodied locations and communicate *to* others, which is why I situate my present voice and this project within my own diasporic Puerto Rican context and personal emergence into the consciousness and space of the Global South. One way to take this call for delinking seriously—in fact, it is almost a requirement of scholars like Maldonado-Torres and Mignolo—is to shift away from the visual/written bias of Western culture and toward a stance emphasizing embodied speech and listening.[93] Maldonado-Torres, for example, stresses the importance of a dialogue that "breaks through Eurocentric [and U.S. American-centric] prejudices and seeks to expand the horizon of interlocutors beyond colonial and imperial differences. The de-colonial attitude seeks to be able to *listen to what has been silenced.*"[94] Listening, here, does not have to be understood literally. Yes, decoloniality would imply that we must actually listen to the voices that have been silenced. Scholars like Lisbeth Lipari, Jeffrey Murray, and Kelly Oliver all point to the importance of the physicality and presence of listening-in-person.[95] With this in mind, I engaged in conversations with former Young Lords to experience and generate a repertoire of embodied knowledge, which has shaped greatly my own understanding of their prior activism. But listening can also be metaphorical; we can understand it as a critical-interpretive strategy for coming to archival and textual material with an openness to the Other that challenges sedimented ways of understanding and acting in the world. Oliver describes this as a "tension between recognizing the familiar in order to confirm what we already know," which would be the modus operandi of coloniality and its concomitant zero-point epistemology, "and listening for the unfamiliar that disrupts what we already know," which is the orienting principle for decoloniality.[96]

Such a willingness to listen, both literally and metaphorically, is predicated on an ethics of critique that goes beyond the skepticism of power. Listening, for Maldonado-Torres, requires something akin to an *ethic of decolonial love*. Here, the critic both struggles "against the structures of dehumanization" and positively expresses "*non-indifference* toward the Other."[97] This is Fanon's love, captured well in the second epigraph of this chapter. It is, in Oliver's assessment of Fanon, "a vision of love . . . that is not self-centered but other-centered. Love for and between those othered by dominant culture opens up new possibilities" that transcend and transgress liberal political logics.[98] The critic-theorist must give the gift of the self, who Maldonado-Torres argues "is only able to *see* (*theros*) and *grasp* (comprehend), because it first *hears* and *gives*. Hearing the 'cry' of the wounded and the afflicted becomes, in this sense, the enlightening act *par excellence*."[99] On a practical level, this means that I must begin *hearing* those accented voices excluded from scholarly theorizing and the discourse communities I study, *internalizing* their thought, and *seeking* ways to delink from coloniality. Love can function, here, Sandoval explains, as "a hermeneutic, a set of practices and procedures" that can move us "toward a differential mode of consciousness."[100] Beyond examining the ways in which love becomes a key principle and practice for some of the Young Lords' own discursive and activist practices, love is my guiding impulse *for engaging* the organization as well as the critical ethic undergirding *how I proceed* with such an engagement.

In short, the task is a challenging one: *scholars must first alter the intellectual terrain from which we as critics and theorists speak and listen.* Guided by an ethic of decolonial love, we have to grapple with the ways in which we have consented to and participated in the reproduction of colonial violence. I have to come to terms, for example, with the ways in which some of my own prior engagements of the Young Lords, including a dissertation guided by my preoccupation with radical democratic theory, enacted forms of colonial violence.[101] In a 2012 interview, the brilliant, award-winning author Junot Díaz draws from U.S. Third World feminists to frame our praxis thusly:

> Because rather than strike at this issue or that issue, this internal bearing of witness raised the possibility of denying our oppressive regimes the true source of their powers—which is, of course, *our* consent, *our* participation. This kind of praxis doesn't attack the head of

the beast, which will only grow back; it strikes directly at the beast's heart, which we nurture and keep safe in our own.[102]

So that is the hard part: we have to be self-reflexive enough to begin challenging our own complicities in modernity/coloniality before we can faithfully and lovingly engage others, which is what I attempt in my encounter with the New York Young Lords in the coming pages.

Delinking, in this way, has to be understood as manifold: as both practice and perspective, as both a *thing* and a *way*. On one hand, it includes practices of dis/articulation, meta-ideologizing, disidentification, and so forth, that challenge the centrality of coloniality and its attendant forms of epistemic privilege to re-accent metaphorical and literal places with a decolonial tone. On another hand, delinking is a set of scholarly and activist perspectives, guided by an ethic of decolonial love, that reorient us toward hearing the voices of the Global South so that we might begin disrupting what we know and how we come to know those things, but not necessarily in ways that are accountable or attempt to answer to the West. Rather, delinking seeks to enact a "preferential option for the condemned of the earth" and calls for a "reactivation of subaltern knowledges" that "transcends and transgresses the imposition of abstract universals while it opens up the path for dialogue among different epistemes."[103] Where appropriate, then, delinking directs us to speak *from* and *with* the Global South as well, to generate spaces for and voices of epistemic disobedience in our varied scholarly contexts. *The New York Young Lords and the Struggle for Liberation* is an effort in this direction—to come to understand better the significance of the Young Lords in terms of their decolonial praxis and to model forms of scholarly decoloniality such that we all can begin more productively taking up the discourses and activisms of Latin@s and others colonized on their own terms, guided always by love.

To this end, the book's Conclusion advances an argument for the importance of considering the Young Lords as a touchstone of decolonial possibility in a world still marked by coloniality and its wounding epistemology and ontology. The conclusion responds to the question "What can decoloniality look like and why should it matter to a U.S. American audience today?" through an extension of my analyses of their rhetorics of "community control" and a turn to the issue of theorizing and practicing democracy. While certain styles, topoi, and sensibilities from the Young Lords can and should be recovered and reworked, it is a mistake to simply mimic their activism in contemporary times. I argue for a rethinking of democracy rooted in decolonial heterogeneities that keeps open the terrain for political contestation, features commitments to racial and gender justice, is guided more by liberation than by recognition, and empowers people to be engaged political subjects who exhibit epistemic disobedience by delinking from coloniality and rejecting neoliberal hegemonies. If Mignolo is right in suggesting that we have reached a "point of no return" in which "the future of the planet, not just Western civilization, can hinge on whether the balance is tilted" toward the decolonial or away,[104] then it is imperative that we come to terms not just with the perspectives and intellectual commitments undergirding decoloniality but also with various practices of delinking that can orient us toward inventing new possibilities grounded in the colonial wound and its persistent mark on our bodies, minds, and places.

I

History and Ideology

1

Origins and Optics

Remembering Colonialism, Nationalism,
and Radicalism with the Young Lords

For centuries, we have been taught that we are a small, quiet,
insignificant, shuffling people who cannot even govern ourselves and
who are very happy having outside governments control our lives. We
have been taught that Puerto Rico is a beautiful island for tourists on
summer vacations. We are taught that revolution is the work of maniacs
and fanatics and has nothing to do with nice, docile spics. Yet we have
not been quiet; the people of Borinquen have struggled for liberation
from the time of the Taino Indians to the present.

—IRIS MORALES, "El Grito de Lares"

Your best defense against the ignorance of bigots and haters is pride in
your own heritage. That's why you must learn your own history. Do it
now. Don't wait until you are in College. You don't need teachers. Go to
the library. Ask your parents and relatives and friends.

—JOSÉ TORRES, "A Letter to a Child like Me"

Puerto Rico, like any nation, is an invention. From a realist perspective, of
course, this is nonsense—Puerto Rico (the land, the place) has always
existed in human history as a land mass roughly thirty-five miles wide by
a hundred miles long, just west of the Dominican Republic, north of Vene-
zuela, and about 1,600 miles south of New York City. What I mean, instead, is
that this place we *call* "Puerto Rico" is an invention. It is the rhetorical product
of Spanish and United States colonialism and the various forms of resistance/
response to that colonialism. It is, to borrow a phrase from journalist and
former Young Lord Juan Gonzalez, the "harvest of empire" reaped by the
United States under the Monroe Doctrine and manifest destiny.[1] In this sense,
economic historian James Dietz argues, "The history Puerto Ricans have made
is thus not solely of their own choosing: the colonial experience has shaped
the boundaries of action and has contributed to the 'rules of the game,' and
always and ominously the colonial power has been ready to back up its material interests with force to defend them."[2] This land, originally called Borikén

(Land of the Brave Lord) by the indigenous Taínos, was claimed by Spain under Columbus's second voyage in 1493, renamed San Juan Bautista by Columbus, and eventually reduced to pure instrumentality through its renaming as Puerto Rico (literally, "rich port"). As a Spanish colony first settled by Juan Ponce de León in the early sixteenth century, the Taínos were nearly exterminated (those remaining alive were enslaved), the colony became reliant on slaves from Africa, and Puerto Rico fulfilled a key role as agricultural producer, trade port, and military post. In 1898, the United States became its new colonial master as Puerto Rico was transformed into a spoil of the Spanish-American War. It remains today, under Supreme Court rulings and congressional affirmation, an "unincorporated territory" of the United States: "Integrated but not assimilated; *part* of but not *of* the United States, U.S. citizens by law but Puerto Ricans first," Dietz argues, "these are the tensions and contradictions that permeate society at all levels."[3] Even (perhaps especially) in the face of political and economic reforms, the legacy of colonialism remains potent both on the island and, through multiple periods of migration, within these United States.

While there are many examples of Puerto Rican resistance to colonial oppression—beginning with Taíno revolts in the sixteenth century, various slave revolts, and the 1868 El Grito de Lares revolt in Puerto Rico and continuing with rebellions on the island and by *independentistas* within the United States, such as the attack (led by Lolita Lebrón) on the U.S. House of Representatives in 1954—widespread resistance by Puerto Ricans, especially second-generation, within the United States was chilled by state repression. In 1968, however, things began to change. Chicago street gang leader José "Cha Cha" Jiménez found himself jailed. While in the Cook County Jail for sixty days on drug charges, Jiménez came to political consciousness via exposure to radical black writings. Through this political conversion, one as affectively powerful as any religious conversion, Jiménez led his Young Lords into a new era of community service and activism aimed at asserting some local control of their community in Chicago. Shortly thereafter, a group of young Puerto Ricans began meeting in New York under the name La Sociedad de Albizu Campos. In search of a model for activism and finding those offered by groups like the Black Panthers to be inadequate for their needs as multiracial Boricuas, these Nuyoricans learned of the Chicago group's existence, made their way to the Windy City, and formally requested to charter a New York chapter of the Young Lords Organization.

Origins are always tricky to navigate, and the origins of the New York Young Lords are no exception. While we can temporally mark the official, chartered beginning of the New York branch of the Young Lords Organization as July 26, 1969, that tells only part of the story. And the whole story, whatever that would look like, might never be told because it is contested, deeply personal, perspectival, and fragmented—the whole exceeds the sum of its parts, which are rooted in the embodied experiences and cultural memories of the many young people involved in its unfolding. There are more or less "official" origin stories for the Young Lords, which consist of histories written by the organization's leadership collective in the early 1970s and by former leaders retrospectively in the 1980s and beyond; but these stories sometimes emphasize different organizational structures and risk marginalizing the voices of the cadre (members who had no defined leadership positions). Furthermore, such origin stories might start too late, insofar as they can fail to address the sociopolitical and historical conditions that generated a context from which the Young Lords emerged. History, however, is never a simple, objective *given*. "There is always a difference between a history as it takes place and its linguistic facilitation. . . . A history does not happen without speaking, but it is never identical with it, it cannot be reduced to it."[4] In this sense, the telling of history is always limited; choices are always made about what to include and exclude. This becomes particularly problematic in the context of the dispossessed, because history, writes Emma Pérez, "is the story of the conquerors, those who have won. The vanquished disappear."[5]

The young people who would form the Young Lords were all too aware of Pérez's point. Iris Morales, whom I quote in this chapter's opening epigraph, underscored the severity of the victors' normative history—a rhetorical move the organization would follow consistently. Another Young Lord, David Perez, put a finer (if more Manichean) point on it: "Puerto Ricans here and in Puerto Rico are taught three things: Puerto Rico is small and the United States is big; Puerto Rico is poor and the United States is rich; Puerto Rico is weak and the United States is strong. Sort of a national inferiority complex."[6] Such dominant narratives of Puerto Rican docility, ineptitude, and powerlessness were magnified in the New York context and within the U.S. American audience. For example, a popular post–World War II guidebook for New York City reflected and reinforced the troubling viewpoints thusly: "Puerto Ricans were not born to be New Yorkers. They are mostly crude farmers subject to congenital tropical diseases, physically unfitted for the northern climate, unskilled, uneducated, non–English speaking, and almost impossible to assimilate and condition for healthful and useful existence in an active city of stone and steel."[7] Faced with what Frantz Fanon called a "crushing objecthood,"[8] Puerto Ricans were reduced in the popular imaginary and official histories to a caricature, a shell devoid of humanity, an image that was more a reflection of the attitudes of the colonizer than of the people themselves. Given a history of consciousness regarding Puerto Ricans that was, at least at the time, thoroughly racist and colonialist, how ought we to proceed? How can one go about getting a sense for the historical context within which the Young Lords emerged?

Rather than attempt to historicize the Young Lords by engaging in some kind of objectivist exercise that solely lays out the historical-material conditions for the organization's emergence, I want to turn the table to explore how the Young Lords themselves imagined their own history—a methodological move that prioritizes the voices of the dispossessed in the production of local history delinked from modernity/coloniality. For the Young Lords and all Third World radicals in the 1960s and 1970s, crafting a usable history was an urgent necessity. As Fanon argued, "The colonized man who writes for his people ought to use the past with the intention of opening the future, as an invitation to action and a basis for hope."[9] From the very beginning, then, the Young Lords set out to authorize a history (stretching from the island to the metropole) that would undergird the analysis of their social situation and buttress their claims for revolutionary action. With that process and purpose in mind, this chapter is both a history *of* the Young Lords and a history *from* the Young Lords—a narrative about the conditions for their emergence generated, in part, through the countermemory that they crafted.

Over the course of this chapter, my story of the Young Lords' emergence unfolds over three sections. First, I explore aspects of Puerto Rican history that were most significant to the Young Lords. I follow the Young Lords' lead in paying the most attention to problems rooted in Spanish and U.S. colonialism (the genocide of Taínos, slavery, lack of self determination, etc.) and exemplars of resistance in the struggle for liberation (e.g., El Grito de Lares and the emergence of nationalism). Second, I turn attention to the U.S. context and examine some of the historical antecedents that enabled the Young Lords' ascendancy. In the diasporic context in New York, I explore briefly the pre— and post–World War II political organizations oriented toward addressing and improving the Puerto Rican condition in the metropole, which opened spaces from which the Young Lords would emerge (even as they had little awareness of many of the prior activists). More significantly, the Young Lords surfaced within an immediate context marked by deleterious economic conditions, widespread rioting, and a rising tide of radicalism across the nation generally and in New York in particular. Finally, I explore the origins and actions of the New York Young Lords, from their initial emergence in 1969, through multiple organizational transformations, to their ultimate demise in 1976.

From the Taínos to Don Pedro: The Puerto Rican Context

At the time of their emergence in the late 1960s, there were few resources on Puerto Rican history available to the budding Young Lords or anyone else interested in learning more about this onetime Spanish, now U.S. colony. Many of those resources that were available had been written from an unabashedly U.S. American perspective, from the perspective of the colonial victors who had "possessed" the island since 1898. Noted author and poet Piri Thomas, whose best-selling autobiography *Down These Mean Streets* (1967) helped thrust Nuyorican literary figures onto the scene, recounted the sad state of affairs in 1970: "I remembered with pain and bitterness several books and articles by non–Puerto Ricans that had presented a distorted and stereotyped image of my people here on the mainland and in Puerto Rico. Like many other Puerto Ricans, I consider these works especially harmful when they appear cloaked in sociological authenticity and reality."[10] Thomas notes that it was not just his generation but also the present generation of "young American-born Puerto Ricans," like those who would become Young Lords, who were "tired of the stereotyped picture of Puerto Ricans as a meek, submissive, or sexually immoral people," and who "have gone through whole lifetimes with almost no opportunity to learn about our roots, our history, our culture, our unique contributions to the history of the world's peoples."[11] It was not until Kal Wagenheim's book, *Puerto Rico: A Profile* (1970), for which Thomas wrote the foreword I just quoted, that a contemporary and ideologically fair survey of Puerto Rican history, culture, and politics was made accessible to an English-speaking audience;[12] but the dearth of scholarship did not stop the Young Lords from assembling a history and marking out their place within it.

In their newspaper, radio program, and in other discourses, the Young Lords assembled what Maylei Blackwell has called "retrofitted memory," by which she means the practices of "drawing from both discarded and suppressed forms of knowledge" to generate "new forms of consciousness customized to embodied material realities, political visions, and creative desires for societal transformation."[13] As a technique of delinking, retrofitted memory functions as a direct challenge to the coloniality of knowledge that crafts new ways of imagining collective pasts, presents, and futures. It is, simultaneously, a *no* and a *yes*—a rejection of myopic constructions of the past that challenges normative and debilitating constructions of nonpersonhood and an embrace of alternative conceptualizations of a people endowed by a shared humanity to act on history in manners inconceivable by dominant players. I chart and enrich, aided by more contemporary sources, this retrofitted memory crafted by the Young Lords so that the reader might gain a sense for the history the organization envisioned itself operating within. I ask the reader, also, to imagine this history as part of the Young Lords' context. We know from Miguel "Mickey" Melendez's account of his time in the organization that, from the start, would-be members were immersed in practices of recovering a history delinked from the coloniality of knowledge.[14] While it would become much more refined as time went on, the Young Lords' retrofitted memory was constitutive of the rhetorical situation within which they emerged and would become central to their discourse and activism.

The Young Lords crafted a history of Puerto Rico that operated in at least four distinctive, yet interrelated modes. One mode was *recovery*, in which they laid out elements of Puerto Rican history (e.g., Taíno culture) that had been omitted from hegemonic narratives. Another mode was *correction*, in which they revised misconceptions of historical events and individuals in order to highlight (a) outright falsehoods perpetrated by those in power and/or (b) politically and ideologically useful information typically excluded from the historical record. A third mode was *reclamation*, wherein they recast the significance of certain events and individuals for their present struggles, animating a revolutionary imagination that could empower and authorize their activism. Finally, the Young Lords engaged in *connection* by articulating linkages between different temporal and/or geographical contexts (e.g., Spain and the United States in the late nineteenth and mid-twentieth centuries). Their story was told oftentimes through multiple modes at once—by, for example, simultaneously recovering the history of the Taínos, correcting misconceptions about them, and reclaiming the significance of their resistance against Spanish colonialism—which enabled them to craft a complex, sometimes cyclical (rather than linear) historical narrative that empowered them to be agentic subjects who could make their own mark on history. Rather than reproduce their entire history of Puerto Rico, I want to focus attention on a few key themes, people, organizations, and events that were most significant to the Young Lords.[15] In its most refined form, which emerged in 1971, the history they trace is based largely on Wagenheim's aforementioned book, from which the Young Lords (primarily Guzmán, in the case of their thirteen-part *Palante* series on the "History of Borikén") drew heavily in order to engage in various acts of recovery, correction, reclamation, and connection.

The Young Lords' telling of history begins with a recovery and reclamation of the Taínos, the peoples indigenous to Puerto Rico/Borikén. They start by historically, geographically, and socially contextualizing the Taínos, which establishes Taíno civilization as advanced, well organized, and the progenitor of recognizable words that we have today (hammock, maize, and more). The Taínos were not perfect, however. For example, the Young Lords were critical of the ways in which Taínos created divisions between men and women, which served as evidence that "oppression of women began before capitalism, that it can exist under socialism, and that to make sure this does not happen, we must work extra hard to eliminate all false divisions based on sex."[16] Nonetheless, they found hope in this pre-Columbian people who numbered approximately 30,000 in 1493, the year that "the peaceful life of the Indians was disturbed by an intrusion from a fool named christopher columbus, while on his second voyage to the Americas."[17] Borikén, renamed by Columbus as San Juan Bautista, was brought fully under colonial control at the dawn of the sixteenth century. Ponce de León's arrival (1508) and renaming of the island as Puerto Rico (1511) ushered in an era of repression and the gradual extermination of the Taínos, first by force but also by illness.[18] The Taínos rebelled in 1510–1511, but the rebellion was met with even more repression when Ponce de León proceeded to massacre 6,000 of the indigenous people. As Roberto Santiago describes the scene, "After that, the genocide continued unabated."[19]

The Spanish continued their conquest of the island for hundreds of years, importing African slaves to work sugar and coffee plantations and denying islanders the right to self-determination. Global democratic transformations in the eighteenth century, however, brought some changes to the island. In the Young Lords' assessment, "When the 13 amerikkkan colonies rebelled against England, they touched off a wave of democratic thinking in europe that bounced back to Latin America. . . . After the french revolution in 1789, france made up a constitution in 1791 that was a model for other democratic revolutions."[20] Such revolutions included the Haitian slave revolts, which began in 1791 and led, ultimately, to France outlawing slavery in 1793 (Puerto Rico would not follow suit until 1873). Greater democratization in Spain, as well, led to a status change for Puerto Ricans who, in 1812, became Spanish citizens—a change that would be mirrored 105 years later when the United States made a similar decision via the Jones Act, something the Young Lords, breaking from norms of linear historical writing, would refer to as "one old dog passing tricks on [to] the new one."[21]

The eighteenth century also saw the emergence of the *jíbaro* in Puerto Rican culture, someone the Young Lords described as "a folk hero whom the people talk about and admire for having certain qualities." According to Guzmán, "Jíbaros first appeared in the 1700's, the result of the Taínos who fled to the hills, joined with Spaniards and later Africans."[22] Over the years, especially in the mid-twentieth century, the figure of the jíbaro would become central in what Arlene Dávila calls a "folklorization of national culture, which constructs the myth of Puerto Rican identity from the building blocks of the racial triad (Taíno, African, Spanish), the idealization of the peasant past, and the 'unifying' Hispanic heritage."[23] This was later extended through a rhetoric of "la gran familia puertorriqueña."[24] Jorge Duany similarly argues that

the founding myth of the three roots provides a partial, incomplete, and biased account of the origins and development of contemporary Puerto Rican culture. To begin, it shuns American culture after 1898 as a "foreign influence" that threatens to corrupt the three main ethnic strands of national identity. Moreover, the Institute of Puerto Rican Culture, as well as other cultural institutions, has often displayed an excessively pro-Hispanic bent that often reifies the Spanish language as the litmus test of Puerto Ricanness. Among other consequences, this restrictive linguistic and territorial definition of Puerto Rican identity has excluded the diaspora in the United States. Finally, cultural nationalism typically underestimates the political and economic dimensions of national identity.[25]

The result has been a cultural nationalism that, while officially embracing a heterogeneous racial democracy (with the Taino and African roots), continuously subverts non-Spanish contributions "vis-à-vis those of the Spanish" and essentializes identity.[26]

While the Young Lords resisted such flawed conceptualizations of racial democracy that privileged the Spanish over Taíno and African roots, they were enamored with the jíbaro as a figure of revolt and rebellion who was central to the emergence of national consciousness in Puerto Rico in the mid-eighteenth century. As Puerto Ricans who were not in a privileged position under Spanish rule began articulating a sense of "imagined community," some directed their attention to developing modes of resistance to colonialism.[27] One key instance of such resistance that the Young Lords turned to repeatedly was a revolt in the mountain town of Lares which later became known as El Grito de Lares (The Cry/Yell of Lares). In this first post-Taíno organized effort to resist colonial domination, Puerto Rican independentistas, led by Dr. Ramón Emeterio Betances, launched an armed revolt against the Spaniards on September 23, 1868. "El pueblo quiere libertades no las espera de nadie" (The people want their freedom), Betances stated matter-of-factly. "De gracia y merced coje *dijo* ¡Y cesaré de estar triste!" (They don't expect it from anyone. By grace and right *I say* take it. And I shall cease to be sad!)[28] While the revolt was brutally quashed, in part because the Spanish authorities had received prior indication of the planned rebellion, the words of Betances, and the spirit of a people bound together for the nation, lived on.[29] The Young Lords would mark Betances and El Grito de Lares as "the first revolutionary action of the Puerto Rican nation . . . when a group of short, quiet, shuffling, machete-carrying spics tired of taking shit picked up arms against spain."[30] The organization would stand "for the intensification of the struggle that began on September 23, 1868,"[31] and they would continuously draw hope and inspiration from the historical event for their own struggle (see Figure 1.1). Such reclamation work served to connect the Young Lords to an extended struggle and simultaneously challenged racist constructions (note their reappropriation of "spics") of Puerto Rican docility and inaction.

In the aftermath of El Grito de Lares and in the context of continuing democratic revolutions throughout Latin America, things began to change in Puerto Rico. In 1897, Spain's hold on the island was weakening, as was the rest of its empire. As calls for independence in Puerto Rico strengthened, Spain gradually conceded control over politicians on the island. On February 11, 1898, Spain "inaugurated the autonomous government" under the Autonomist Charter.[32] According to Dietz, "The Autonomist Charter gave Puerto Rico full representation in the Cortes and extensive rights to make treaties and to control trade and tariffs."[33] Over the next few months, Puerto Rico gradually exercised more autonomy, and on July 17, 1898, the first and only session of the Autonomous Parliament of Puerto Rico was convened.[34] Unfor-

Figure 1.1   Illustration from the front cover of *Palante* 2, no. 15 (September 11–23, 1971).

tunately, it was too little, too late. Under the authority of the Monroe Doctrine, the United States was increasing its sphere of influence in Latin America and the Caribbean. On July 25, 1898, on the basis of claims of provocation brought on by Spain's alleged attack on the USS *Maine*, the United States invaded Puerto Rico and brought an end to the autonomous government, which held a closing meeting on July 28.[35]

Puerto Rico has remained a U.S. colony since 1898. Initially under military control, on April 12, 1900, the U.S. Congress passed and President McKinley signed the Foraker Act, establishing a civilian government giving "Puerto Ricans less self-government than they had enjoyed under Spain."[36] Additionally, in the 1901 *Downes v. Bidwell* decision, the U.S. Supreme Court, reports

Gonzalez, "ruled that 'the island of Porto Rico is a territory appurtenant and belonging to the United States within the revenue clauses of the Constitution.' Since the island was not an incorporated territory of the United States, as the frontier territories had been, the Court ruled that the Constitution did not automatically apply in Puerto Rico unless Congress granted Puerto Ricans citizenship."[37] Thus, the law became a "constitutive part of the relationship between the United States and Puerto Rico," argues Efrén Rivera Ramos, "and has had a significant role in the production of American hegemony in Puerto Rican society"—a hegemony that continues to legitimate the exercise of colonial power over Puerto Rican subjects.[38]

In 1914, the full Puerto Rican House of Delegates, frustrated with the U.S. policy of colonial domination and exploitation, asked Congress to grant the island independence. According to Gonzalez, "Congress responded instead with the Jones Act in 1917, imposing U.S. citizenship on all Puerto Ricans over the *unanimous* objection of their House of Delegates."[39] Consequent to the Jones Act (which codified into law what the Supreme Court had already ruled),[40] the United States declared Puerto Ricans to be citizens who, as long as they remained on the island, could not vote for president and could not have voting representation in Congress.[41] The Jones Act also established a new, bicameral, elected legislature on the island but reinforced the U.S. president's power to veto all legislation.[42] While islanders may not enjoy the full rights of citizenship (or the rights of full citizenship), they may exercise those formal, legal rights in any state to which they relocate. Importantly, then, the Jones Act had (and still has) broad constitutive effects in Puerto Rican society that reinscribe the colonial relationship, allowing the United States to continue to dominate the Puerto Rican people.[43] The next significant change in status occurred in 1948, when Puerto Rico was granted the power to elect its own governor. Finally, in 1952, Puerto Rico was granted "Commonwealth" status (*Estado Libre Asociado*, literally "Free Associated State"), a form of limited self-rule. To this day, Puerto Ricans living on the island cannot vote for president, do not have voting representation in Congress, and succumb to all U.S. federal laws imposed on the island.

Although there were elements of an emergent national identity in Puerto Rico before the late 1920s (e.g., El Grito de Lares), the Young Lords' key starting point for a discussion of Puerto Rican nationalism was the Nationalist Party and Pedro Albizu Campos. "Born on September 12, 1891, Albizu represents, in the homeland of the Puerto Ricans," according to José Manuel Torres Santiago, "the most valuable symbol of liberty for his dedication to the historical revindication of his country and all Latino nations."[44] Of mixed African and Spanish ancestry, Albizu Campos earned an advanced education at Harvard and served in the U.S. Army during World War I. Albizu Campos then returned to Puerto Rico and actively involved himself in politics. In 1924, he joined the Nationalist Party and was elected its vice president;

in 1932, he was elected its president. Thus began his formal struggle for the independence of Puerto Rico. Torres Santiago writes, "Albizu thought the incorporation of Puerto Rico to the American way of life would destroy the Puerto Rican identity and nationality."[45] As such, Albizu Campos committed himself to political and cultural independence of Puerto Ricans, advancing a separatist agenda that located the only possibility for authentic Puerto Rican-ness in an independent Puerto Rican nation-state—an island-based ideology of Puerto Rican purity that the Young Lords would come to reject.

Under the leadership and guidance of "Don Pedro," the Puerto Rican nationalists would lead numerous protests and armed revolts and face insurmountable repression from the United States and U.S.-backed government of Luis Muñoz Marín (the first elected governor of Puerto Rico, whom the Young Lords would refer to as "the most treacherous snake of all that the amerikkkans produced").[46] Nationalist revolts—for example, the October 30, 1950, Jayuya uprising led by Blanca Canales; the November 1, 1950, attempted assassination of President Truman by Oscar Collazo and Griselio Torresola; and the March 1, 1954, attack on the U.S. Congress led by Lolita Lebrón and including Rafael Cancel Miranda, Irving Flores, and Andrés Figueroa Cordero—would become key sources of inspiration for the Young Lords decades later. No less important to the Young Lords were the instances of repression the nationalists faced—including Albizu Campos's numerous jailings; the March 21, 1937, Ponce Massacre; and the massive crackdown on the Nationalist Party following the rebellions and armed revolts of the 1950s—which, when combined with the material and symbolic successes of nationalist resistance, brought about a "critical moment" where "u.s. rule was in its most contested stage." Unfortunately, the Nationalist Party, in the Young Lords' assessment, "did not rely primarily on analyzing conditions surrounding and within our people's freedom movement, so they did not make best use of the 'critical moment' period."[47] As such, nationalists and their progenitors (like the Movimiento Pro-Independencia [MPI], which formed in 1959) provided resources for resistance against U.S. colonialism, but they were resources that were historically and symbolically valuable as lessons of what *not* to do (e.g., to not replicate what the Young Lords diagnosed as the independentistas' classism and elitism) as much as direct guides for the Young Lords' activism.

From los Pioneros to Black Power: The U.S. Context

Beyond the history of colonialist oppression by Spain and the United States, and concomitant acts of resistance both on the island and mainland, the context for the Young Lords' emergence in New York is complicated and significant—even if less explicitly acknowledged by the organization and its members. Correcting occasional misconceptions about the Black Panthers, for example, Nikhil Pal Singh underscores that "groups like the Panthers did not simply arise ex nihilo out of the general madness of 1968; they were products of an older and wider black radical and revolutionary imagination."[48] The same can be said about the Young Lords, but with some important qualifications. While the conditions of their emergence certainly owe a debt to earlier generations of Puerto Ricans in the United States, they did not always know about those earlier generations because there was no archive, no readily available collection of those prior voices. Asked about influences from and experiences with the Old Left, for instance, Iris Morales responded, "No. No. No. It was almost . . . starting all over again. I may have met people and not known it. But what I was conscious of was like, 'This was it,' what we were doing was it."[49] What they were doing was not "it," of course; but in the consciousness of those who would form the Young Lords, direct influences were more likely to arise out of their immediate socioeconomic conditions and exemplars of radicalism in adjacent and affiliated communities. Nonetheless, prior generations of activists generated conditions of possibility that are important to understanding the Young Lords' own emergence.

By all accounts, the post–World War II years saw a great migration of Puerto Ricans from the island to established cultural centers in New York City; but the U.S. mainland proved to be anything but the "land of opportunity" of which many in the Puerto Rican diaspora dreamed. By most estimates, Puerto Ricans were worse off economically than any other national minority or ethnic group in New York. According to Clara Rodríguez, between 1950 and 1970, Puerto Ricans were inferior to white or black people in terms of employment, occupying a disproportionately high number of blue-collar positions and taking home the least pay.[50] Throughout this period, such economic hardships served as the impetus for various forums for community organization and empowerment. Longtime community activist Antonia Pantoja identified this as a "legacy of political effectiveness" and further singled out the different ways in which Puerto Ricans formed and retained a "community consciousness" in New York through the development of numerous community organizations.[51]

In the Nuyorican diasporic context, two developments deserve particular attention. First, as Pantoja suggests, Puerto Ricans in New York have a fairly lengthy history of community political involvement. Initially, there came *los pioneros*—"the pioneers," who were the first generation of Puerto Rican political participation from the turn of the twentieth century through the 1940s—who formed what Virginia E. Sánchez Korrol calls *colonias*, "geographic, urban centers marked by dense settlement; they provided outlets for Puerto Rican interests, creating institutions which affirmed social identity and fostered internal activities while coping with problems stemming from contacts with the host society."[52] It is within these colonias that Puerto Rican migrants further mobilized and formed trade labor groups, cultural collectives, and political organizations that served to identify and unite the diaspora and fight for specific goals like health, education, and employment equity. According to Roberto Rodriguez-Morazzani, these community organizations operated in "the tradition established by European immigrants . . . [to] provide the different mechanisms of support and forge the spaces necessary in order to strive in an oppressive and hostile environment."[53] In addition to the specifically Puerto Rican organizations, early migrants participated in other "Hispanic" groups and broader based political organizations like the Democratic, Republican, and Communist and other leftist political parties.[54] Unfortunately, the pioneros, "while important for providing political, social and cultural cohesion, were not organizations capable of adequately providing direct social service delivery to an increasingly impoverished community."[55] The Young Lords, eventually cognizant of these earlier groups, (mis)characterized them principally as "social clubs" and "mostly all democratic," speaking to liberal principals of inclusion but not to significant currents of social transformation.[56] This perceived failure on the part of the pioneros created a vacuum to be filled by a new generation of leaders.

During the McCarthy era in the 1950s, "the early left-wing Puerto Rican organizations had ceased to exist, and therefore, there was no radical opposition to the neo-colonial mainland elite who exercised political hegemony in the community, or alternative political outlook with which the emergent leadership would be confronted."[57] Founded in the 1950s and 1960s, Puerto Rican social service agencies originated with a group of young, college-educated, second-generation, U.S.-born Puerto Ricans. These young leaders, known in scholarly literatures as the "young turks," challenged the existent leadership of the pioneros because the latter were too focused on island politics.[58] The young turks, conversely, were guided by an optimistic philosophical liberalism that was fundamentally reformist in character. They became "'resident' critics of monopoly capitalism, criticizing its more brutal aspects, but never questioning the underlying assumptions of capitalism." They "thought that the interests of Puerto Ricans could be served within the existent structural arrangements of liberal capitalism and could themselves serve as instruments of reform through their activities."[59]

While some of the pioneros tended to be more radical/leftist in their views, the young turks were thoroughly embedded in a philosophy of liberalism, limiting them primarily to reformist activities.[60] The young turks were guided, furthermore, by a "uniquely North American notion of individualism," which ran counter to previously collectivist or communitarian models of leadership and community development among the Puerto Rican diaspora. The result was a professionalization of social, cultural, and political groups, which privileged the voices of experts and paid employees rather than the community collectively.[61] This tendency was exacerbated further by the second development to which one ought to be attentive: the failure of 1960s Great Society reforms in El Barrio. According to Carlos Rodriguez-Fraticelli and Amilcar

Tirado, the influx of antipoverty funds was a promising development that should have solved some of the economic problems in El Barrio, but ultimately, "the socio-economic conditions of minorities changed little."[62]

The widespread frustration with socioeconomic conditions in El Barrio and throughout urban communities of color, especially when combined with racist constructions of black and Latin@ people, heightened political tensions and "paved the way for the resurgence of radical movements, which rejected liberal reformist solutions."[63] Such radicalism became anchored in the development of racialized enclaves within cities nationwide. "Throughout the 1950s and 1960s," Joseph Boskin argues, "television portrayed the city as a violent, unhealthy, dirty, corrupt, lonely, unseemly place for people to live, develop, and grow."[64] White flight led to a boom of suburban development and further marginalization and vilification of city life. "By the 1960s," Boskin continues, "all major and most smaller cities had sizable numbers of various ethnic groups in the downtown areas, living in slum ghettos, breathing the increasingly foul urban air, and becoming increasingly alienated. They gradually developed an urban consciousness—a consciousness of the entrapped underclass."[65] In New York and across the nation, feelings of hopelessness peaked in the form of riots in the mid-1960s that "directed attention to the anguished plights of millions of Negros, Puerto Ricans, and Mexican-Americans living in the urban centers of the country."[66]

While much scholarly attention has focused on the relevance of riots as both evidence of and influence in the radicalization of black communities, they were immensely important in the cultivation and emergence of radical consciousness in Puerto Rican communities as well. Wagenheim, for example, points to the significance of "Puerto Rican riots" in New York beginning in 1966, as an expression of "frustration."[67] The Young Lords themselves, however, pointed to the territorial and political importance of riots: "For example, in '65, the time of the East Harlem riots, we held East Harlem for two days. We had the roof-tops, the streets and the community—no pigs could go through."[68] Unfortunately, in the Puerto Rican community, such rioting ushered in reformist solutions. "To end it," observed Young Lords Minister of Information Pablo Guzmán, "they shipped in anti-poverty. They brought it in full-force, and they bought out a lot of the young cats who were leading the rebellions."[69] Therefore, argues Luis Aponte-Parés, "While Puerto Ricans were knitting a community in the ghetto, slum clearance and urban renewal were unweaving the work of a generation: the deterritorialization of a whole community."[70] In black communities, however, "militant groups fashioned a framework of sociopolitical objectives essentially absent in the earlier period of protest"[71] and, Singh adds, framed the riots as "revolts or uprisings," which transformed them into a "rallying point for a black power imaginary" that helped solidify and extend the era of Black Power activism.[72]

Black Power, Lorrin Thomas argues, was not the sole "progenitor of radical politics in the United States, a singular force in the radicalization of other identity-based activist groups—Chicanos, Asian Americans, Puerto Ricans, feminists, gay liberationists"—as many dominant narratives would have it;[73] however, it was still a significant influence on the Young Lords because it was the most readily available and visible form of radical activism within their community. They learned of the original Chicago chapter of the Young Lords, for example, by reading an interview of their leader in the Black Panthers' newspaper.[74] The Students for a Democratic Society (SDS), the Student Non-violence Coordinating Committee (SNCC), and the mainstream civil rights movement surely helped set a leftist, activist tenor in the national political arena and, in the case of SDS, locally in New York; however, it was the radicalism and nationalism of groups like the Black Panther Party that encouraged most immediately the choices that the New York Young Lords would make.[75] Writing about the origins of the organization, Guzmán pointed to the Black Panthers as the only initial "model we had to go on in this country," even as they were influenced further by "Che, Fidel, Fanon, Marx, Lenin, Jefferson, the Bill of Rights, Declaration, [and] Constitution."[76] Although Guzmán certainly speaks to the broad, heterogeneous traditions within which the Young Lords operated, Black Power was the most important antecedent.

On the significance of the history of black radicalism generally and black nationalism in particular, Guzmán recounted his early education in the politics of race. "So early in my life I learned about this country's history," Guzmán wrote. "I was further influenced by reading the stories of Nat Turner, Harriet Tubman, and Fredrick Douglass, by learning of W.E.B. DuBois and Marcus Garvey, by studying the life and works of Malcolm X and the southern civil rights movement, of Stokely Carmichael, H. Rap Brown, and the Black Panther Party."[77] Similarly, Denise Oliver (who would become a member of the Young Lords' Central Committee) had the experience of being a roommate with various Black Power advocates while a student at Howard University in the 1960s. She also came of age politically in Harlem, working at the Truth Café and literally having her life saved by Malcolm X.[78] These interactions with black radicals were not isolated cases; rather, they were constitutive of the political consciousness of radical Puerto Ricans like the Young Lords.[79] So significant were they, posits Rodriguez-Morazzani, that the legacy of Malcolm X came to occupy a place equal to Albizu Campos in the radical Puerto Rican imaginary.[80] The assassination of Malcolm X, in particular, was a pivotal moment because it served the dual purpose of radicalizing further African Americans and exposing the continued severity of racism. Furthermore, posits Rodriguez-Morazzani, "Exposure to the African American political and literary culture led many Puerto Rican youth to seek out resources for the exploration of their own identity."[81] For example, the first biographical sketch published in the Young Lords' newspaper, *Palante*, was not of another Latino; rather, it was a brief essay on Malcolm X that tied his radicalism to theirs.[82]

Also influential in the Young Lords' intellectual development, along with the Panthers and other Black Power advocates, were the writings of psychologist and decolonial activist Frantz Fanon. Fanon was one of the most central voices in the global struggle for decolonization, and as Singh argues, his *The Wretched of the Earth* (published in French in 1961 and translated into English in 1963) was "the most important theoretical influence on . . . late 1960s radicals" like the Black Panthers, the Revolutionary Action Movement (RAM), and the Young Lords.[83] Fanon's significance resides in his uncompromising critique of racist, colonialist dehumanization and forceful calls for radical systemic and (inter)personal change. "As Frantz Fanon—the most perceptive and articulate writer speaking for the colonized, not the colonialists—has pointed out," observed Puerto Rican scholar Manuel Maldonado-Denis in 1969, "colonialism creates in the minds of colonial peoples a sense of inferiority, a feeling of impotence and self-destruction, a desire to negate themselves by becoming more like the colonialists."[84] From Fanon, the Black Panthers, Young Lords, and others would cull attentiveness to the lumpenproletariat (in Fanon's words, "that horde of starving men, uprooted from their tribe and from their clan, constitutes one of the most spontaneous and the most radically revolutionary forces of a colonized people")[85] and what Singh calls "a sharply dialectical view, in which race and nation—as manifestations of the particular and universal—could only be harmonized through an agonistic transvaluation of the local and global hierarchies in which they were embedded."[86] As we will see in the next chapter, such a dialectical view worked itself into the Young Lords' formulation of revolutionary nationalism and attendant critique of coloniality.

The Origins and Actions of the New York Young Lords

Born of this complex history, the New York Young Lords were formed by a multitude of young men and women with varied interests and experiences. People who were drawn to the Young Lords came from diverse backgrounds: some were students with experience in late 1960s radicalism; others had been community activists in New York City; still others had little political experience outside their homes and/or jobs. The organization attracted individuals with varying levels of experience and political consciousness. This is one of the practical reasons the Young Lords featured political education as a core activity of the group in which all members and "friends of the Lords" (trainees) were expected to participate. But despite such disparate experiences and backgrounds, the young people who would become founders and members of the organization shared some commonalities. They were influenced by and drew inspiration from social justice activism and freedom struggles of the 1960s, especially the civil rights movement, Black Power, Students for a Democratic Society, and other New Left organizations. They were inspired by the later King (whose voice on economic justice became more radical) and by Malcolm X. And they were impressed by other peoples' struggles against the colonial matrix of power occurring worldwide. Carlos "Carlito" Rovira, an early member of the organization, recalls, "There was a sense of empowerment in the movements of the oppressed."[87]

The activism of the time and the growing sense of racial and economic inequality compelled these young people to seek avenues for social change. Some began by helping their families negotiate racist social service organizations. Others got involved in organizing community members around welfare rights and other aspects of antipoverty activism. Others joined groups like the United Bronx Parents Youth Leadership Program and the Real Great Society. Still others sought ways to cultivate a sense of Puerto Rican and Latin@ historical and racial consciousness. While there were multiple paths to activism for these young Puerto Ricans, it seems that one of the defining moments for all of them was the birth of an awareness (reached in different ways and contexts) that they needed to begin organizing to address the unique situations they faced as Puerto Ricans in New York.

Guzmán, one of the founding leaders of the New York Young Lords, has reflected on his own consciousness shift and reorientation to Puerto Rican activism. "To be 'Puerto Rican' or 'Latino' before 1969 in New York, for those of us raised there and not recent immigrants from the islands, was not clearly understood. Or appreciated yet. . . . My entire life experience, then, pointed towards me joining the Black Panther Party."[88] Guzmán's experience was not, in some regards, unique; others with whom I have conversed shared similar experiences of looking to the Black Panthers for leadership and attending their rallies because the Panthers were the closest fit for them racially and ideologically. Ultimately, although the Young Lords would be allied closely with the Black Panthers, many young Puerto Ricans felt out of place within the Panthers and sought other outlets and models for political involvement.

Luis Garden Acosta, who joined the Young Lords cadre at the end of 1969, shared with me a similar story, but from a different angle. He recalled some of his activist work in the mid-1960s, which included helping to create the National Welfare Rights Organization and antiwar activism with the Catholic Worker Movement. Garden Acosta grew dissatisfied with the whiteness of these organizations and felt an increasingly strong need to engage Puerto Rican social justice issues. He recounted to me, "I tried to go to La Misión Vito Marcantonio, which was a mission of the MPI here. Now, that's how they looked upon us here—Puerto Ricans born and raised here—as a place where they could come and create a *mission* to support the 'real deal,' which was the independence of Puerto Rico . . . not to deal with the self-determination of Puerto Ricans here."[89]

Garden Acosta felt uncomfortable at La Misión and with the MPI, which was an island-based organization, because they did not address his needs and experiences as a second-generation Puerto Rican in New York—one who could not speak Spanish fluently and who came from a working-class background that contrasted with the more upper-class roots of the MPI members.

Faced with insufficient alternatives, young Puerto Ricans in New York who would eventually form the Young Lords began meeting in several different configurations.[90] The first grouping, from which several early leaders of the organization emerged, was La Sociedad de Albizu Campos (SAC). SAC formed and eventually took its name (though it is unclear when precisely) when a group of mostly Puerto Rican college students began meeting in January 1969 at the State University of New York at Old Westbury, "because they felt something had to be done to connect them with the people they had left behind in the ghetto."[91] Reading about and discussing issues of Puerto Rican race, class, nation, history, politics, and revolution, this group struggled with this new knowledge that had been denied many of them. After some time, the group began meeting in El Barrio, sometimes in the offices of the Real Great Society (more on them below) and other times in Oliver's apartment (she was another Old Westbury student), and included regular members Mickey Melendez (who was a principal organizer of SAC), David Perez (an Old Westbury student from Chicago), Juan Gonzalez (a Columbia student with community organizing experience and ties to SDS), and Felipe Luciano (an activist and member of the original Last Poets). Guzmán, who was a student at Old Westbury, joined the now-named SAC in May 1969, after returning from an immersive educational trip to the Centro Intercultural de Documentación in Cuernavaca, Mexico—a research center founded and run by Ivan Illich, a radical priest and critic of Third World developmentalism.[92]

Contemporaneous to SAC, three other groups central to the Young Lords' beginnings were meeting in El Barrio and the Lower East Side of Manhattan. First, the Real Great Society (RGS; which originated as an antipoverty organization in the Lower East Side in 1964) established an East Harlem branch under the leadership of Angelo "Papo" Giordani in 1967.[93] Joining forces with the Urban Planning Studio (UPS) in early June 1969, RGS/UPS combined youth activists and urban planners who diagnosed El Barrio as "an underdeveloped country" that was "awakening in its rights and abilities for self control and self determination"; and they believed the "balance of power [was beginning] to shift towards the people."[94] RGS provided space to SAC for meetings but also engaged in activism in their own right, such as garbage protests that would later be an unacknowledged model for the Young Lords.[95] Second, and also in contact with RGS, there was a group of New Left activists in the Lower East Side under the leadership of José Martinez. Martinez and others had attended the March 1969 National Youth and Liberation Conference in Denver and the May 1969 SDS meeting in Chicago.[96] There they met Jose "Cha

Cha" Jiménez, leader of the Chicago-based Young Lords Organization, and returned to New York on an unsanctioned mission to organize Young Lords.[97] Martinez's group linked up with RGS when they learned of their garbage activism in June 1969. Third, there was a youth photography workshop, led by Hiram Maristany, which was based in El Barrio. Recalls Guzmán, "Hiram's guys were also different from the other two groups in that they were *of* the barrio and destined to *remain* in the barrio, whereas guys like me had either punched a ticket to college or the service *out* of the barrio, or else weren't from the barrio at all."[98] While all of these groups had varying levels of contact with one another, SAC took a leadership role in chartering a Young Lords chapter in East Harlem.

In early June 1969, members of SAC began talking about ways to move from consciousness raising within the group to action out in the community. According to one member of SAC and an early Young Lords cadre, "We didn't have a system, a function. Nobody was a boss. Nobody was a leader. We were just a group of people trying to do something for the community we lived in."[99] Soon, when perusing the June 7 issue of *The Black Panther*, they found a model for their activism in the Young Lords Organization, a street gang "turned political" in Chicago.[100] José "Cha Cha" Jiménez had been in the Young Lords gang since 1959, when it emerged in response to manifold forms of abuse Puerto Ricans faced from white neighborhood gangs. Spending time in and out of jail, Jiménez again found himself incarcerated in 1968. While in the Cook County Jail on drug charges, Jiménez befriended a Black Muslim librarian and began reading widely. Central to his emergent consciousness were the works of Martin Luther King Jr., Malcolm X, and the American Catholic Thomas Merton, from whose *Seven Storey Mountain* Jiménez drew a vocabulary for conversion.[101] "When Cha Cha got out of jail," recounted Iris Morales, "he returned to his neighborhood and organized the Young Lords to protest the city's urban renewal plans that would have uprooted the Puerto Rican/Latino community."[102] In the fall of 1968, Jiménez transformed the gang into the Young Lords Organization, which operated in coalition with the Black Panthers and Young Patriot Organization (a radical white group) under the banner of the original Rainbow Coalition.

Resolved to follow the Young Lords' lead, members of SAC first sought to unify the groups in New York. The precise ways in which this unfolded are unclear. In their official narrative, the New York Young Lords claimed that Martinez's Lower East Side group merged with those who had led the garbage activism in El Barrio, but accounts from RGS members (who originated that activism) would cast doubt on this claim.[103] Perhaps specific people who had been involved in the garbage protests joined forces with Martinez's group, but RGS remained active and independent. Furthermore, there is little evidence that Martinez himself joined the Young Lords, but others from the Lower East Side group most definitely did. Regardless of the precise mechanisms by which it was accomplished, SAC, Maristany's group, and the Lower East Side group joined forces as a unified organization to be based out of a reappropriated East Harlem storefront, between 111th and 112th Streets on Madison Avenue.

Shortly thereafter, Guzmán, Perez, and one other person hopped in Mickey Melendez's Volkswagen Beetle and made their way to Chicago to meet with Jiménez and formally request a charter for a New York chapter of the Young Lords Organization.[104] Jiménez granted the charter and was flown out to New York to meet with the nascent organization, which initially functioned under the leadership of Diego Pabón as deputy chairman.[105] Guzmán recalls Jiménez instructing them, "Our people in the community are going to join us only through *observation* and *participation*. We can preach 'till we're blue in the face. But at some point, they're only going to understand after they see us throw down and after we move them to throw down themselves."[106] On July 26, 1969, the New York chapter of the Young Lords Organization announced itself to the world at a Tompkins Square Park rally organized, according to Agustín Laó, "in solidarity with the attack on the Moncada Barracks by Cuban rebels in 1953." There, Felipe Luciano (now the deputy chairman of the organization) started "'rapping' on the 'need for more revolutionary action' and performing his poem 'Jíbaro, My Pretty Nigger,' accompanied by Conga sounds, as well as by Black Panthers, Newsreel, and Youth Against War and Fascism."[107] Within twenty-four hours, they shut down the streets of El Barrio with their first major political offensive.

Phase One: Young Lords Organization (YLO)

The Young Lords in New York functioned, in their first phase of development, as a chapter of the national organization based in Chicago. In the beginning, the Young Lords were filled with revolutionary desires—they wanted nothing short of a different world, an almost utopian world in which their people (and all "the people") could coexist peacefully and equally. The older members of the group (the ones who had some college education and had founded SAC before the Lords) were especially well read. "Toiling at our studies," recounts Melendez, "we developed a good sense of what the people needed and how to proceed in order to succeed in political struggles . . . or so we thought."[108] They were academic revolutionaries at the beginning: well read with little practical experience.[109] Quickly, however, the Young Lords learned that these different theoretical perspectives offered little solace to the (poor and often uneducated) people in El Barrio, as most people simply did not see the relevance of such theories in practice. Therefore, following Jiménez's leadership, the YLO sought to better connect ideas to action in their community. The activists decided they would have to go to the people to figure out what they needed if it was not revolution.

Such community-based organizing and outreach led the YLO to launch their garbage offensive, which is the subject of Chapter 4. Their first "offensive" (the name they gave to significant instances of direct action), the garbage offensive, emerged in mid-July 1969, as they were structurally cementing themselves as the new YLO chapter in New York. Modeled after the RGS's garbage activism in 1968 and 1969 but emerging directly from community demands, they began initially by cleaning the streets each Sunday. On July 27, one day after officially becoming the New York chapter of the Young Lords Organization and two weeks after starting to clean the streets, the first point of social discord surfaced when some members attempted unsuccessfully to procure new supplies (brooms, cans, etc.) from the local sanitation department. It was at this point that the YLO came face to face with the bureaucracy of the liberal capitalist system and subsequently advanced a revolt in El Barrio. The YLO, together with a variety of community members who had been helping them pick up garbage, took heaped trash collections and placed them in several busy intersections, blocking significantly the traffic coming into and going out of Manhattan. The tactical placement of garbage peaked on August 17 when hundreds of Barrio Boricuas expanded their rebellion to include overturning cars, lighting fire to the trash, and damaging police property. The Sunday garbage offensives continued until September 2, with Young Lords and other community members engaged actively in dissent.

By September, the New York YLO, based out of their office on Madison Avenue in East Harlem, had taken on a clear organizational structure. The Central Staff, which answered to the YLO national office in Chicago, was composed of five people: Felipe Luciano, deputy chairman; David Perez, deputy minister of defense; Pablo "Yoruba" Guzmán, deputy minister of information; Juan Gonzalez, deputy minister of education; and Juan "Fi" Ortiz, deputy minister of finance. Emboldened by the successes of the garbage offensive, the YLO resolved to shift focus "from street fighting to programs which served our people and which would also build the organization's theoretical level."[110] Borrowing from the models offered by the YLO in Chicago and the Black Panthers nationwide, the New York YLO addressed change at the local level in their immediate community through "serve the people" programs.[111] Such programs included a free breakfast program (modeled after the Black Panthers' successful nationwide program) and a lead poisoning detection program that enlisted the help of medical students who went door to door in Puerto Rican neighborhoods to test children for lead poisoning.[112] They also started the process of organizing hospital workers (something that would result in the formation of the closely allied Health Revolutionary Unity Movement [HRUM]), supporting the struggles of mothers on welfare, and educating members and supporters about the revolutionary struggles of others worldwide (eventually, they would develop different, detailed curricula for "friends of the Lords," cadre, and members of Central Staff).

In October 1969, the New York YLO wrote the first version of its "13 Point Program and Platform" (see Figure 1.2); in November 1970, the Young Lords revised the document (see Figure 1.3). Following the lead of the Black Panthers, who had their own "platform and program" consisting of ten points, the

13 POINT PROGRAM AND PLATFORM
YOUNG LORDS ORGANIZATION
OCTOBER 1969

THE YOUNG LORDS ORGANIZATION IS A REVOLUTIONARY
POLITICAL PARTY FIGHTING FOR THE LIBERATION OF ALL
OPPRESSED PEOPLE

1. WE WANT SELF-DETERMINATION FOR PUERTO RICANS—LIBERATION ON THE ISLAND AND INSIDE THE UNITED STATES

For 500 years, first spain and then the united states have colonized our country. Billions of dollars in profits leave our country for the united states every year. In every way we are slaves of the gringo. We want liberation and the Power in the hands of the People, not Puerto Rican exploiters.
QUE VIVA PUERTO RICO LIBRE!

2. WE WANT SELF-DETERMINATION FOR ALL LATINOS

Our Latin Brothers and Sisters, inside and outside the united states, are oppressed by amerikkkan business. The Chicano people built the Southwest, and we support their right to control their lives and their land. The people of Santo Domingo continue to fight against gringo domination and its puppet generals. The armed liberation stuggles in Latin America are part of the same war of Latinos against imperialism.
QUE VIVA LA RAZA!

3. WE WANT LIBERATION OF ALL THIRD WORLD PEOPLE

Just as Latins first slaved under spain and then the yanquis, Black people, Indians, and Asians slaved to build the wealth of this country. For 400 years they have fought for freedom and dignity against racist Babylon (decadent empire). Third World people have led the fight for freedom. All the colored and oppressed peoples of the world are one nation under oppression.
NO PUERTO RICAN IS FREE UNTIL ALL PEOPLE ARE FREE!

4. WE ARE REVOLUTIONARY NATIONALISTS AND OPPOSE RACISM

The Latin, Black, Indian and Asian people inside the u.s. are colonies fighting for liberation. We know that washington, wall street, and city hall will try to make our nationalism into racism; but Puerto Ricans are of all colors and we resist racism. Millions of poor white people are rising up to demand freedom and we support them. These are the ones in the u.s. that are stepped on by the rulers and the government. We each organize our people, but our fights are the same against oppression and we will defeat it together.
POWER TO ALL OPPRESSED PEOPLE!

5. WE WANT COMMUNITY CONTROL OF OUR INSTITUTIONS AND LAND

We want control of our communities by our people and programs to guarantee that all institutions serve the needs of our people. People's control of police, health services, churches, schools, housing, transportation and welfare are needed. We want an end to attacks on our land by urban removal, highway destruction, universities and corporations.
LAND BELONGS TO ALL THE PEOPLE!

6. WE WANT A TRUE EDUCATION OF OUR CREOLE CULTURE AND SPANISH LANGUAGE

We must learn our history of fighting against cultural, as well as economic genocide by the yanqui. Revolutionary culture, culture of our people, is the only true teaching.
LONG LIVE BORICUA!   LONG LIVE EL JIBARO!

7. WE OPPOSE CAPITALISTS AND ALLIANCES WITH TRAITORS

Puerto Rican rulers, or puppets of the oppressor, do not help our people. They are paid by the system to lead our people down blind alleys, just like the thousands of poverty pimps who keep our communities peaceful for business, or the street workers who keep gangs divided and blowing each other away. We want a society where the people socialistically control their labor.
VENCEREMOS!

8. WE OPPOSE THE AMERIKKKAN MILITARY

We demand immediate withdrawal of us military forces and bases from Puerto Rico, Vietnam, and all oppressed communities inside and outside the us. No Puerto Rican should serve in the u.s. army against his Brothers and Sisters, for the only true army of oppressed people is the people's army to fight all rulers.
U.S. OUT OF VIETNAM, FREE PUERTO RICO!

9. WE WANT FREEDOM FOR ALL POLITICAL PRISONERS

We want all Puerto Ricans freed because they have been tried by the racist courts of the colonizers, and not by their own people and peers. We want all freedom fighters released from jail.
FREE ALL POLITICAL PRISONERS!

10. WE WANT EQUALITY FOR WOMEN. MACHISMO MUST BE REVOLUTIONARY...NOT OPPRESSIVE

Under capitalism, our people have been oppressed by both the society and our own men. The doctrine of machismo has been used by our men to take out their frustrations against their wives, sisters, mothers, and children. Our men must support their women in their fight for economic and social equality, and must recognize that our women are equals in every way within the revolutionary ranks.
FORWARD, SISTERS, IN THE STRUGGLE!

11. WE FIGHT ANTI-COMMUNISM WITH INTERNATIONAL

Anyone who resists injustice is called a communist by "the man" and condemned. Our people are brainwashed by television, radio, newspapers, schools, and books to oppose people in other countries fighting for their freedom. No longer will our people believe attacks and slanders, because they have learned who the real enemy is and who their real friends are. We will defend our Brothers and Sisters around the world who fight for justice against the rich rulers of this country.
VIVA CHE!

12. WE BELIEVE ARMED SELF-DEFENSE AND ARMED STRUGGLE ARE THE ONLY MEANS TO LIBERATION

We are opposed to violence—the violence of hungry children, illiterate adults, diseased old people, and the violence of poverty and profit. We have asked, petitioned, gone to courts, demonstrated peacefully, and voted for politicians full of empty promises. But we still ain't free. The time has come to defend the lives of our people against repression and for revolutionary war against the businessman, politician, and police. When a government oppresses our people, we have the right to abolish it and create a new one.
BORICUA IS AWAKE!   ALL PIGS BEWARE!

13. WE WANT A SOCIALIST SOCIETY

We want liberation, clothing, free food, education, health care, transportation, utilities, and employment for all. We want a society where the needs of our people come first, and where we give solidarity and aid to the peoples of the world, not oppression and racism.
HASTA LA VICTORIA SIEMPRE!

Figure 1.2   Original "Young Lords Party 13 Point Program and Platform," October 1969, as published in *Palante*.

YOUNG LORDS PARTY

TENGO PUERTO RICO EN MI CORAZON

13 POINT PROGRAM

AND PLATFORM

YLP

THE YOUNG LORDS PARTY IS A REVOLUTIONARY POLITICAL PARTY FIGHTING FOR THE LIBERATION OF ALL OPPRESSED PEOPLE

1. WE WANT SELF-DETERMINATION FOR PUERTO RICANS, LIBERATION ON THE ISLAND AND INSIDE THE UNITED STATES.

For 500 years, first spain and then the united states have colonized our country. Billions of dollars in profits leave our country for the united states every year. In every way we are slaves of the gringo. We want liberation and the Power in the hands of the People, not Puerto Rican exploiters. QUE VIVA PUERTO RICO LIBRE!

2. WE WANT SELF-DETERMINATION FOR ALL LATINOS.

Our Latin Brothers and Sisters, inside and outside the united states, are oppressed by amerikkkan business. The Chicano people built the Southwest, and we support their right to control their lives and their land. The people of Santo Domingo continue to fight against gringo domination and its puppet generals. The armed liberation struggles in Latin America are part of the war of Latinos against imperialism. QUE VIVA LA RAZA!

3. WE WANT LIBERATION OF ALL THIRD WORLD PEOPLE.

Just as Latins first slaved under spain and the yanquis, Black people, Indians, and Asians slaved to build the wealth of this country. For 400 years they have fought for freedom and dignity against racist Babylon. Third World people have led the fight for freedom. All the colored and oppressed peoples of the world are one nation under oppression. NO PUERTO RICAN IS FREE UNTIL ALL PEOPLE ARE FREE!

4. WE ARE REVOLUTIONARY NATIONALISTS AND OPPOSE RACISM.

The Latin, Black, Indian and Asian people inside the u.s. are colonies fighting for liberation. We know that washington, wall street, and city hall will try to make our nationalism into racism; but Puerto Ricans are of all colors and we resist racism. Millions of poor white people are rising up to demand freedom and we support them. These are the ones in the u.s. that are, stepped on by the rulers and the government. We each organize our people, but our fights are the same against oppression and we will defeat it together. POWER TO ALL OPPRESSED PEOPLE!

5. WE WANT EQUALITY FOR WOMEN. DOWN WITH MACHISMO AND MALE CHAUVANISM.

Under capitalism, women have been oppressed by both society and our men. The doctrine of machismo has been used by men to take out their frustrations on wives, sisters, mothers, and children. Men must fight along with sisters in the struggle for economic and social equality and must recognize that sisters make up over half of the revolutionary army; sisters and brothers are equals fighting for our people. FORWARD SISTERS IN THE STRUGGLE!

6. WE WANT COMMUNITY CONTROL OF OUR INSTITUTIONS AND LAND.

We want control of our communities by our people and programs to guarantee that all institutions serve the needs of our people. People's control of police, health services, churches, schools, housing, transportation and welfare are needed. We want an end to attacks on our land by urban renewal, highway destruction, and university corporations. LAND BELONGS TO ALL THE PEOPLE!

7. WE WANT A TRUE EDUCATION OF OUR AFRO-INDIO CULTURE AND SPANISH LANGUAGE.

We must learn our long history of fighting against cultural, as well as economic genocide by the spaniards and now the yanquis. Revolutionary culture, culture of our people, is the only true teaching. JIBARO SI, YANQUI NO!

8. WE OPPOSE CAPITALISTS AND ALLIANCES WITH TRAITORS.

Puerto Rican rulers, or puppets of the oppressor, do not help our people. They are paid by the system to lead our people down blind alleys, just like the thousands of poverty pimps who keep our communities peaceful for business, or the street workers who keep gangs divided and blowing each other away. We want a society where the people socialistically control their labor. VENCEREMOS!

9. WE OPPOSE THE AMERIKKKAN MILITARY.

We demand immediate withdrawal of all u.s. military forces and bases from Puerto Rico, VietNam, and all oppressed communities inside and outside the u.s.. No Puerto Rican should serve in the u.s. army against his Brothers and Sisters, for the only true army of oppressed people is the People's Liberation Army to fight all rulers. U.S. OUT OF VIETNAM, FREE PUERTO RICO NOW!

10. WE WANT FREEDOM FOR ALL POLITICAL PRISONERS AND PRISONERS OF WAR.

No Puerto Rican should be in jail or prison, first because we are a nation, and amerikkka has no claims on us; second, because we have not been tried by our own people (peers). We also want all freedom fighters out of jail, since they are prisoners of the war for liberation. FREE ALL POLITICAL PRISONERS AND PRISONERS OF WAR!

11. WE ARE INTERNATIONALISTS.

Our people are brainwashed by television, radio, newspapers, schools and books to oppose people in other countries fighting for their freedom. No longer will we believe these lies, because we have learned who the real enemy is and who our real friends are. We will defend our sisters and brothers around the world who fight for justice and are against the rulers of this country. QUE VIVA CHE GUEVARA!

12. WE BELIEVE ARMED SELF-DEFENSE AND ARMED STRUGGLE ARE THE ONLY MEANS TO LIBERATION.

We are opposed to violence - the violence of hungry children, illiterate adults, diseased old people, and the violence of poverty and profit. We have asked, petitioned, gone to courts, demonstrated peacefully, and voted for politicians full of empty promises. But we still ain't free. The time has come to defend the lives of our people against repression and for revolutionary war against the businessmen, politicians, and police. When a government oppresses the people, we have the right to abolish it and create a new one. ARM OURSELVES TO DEFEND OURSELVES!

13. WE WANT A SOCIALIST SOCIETY.

We want liberation, clothing, free food, education, health care, transportation, full employment and peace. We want a society where the needs of the people come first, and where we give solidarity and aid to the people of the world, not oppression and racism. HASTA LA VICTORIA SIEMPRE!

Figure 1.3 Revised "Young Lords Party 13-Point Program and Platform," November 1970, as published in *Palante*.

YLO's Program and Platform helped the group secure and clarify a direction and orientation for the organization, while also serving as a guideline for key talking points. Written as a collection of thirteen programmatic points, each coupled with longer explanations and accompanying exclamatory slogans, the Program and Platform helped guide their community service and activism. As is evident from photographs of the New York YLO, the Program and Platform also served as a concrete link between their actions and their ideology; for example, one photograph by Michael Abramson shows a sign that reads "#13 We Want a Socialist Society" next to another sign reading "Free Clothes for Our People" at a clothing drive in July 1970.[113] Also in October, the YLO created the thirty-point "Rules of Discipline of the Young Lords Organization" (revised in December 1970), which began with the reminder "You are a Young Lord 25 hours a day" and prohibited members from committing "crimes against the people" or gossiping and required that they memorize and understand the Program and Platform (see Figure 1.4).[114] Although the rules of discipline included a prohibition on drug use (point 4), this seemed directed more at hard drugs (like heroin, which they actively campaigned against) and not marijuana, use of which was commonplace amongst many radicals of the era. Both documents would eventually be published in nearly every issue of their biweekly newspaper, *Palante*, once production moved to New York.[115]

October 1969 also brought two other significant changes to the organization. First, the New York chapter expanded operations to Newark, which also had a large Puerto Rican population. With this expansion, the national Young Lords Organization began recognizing the New York chapter as the head of the "East Coast Region" of the YLO. The second major change was their reentry into direct action through the "church offensive" (their second major offensive, which is the focus of Chapter 5). The church offensive targeted the First Spanish Methodist Church, which was chosen, argued Guzmán, "because it was right smack dead in the center of the Barrio. It's a beautiful location right in the middle of the community. It was also chosen because it is the one church . . . that has consistently closed itself up to the community."[116] Over the course of several weeks, the YLO sought unsuccessfully to negotiate use of the space for their breakfast program as well as community health and education needs. Appealing directly to the parishioners on Sunday, December 7, police and YLO members clashed, resulting in several injuries and fourteen arrests. Three weeks later, on December 28, the YLO took control of the church, renamed it "the People's Church," and maintained control for eleven days. The People's Church became a site of community building, education, arts, and health. It came to a close on the morning of January 7, 1970, when 105 YLO and community members submitted peacefully to arrest.

In the aftermath of the church offensive, membership and community support boomed. According to the organization's own accounts, in the months

RULES OF DISCIPLINE OF THE YOUNG LORDS ORGANIZATION

Every member of the YOUNG LORDS ORGANIZATION must follow these rules. CENTRAL COMMITTEE members, CENTRAL and BRANCH STAFFS, including all captains, will enforce these rules.

Every member of the party must memorize these rules, and apply them daily. Any member found violating these rules is subject to suspension by the ORGANIZATION.

THE RULES ARE:

1. You are a YOUNG LORD 25 hours a day.
2. Any ORGANIZATION member busted on a jive tip which that member brought down on himself or others, can swim alone.
3. Any member found shooting drugs will be expelled.
4. No member may have any illegal drug in his or her possession or in their system while on duty. No one may get drunk on duty.
5. No member will violate rules relating to office work or general meetings of the ORGANIZATION ANYWHERE'
6. No one will point or fire a weapon of any kind unnecessarily or accidentally at anyone.
7. No member can join any army force other than the People's Army of Liberation.
8. No ORGANIZATION member will commit crimes against the people.
9. When arrested, YOUNG LORDS will give only name, address, and will sign nothing. Legal first aid must be under—stood by all members.
10. No member may speak in public unless authorized by the Central Committee or Central Staff.
11. The 13 Point Program must be memorized and the Platform must be understood by each member.
12. ORGANIZATION communications must be nation—al and local.
13. No member may speak about another member unless he or she is present.
14. All ORGANIZATION business is to be kept within the ORGANIZATION.
15. All contradictions between members must be re—solved at once.
16. Once a week all Chapters and Branches will conduct a criticism and self-criticism session.
17. All members will relate to Chain of Command. Officers will discipline officers, cadre, and so on. The O.D. is the final authority in the office.
18. Each person will submit a daily report of work to the O.D..
19. Each YOUNG LORD must learn to operate and service weapons correctly.
20. All Leadership personnel who expel a member, must submit this information, with photo, to the Editor of the newspaper, so that it will be published in the paper, and known by all Chapters and Branches.
21. Political Education classes are mandatory for general membership.
22. All members must read at least one political book a month, and at least two hours a day on contemporary matters.
23. Only assigned ORGANIZATION personnel should be in office each day. All others are to sell papers and do political work out in the community, including captains, section leaders, etc..
24. All Chapters must submit weekly report in writing to National Headquarters.
25. All Branches must implement First Aid/Medical Cadres.
26. All Chapters and Branches must submit a weekly finan—cial report to the Ministry of Finance.
27. No Chapter or Branch shall accept grants, poverty funds, money, or any aid from any government agency.
28. All Traitors, Provacateurs, and Agents will be subject to Revolutionary Justice.
29. At all times we keep a united front before all forms of the man. This is true not only among LORDS, but all Revolutionary Companeros.
30. All Chapters must adhere to the policy and ideology put forth by the Central Committee of the YLO. Likewise, all members will know all information published by the ORGANIZATION.

Figure 1.4   Original "Rules of Discipline of the Young Lords Organization," as published in *Palante*.

following the People's Church takeover, the YLO engaged in daily organizing programs and outreach in the community. In March, they began a community radio program on WBAI-FM, called *Palante*, which helped them reach an even wider audience. The radio program, however, did not come out of the blue. Starting with the garbage offensive and refined through the church offensive, the YLO proved to be incredibly media savvy and adept at garnering media attention. According to José Ramón Sánchez, the YLO was the focus of 40 percent of all *New York Times* reporting on Puerto Ricans during and immediately following the church offensive. From December 1969 to December 1970, the Young Lords were the focus of one-third of all *New York Times* reporting on Puerto Ricans. Importantly, Sánchez argues, the Young Lords "taught Puerto Ricans that the media had become not just a channel but also a major object of power. . . . They introduced the Puerto Rican community to the heights of what was possible. They placed the Puerto Rican community at center stage and pushed it to dance to the larger society's media-driven style."[117] Garnering public support from major figures like Jane Fonda and

THE YOUNG LORDS ARE HERE!

THE YOUNG LORDS ARE HERE AT LAST!

AFTER WAITING AS LONG AS POSSIBLE, UNTIL FINALLY PEOPLE
FROM THE SOUTH BRONX TRAVELED TO EL BARRIO TO TELL US THAT WE WERE
NEEDED, THE YOUNG LORDS ORGANIZATION (YLO) HAS OPENED UP A BRANCH OF THE
NEW YORK CHAPTER AT 949 LONGWOOD AVENUE, CORNER KELLY. WE WILL SERVICE
THE BRONX WHEREVER OUR PEOPLE ARE AT. WHERE ARE PEOPLE ARE, WE ARE.

THE YLO IS A REVOLUTIONARY POLITICAL PARTY THAT FIGHTS FOR
THE LIBERATION OF ALL OPPRESSED PEOPLE. YOU MAY OR MAY NOT KNOW IT, BUT
WE ARE ALL OPRESSED. WE ARE OPRESSED BECAUSE WE ARE PUERTO RICAN; WE ARE
OPRESSED BECAUSE WE ARE BLACK; WE ARE OPRESSED BECAUSE WE LIVE IN ROTTEN
HOUSING; WE ARE OPRESSED BECAUSE WE ARE HUNGRY. TO FIGHT THIS, THE YLO
TEACHES US HOW, TOGETHER, WE CAN BEAT THE SYSTEM AND KNOCK THE MAN DOWN.
THEN WE CAN BEGIN BUILDING A TRUE DEMOCRACY, A TRUE GOVERNMENT BY OUR
PEOPLE, FOR OUR PEOPLE, AND OF OUR PEOPLE.

TO DO THIS, WE HAVE CERTAIN PROGRAMS, SUCH AS THE 13-POINT
PROGRAM, FREE BREAKFAST PROGRAMS, LEAD POISONING PROGRAMS, AND
COMMUNITY EDUCATION PROGRAMS. IF YOU HAVE ANY IDEAS AS TO WHAT KIND OF
PROGRAMS YOU THINK ARE NEEDED, STOP BY THE OFFICE.

THE OFFICE WILL ALSO BE AN INTERNATIONAL LATIN INFORMATION
CENTER THAT WILL COLLECT INFORMATION FROM ALL AROUND THE WORLD AND SEND
IT OUT HERE, IN THE FORM OF A BRAND NEW COMMUNITY NEWSPAPER.

¡QUE VIVA EL SUR DE BRONX!   LIBERATE PUERTO RICONOW!

Figure 1.5   Flyer announcing the opening of the Bronx community office. (New York University Tamiment Library and Robert F. Wagner Labor Archives, Printed Ephemera Collection on Organizations, PE 036, box 115, folder Young Lords Party 2.)

Sammy Davis Jr. and from Puerto Rican musicians throughout the community, the YLO was "able to capture the public's attention and imagination to a degree that no Puerto Rican politician or leader has been able to do since then."[118] With membership growing, the YLO opened another branch in the Bronx in April (see Figure 1.5), where they located their information center and taught community education courses, in addition to other regular organizing and outreach.

May 1970 was a key period of transition and transformation for the organization. First, the New York YLO began full-scale publication of their newspaper, *Palante*. Oliver, in her new role as "communications secretary" (and eventually, in July, minister of finance), handled artwork and layout, while Guzmán claimed the role of editor and Gonzalez the role of production manager. The newspaper functioned as a news and propaganda service and, sold for 25 cents per issue, became the most important fund-raising device for the organization. According to Guzmán, "During our peak period of 1970–71, we were selling most of the 10,000 (occasionally 20,000) copies of each issue we were printing up every other week."[119] Second, the now-named "Central Committee" of the East Coast regional chapter went on a retreat that addressed two key issues. The committee decided, in principle, to address the issue of machismo within the organization. As I discuss further in Chapter 3, however, significant change did not come until July through September, when a grassroots movement within the organization led to substantial transformation. The committee also discussed relations with Chicago, which had become strained. By the end of the month, they reached a decision: they would split from the Chicago-based organization, change their name slightly, and take on the mantle of a new national party, the Young Lords Party (YLP). There were various reasons for the split, some having to do with differences of opinion and vision, others having to do with the New York group not feeling as though they were respected enough given the amount of work they were accomplishing (running the newspaper, leading a larger membership, etc.), still others related to the New York Young Lords believing Chicago had a hard time leaving their gang past behind, and yet others related to what the New York chapter felt was a need to have a truly national party.[120] Whatever the reasons, the Young Lords Party announced itself to the world with a new masthead on the cover of their June 5, 1970, issue of *Palante* (see Figure 1.6).

Phase Two: Young Lords Party (YLP)

Continuing various community programs (and, by this time, having branches throughout the Northeast, adding Philadelphia in August), the YLP adopted a more explicitly political structure that was better aligned with their stated goals. Specifically, the YLP developed "mass people's organization[s, which] involve[d] the Puerto Rican people wherever they [were] at any level of struggle."[121] There were five different organizations within the YLP during this stage. First, the Puerto Rican Workers Federation took the struggle into places of employment in an attempt to challenge and, eventually, overthrow capitalist economics. Second, the Lumpen Organization enlisted the class below the workers, including those in jail, drug users, and the unemployed, in the struggle.

Figure 1.6   Front cover of *Palante* 2, no. 4 (June 5, 1970), announcing the "Young Lords Party."

This wing of the YLP was largely responsible for the (in)famous Attica prison uprising.[122] Third, the Women's Union sought to organize women in the struggle and challenged misconceptions about gender, sex, and sexuality. Fourth, the Puerto Rican Student Union (PRSU) mobilized students in high schools and colleges. Finally, the Committee for the Defense of the Community dealt most directly with different community issues, such as health, land use, and breakfast programs. In all, according to Juan Gonzalez in a speech to Hawaiian students in November 1971, the YLP believed they were "trying to build a structure to involve our people in whatever level they wanted to involve themselves. . . . So, we see those people's organizations as the beginning, the seed of the people's self-government where the people train themselves to be involved in the revolutionary process and exercise their political power."[123]

During this phase of development (from May 1970 to July 1972), the YLP expanded operations, membership, and scope. In July 1970, the YLP worked in coalition with HRUM and the Think Lincoln Committee on their third offensive: the Lincoln Hospital offensive, which saw the takeover of the condemned Bronx hospital, with the goal of improved health care and working conditions.[124] In August 1970, Felipe Luciano was demoted to cadre (he would leave the organization two months later) for numerous reasons related to his leadership style and accusations of machismo. In September 1970, the YLP successfully integrated its cadre and leadership along gendered lines, started the process of revising their Program and Platform to explicitly reject sexism and machismo (a change that is first reflected in a November issue of *Palante*), and placed women in more leadership roles (e.g., the addition of Gloria Gonzalez as field marshal)—all of which will be discussed at length in Chapter 3. They also began recognizing and tackling heterosexism in the organization. September also saw Richie Perez (a former school teacher who joined the YLO during the church offensive) take over *Palante* newspaper production and the YLP's involvement in a conference for Puerto Rican students, organized principally by the PRSU, at Columbia University.

October 1970 brought more expansion of YLP programs and direct action. To begin, the YLP expanded its reach into prison populations and joined forces with the Inmates Liberation Front (ILF), which became an official section of the YLP in prisons. On October 15, the need for prison activism and transformation hit home when jailed Young Lord Julio Roldan was found hanged in his jail cell in the Tombs (the Manhattan House of Detention). Officials ruled it a suicide, but Young Lords were in disbelief.[125] "We knew we were being taken for a ride. Julio was a Young Lord, and we were not about useless, wasteful suicide. There had to be some action taken to provide an example for our people; a demonstration just wasn't going to make it."[126] Three days later, the YLP engaged in its fourth offensive, staking claim to the People's Church once again, at the completion of a 2,000-person funeral march that ended at the church; but this time, they did so with guns and established the Julio Roldan Memorial Defense Center. The YLP maintained control of the People's Church until peacefully succumbing to a court order to vacate on December 9—but not before drawing enough attention to garner multiple investigations of Roldan's death (including two autopsies). While they held the church, the YLP also led a 10,000-person march to the United Nations, on October 30 (the twentieth anniversary of the 1950 Nationalist Party rebellion in Puerto Rico), to demand self-determination for Puerto Ricans on the island and everywhere.[127] By the close of 1970, they had also opened an office in the Lower East Side and, according to one tally, had core membership that totaled over one thousand.[128] Based on numbers from rallies, it is safe to say that their supporters further numbered in the thousands, if not tens of thousands; but no official counts or rosters were ever kept, and there is reason to believe that core membership across the multiple branches (those who were, per the first rule of discipline, "a Young Lord 25 hours a day") was in the hundreds rather than a thousand.

In March 1971, they expanded their operations again. First, they opened an office in Bridgeport, Connecticut, to serve and organize the Puerto Rican population there. Additionally, through much internal conflict (that led to the departure of Oliver, then minister of economic development), the YLP decided to expand operations to Puerto Rico, launching the "Ofenciva Rompecadenas" (Break-the-Chains Offensive) by opening branch offices in El Caño and Aguadilla and coming under the strict scrutiny of the Federal Bureau of Investigation's Counterintelligence Program (COINTELPRO).[129] The expansion, however, was short-lived, as all the members of the Aguadilla branch resigned in April 1972.[130] According to Morales, the move to the island was one of the organization's biggest mistakes. She writes:

> The move to Puerto Rico was a disaster for the organization and the biggest mistake it ever made. The group lost its relationship to the Puerto Rican community in the United States. Simultaneously, the organization became increasingly dogmatic as members spent most of their days in endless debates about Marxist-Leninist-Maoist philosophy. Isolated from reality of the Puerto Rican/Latino community, the organization became irrelevant.[131]

The YLP left the island completely, but the damage was already done. Disagreement over Ofenciva Rompecadenas had fractured the organization, and some of the core New York members (like Morales and Richie Perez) were shipped off to branch offices outside of the city. Throughout the Puerto Rican experiment, furthermore, the Central Committee consolidated, and Gloria Fontañez (formerly Gonzalez) emerged as an influential leader within the organization. Through 1972, membership was in decline and public support began to falter. As the Young Lords Party completed their withdrawal from Puerto Rico, they concretized a shift in focus and mission, which became clarified in the First Party Congress (it would also be their last), which was held June 30 to July 3, 1972.

Phase Three: Puerto Rican Revolutionary Workers Organization (PRRWO)

As a result of the Party Congress, the Young Lords entered their third and final phase, becoming the Puerto Rican Revolutionary Workers Organization. "Though the Lords had substantially declined in size from their high-point of 1,000-plus members in 1970–71," posits Max Elbaum, "the organization still retained considerable prestige and influence. The Puerto Rican Student Union merged into the new PRRWO [in 1972], and PRRWO continued to publish the YLP-launched bilingual newspaper *Palante*."[132] The PRRWO represented a radical shift from the YLO and the YLP. One of the most telling examples of the differences between the earlier iterations of the Lords and this final stage is found in their respective icons. Where for the YLO and YLP, iconic figures such as Che Guevara, Albizu Campos, and Malcolm X were featured prominently in *Palante* and on posters, the PRRWO (on the back cover of the publication that emerged out of its First Party Congress) featured Karl Marx, Friedrich Engels, Vladimir Lenin, Joseph Stalin, and Mao Zedong (see Figure 1.7). According to Laó, "To a significant extent, the leadership had changed and public support diminished. The Lords were not anymore a vibrant local force (let's say in East Harlem or the South Bronx); from a popular radical left, they degenerated into the strict ideological left."[133] The PRRWO closed its community offices and organizations and directed full attention to the workers' struggle from an internationalist perspective. Gone were the featured concerns for immediate community problems and the need to educate the people. The membership declined sharply, and those who remained were sent to work in factories to aid in developing a workers' consciousness through unionization.[134]

The PRRWO worked in close alliance with other Third World Marxist organizations in this time period. Central to this new organization was a coalition of several other organizations working under the banner of the National Liaison Committee (NLC), which was an arm of the Revolutionary Union (RU). According to Elbaum,

> The NLC had been formed in July 1972 by representatives of the RU, IWK [I Wor Kuen], BWC [Black Workers Congress] and PRRWO at the New York meeting where the Young Lords Party changed their name to the Puerto Rican Revolutionary Workers Organization. Not a public organization, the NLC was designed to serve as a vehicle for

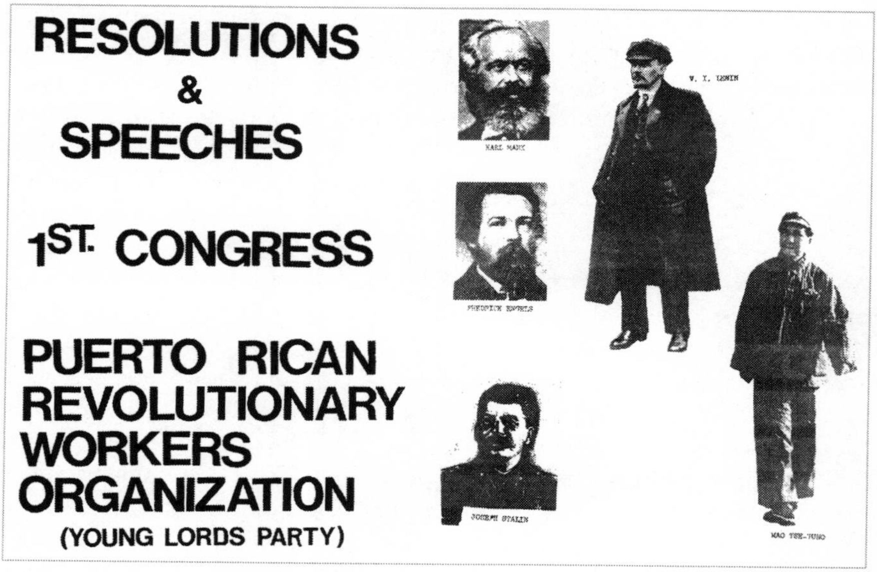

Figure 1.7   Front and back covers of the Puerto Rican Revolutionary Workers Organization's "Resolutions and Speeches, First Congress," July 1972.

discussions and common work aimed at uniting participant groups. RU was the NLC's driving force. It had functioned as a Marxist-Leninist group longer than the other organizations, had a clearer strategy, and believed itself to be the key nucleus of the future New Communist party.[135]

The coalition with the NLC and RU, however, became increasingly tense. In 1973, the PRRWO, IWK, and BWC "began to criticize the predominantly white RU for trying to submerge people of color groups in a merger process destined to produce a white-dominated party." The RU responded by attacking the groups for "narrow nationalism," and the NCL began disintegrating in the fall of 1973, with the PRRWO departing in 1974.[136]

Toward the end of 1975, the PRRWO would align itself with the Revolutionary Workers League (RWL) as part of the "Revolutionary Wing," which grew preoccupied with attacking "everyone else for being insufficiently anti-revisionist and for focusing on mass work instead of doctrinal purification campaigns."[137] By this point, the PRRWO had left behind its concerns for democracy in the organization and eventually devolved into a protoauthoritarian regime under the leadership of Fontáñez. Loyal members were accused of being "spies" for COINTELPRO, some were placed on house arrest, and others were threatened and beaten. According to Elbaum, "The PRRWO and RWL remained allied for a time before collapsing altogether amid purges, reports of violence and physical intimidation against ex-members, and charges that various individuals were police agents."[138] Only a handful of members remained when the PRRWO went defunct in 1976.

From its emergence in 1969, to its peak in 1971, to its ultimate demise in 1976, the Young Lords transformed Puerto Rican politics in the diaspora, especially New York City. They were not the only organization struggling for radical change, but they were probably the most significant insofar as their emergence ushered in a distinctly New York perspective on the Puerto Rican struggle that continues to have influence and relevance today—influences we can see in examples like the late 1990s restructuring of the Almighty Latin King and Queen Nation into a "street political organization" modeled on the Young Lords and Black Panthers, in UNIVERSES' critically acclaimed play, *Party People*, based on the Young Lords and Black Panthers, and in Sonia Manzano's recent young adult novel *The Revolution of Evelyn Serrano*, which is based on Young Lords history.[139] Laó is quite apt in his assessment that the "memory of the Young Lords can give us, to use Raymond Williams' expression 'resources of hope,' tools for the theory and practice of social change, a counter-memory of resistance, along with resources of utopia, enabling visions of a post-colonial future of more equality and freedom."[140] As we will see in the coming chapters, various "resources of hope" can be drawn from such diverse areas as the Young Lords' engagement of questions of gender, to their (re)tropicalization of space in El Barrio, to their rearticulation of "the people." In their own time as well, however, the Young Lords' practices of retrofitted memory generated a similar "countermemory of resistance" that challenged the coloniality of knowledge and anchored their activism in a long (recovered) history of decolonial resistance.

Just as we can draw "resources of hope" from the Young Lords, they drew their own from prior generations of Boricuas, other Latin@s, and others in the Global South who resisted coloniality in their times and places. Building on the historical work in this chapter, then, I next turn my attention to the ways in which the Young Lords engaged questions about the relationship between coloniality and nation through their concept of "revolutionary nationalism," which is a distinctive form of nationalism informed by Puerto Rican nationalism but not beholden to it. Within their unique diasporic context, the Young Lords' revolutionary nationalism avoided some of the problematic qualities of island-based nationalism by focusing on the interrelationship between colonialism, capitalism, racism, and sexism. This conceptual innovation led them to craft an ideologically inventive concept that was fitting to their social and historical context and facilitated a delinking from modern coloniality.

2

Figural, Not Foundational

The Young Lords and Revolutionary Nationalism

Revolution is mankind's way of life today. This is the age of revolution: the "age of indifference" is gone forever. But the latter age paved the way for today; for the great masses of mankind, while still suffering the greatest oppression and the greatest affronts to their dignity as human beings, never ceased to resist, to fight as well as they could, to live in combat.

—FRANTZ FANON, *A Dying Colonialism*

Decolonization never takes place unnoticed, for it influences individuals and modifies them fundamentally. It transforms spectators crushed with their inessentiality into privileged actors, with the grandiose glare of history's floodlights upon them. It brings a natural rhythm into existence, introduced by new men, and with it a new language and a new humanity.

—FRANTZ FANON, *The Wretched of the Earth*

Colonialism as an institution is dead the world over. Puerto Rico cannot—will not—be the exception to this rule.

—MANUEL MALDONADO-DENIS, "The Puerto Ricans: Protest or Submission?"

t is entirely possible that the topic of nationalism is the most studied theme engaged in relation to Puerto Rican society. Animated by broader historical and cultural questions about the rise of the Puerto Rican Nationalist Party (PNP), key figures like Pedro Albizu Campos and Lolita Lebrón, state cultural policy, the formation of national identity, and even tensions between island-based and mainland-based community activists, there is an abundance of excellent scholarship on nationalism in various Puerto Rican contexts.[1] That said, much of the scholarship is focused on independence and identity in the Puerto Rican nation, with far less sustained attention directed to the Puerto Rican diaspora generally and U.S.-based social movements in particular. The dearth of scholarship has been obvious for some time; and despite the call for more scholarship at the heart of Andrés Torres and José Velázquez's *The Puerto Rican Movement* a decade and a half ago and Carmen Teresa Whalen and Víctor Vázquez-Hernández's edited *The Puerto Rican Diaspora: Historical Perspectives* a decade ago, few have taken up the task.[2] This chapter aims to draw from and complicate some of the existent scholarship by focusing on the ways in which the Young Lords advanced a particular kind of nationalist politics, revolutionary nationalism, in El Barrio and beyond.

In the previous chapter, I demonstrated some of the ways in which the Young Lords arose in response to complex historical and sociopolitical contexts marked by multiple experiences of nationalism, both on the island and in the mainland United States. This history found its roots in the conflict-ridden production of the Puerto Rican nation from without and within—as a product of direct colonial administration, first by Spain, then by the United States; as a response to that colonialism (e.g., El Grito de Lares); and through state cultural policy that crafted a problematic racial democracy through the rhetorical trope of "la gran familia puertorriqueña." Struggles against myopic constructions of the nation and colonial subjectivity spilled over into diasporic contexts as organizations with ties to nationalists and independentistas worked within the United States to advance the cause of Puerto Rican independence. Many people involved with these different U.S.-based organizations and U.S. extensions of Puerto Rican organizations were migrants with allegiances to Puerto Rico first. But in the aftermath of the Red Scare and crackdowns on Puerto Rican nationalists in the 1950s, U.S.-based political activism surrounding Puerto Ricans became professionalized, liberalized, and bureaucratized. By the late 1960s, in the wake of the civil rights movement, widespread riots, and increased militancy by people of color, "politicized young Puerto Ricans began to challenge the moderate, liberal approach of the older second generation and embrace a more radical agenda that would shift the balance of Puerto Rican activism in New York by 1970."[3]

The Young Lords arose in a manner and with a set of perspectives that complicated the dominant nationalist narrative and telos in a number of ways. First, most members were not from the island and had no particularly strong desire to repatriate. As a consequence, their allegiances were to the communities in which they were raised and came to sociopolitical consciousness. Second, the Young Lords were disaffected youth, totally disillusioned with the political process and liberal democratic proceduralism. They had no faith in the government or electorate and had little confidence that governments and nation-states were the answers to their problems or the problems of anyone from the Global South. Even the successes of Italian American East Harlem congressman Vito Marcantonio, a champion of Puerto Rican issues and leftist anti-imperialism, were a distant memory that rarely received mention. Third, the Young Lords were steeped in the radicalism of the Third World Left both domestically and abroad. Although I think some scholars overstate the case by implying that the Young Lords merely mimicked the Black Panthers,[4] there is little doubt that black radicals in the United States like the Panthers, Malcolm X, and Harold Cruse and global figures like Frantz Fanon and Mao Zedong had a strong influence on the Young Lords' complex ideological perspectives, rhetorical performances, and modes of activism. As a result, the Young Lords supported nationalist politics and demands for independence, but they did so through different rhetorics that were attentive to their social, historical, political, and geographic positionality outside of the island. For example, "rather than asking for recognition in a liberal discourse of inclusion-as-equals, militant youth [like the Young Lords]," writes Lorrin Thomas, "framed their demands . . . in more challenging terms, insisting on the legitimacy of their claims for sovereignty—'self-determination' and 'liberation'— both for Puerto Ricans in the metropole and for their homeland itself."[5] The Young Lords linked together such calls for "self-determination," "liberation," and "community control" through a rhetoric of "revolutionary nationalism."

Revolutionary nationalism was not the same stale nationalism of prior years. Rather than merely parrot the political nationalism of the Puerto Rican Nationalist Party or other independentistas, the Young Lords advanced what Jeffrey Ogbar calls a "new brand of nationalism [that] recognized the centrality of race to Puerto Rican political discourse in ways unseen in the politics of earlier forms of nationalism."[6] They were "animated by the Cuban revolution, by decolonization struggles across Africa and southeast Asia, and by their opposition to the United States' war in Vietnam" in addition to Puerto Rican nationalist stalwarts like Pedro Albizu Campos, Lolita Lebrón, and the PNP.[7] But, Thomas argues, they were powerfully and "deeply influenced by their local context—weaving together a diasporic version of nationalist ideals that was inclusive and antiracist with a radical grassroots antipoverty agenda," and they "saw island nationalists' agenda as too narrowly focused on Puerto Rican politics" at the expense of local concerns in New York.[8] As a result, the Young Lords' revolutionary nationalism emerged as an organic product of their lived reality in the metropole—a geographically located and biopolitically grounded concept that spoke to the needs of Nuyoricans linked to global struggles for Third World liberation.

Ironically, the two scholars who have published on the Young Lords and nationalism pay scant attention to the uniqueness of the organization's specific formulation of "revolutionary nationalism." Thomas's excellent historical work rightly grounds the Young Lords' nationalism in critiques of "internal colonialism" extending to Latin America, Puerto Rican nationalists and independentistas, and Black Power advocates, while simultaneously complicating the Young Lords' relationship to island-based nationalist claims; but she never once uses the term "revolutionary nationalism," which was central to the Young Lords' formulation. Ogbar calls the Young Lords' nationalism "radical ethnic nationalism" to underscore the idea that "this form does not limit its nationalist agenda exclusively to its own group." He explores the ways in which the Young Lords' and Black Panthers' nationalisms allowed the groups to "work intimately with members from other ethnic groups in various contexts in symbiotic struggle."[9] But Ogbar's formulation avoids almost entirely the rich articulation of nationalism coming from New York—focusing some attention on the discourse of the Chicago chapter and rooting his analysis in an abstracted formulation of nationalism (based in his scholarship on the Black Panther Party) at the expense of the myriad symbolically rich spoken and written rhetorics of the New York branch. Furthermore, neither Thomas nor Ogbar take the full significance of the coloniality of knowledge, power, and being into consideration. While Thomas does well to direct attention to the Young Lords' critical engagement of "internal colonialism" and their complex relationship to orthodox nationalist claims, she interprets the Young Lords' rhetoric through the lens of "recognition" and risks missing the significance of their decolonial calls for *liberation*, which is a topic I take up in Chapter 3. Conversely, Ogbar's inattention to decoloniality is more significant. He is certainly aware of Puerto Rico's history of colonialism; but formulating it as a question of historicity, Ogbar does not address the ways in which coloniality continued beyond contexts of direct rule and framed in fundamental ways the manner in which the Young Lords engaged their epistemic, political, and rhetorical situation.[10]

Approaching the Young Lords from a perspective more attuned to both their situated public discourses and the ways in which those discourses invoked de/coloniality, I aim in this chapter to enrich our understanding of the Young Lords' rhetoric of revolutionary nationalism. Any reading of the Young Lords' discourse and activism must be attentive to the colonial difference—to the ways in which their politics are a response to the lived experience of coloniality in the metropole and the relationships between that experience of coloniality and anticolonial struggles on the island and throughout the Global South. In being attentive to coloniality, I believe it is a mistake to simply graft abstract theoretical frameworks for nationalism onto the Young Lords. We must, to a certain extent, meet them on their own terms and understand better the historical context that prefigures the emergence of revolutionary nationalism as a unique articulation for the organization. In contextualizing their discourse, I argue that the New York Young Lords' rhetoric of revolutionary nationalism advanced a decolonial critique that disarticulated or delinked their political program from the modern/colonial system, while staking out an alternative to the two extremes of political nationalism and cultural nationalism. Rather than centering a modern/colonial construction of the nation, the Young Lords' rhetorical "nationalism" functioned differentially as a "symbolic agency"—a signifying *means*—through which the group decolonized their imaginary, reformulated political subjectivity, and opened the space for radical possibility.[11] Nationalism functioning in a figural register challenges commonplace understandings of nationalism and nation, even those prominent within decolonial scholarship,[12] while also highlighting the need for stronger rhetorical sensibilities in the scholarship we do.

This chapter develops over four main sections. First, I return to Ogbar as a starting point from which I develop my argument. Ogbar's inattentiveness to the actual language of the Young Lords is a problem of both method (because he applies theories that are ill suited) and history (because he never captures what the Young Lords, in fact, said and did) and invites a decolonial response. Next, I lay the historical and theoretical groundwork for the emergence of the Young Lords' articulation of revolutionary nationalism. Examining the historiography on internal colonialism and revolutionary nationalism and contemporaneous engagements of nationalism in Puerto Rican contexts in the 1960s, this section of the chapter is both descriptive of the Young Lords' context and prescriptive of how we ought to examine their discourse. Third, turning my attention back to the Young Lords, I show how these young radicals crafted coloniality as an exigence to address—one that was responsible for the production of a colonial mentality, racism, and sexist machismo. Finally, I entertain the ways "revolutionary nationalism" functioned as a response to their colonial exigence. Revolutionary nationalism enabled the Young Lords to develop an anticapitalist, antiracist, antisexist liberation politics responsive to the intersectionality of oppressions under modernity/coloniality.

Misrecognizing Nationalism

Early in my research on the Young Lords, I was in New York City for a combined trip to the archives and the biennial Puerto Rican Studies Association convention, which was being held at the City University of New York Graduate Center. After the main conference activities had completed for the day, I boarded the subway to head back to my hotel. Traveling with a friend from the Center for Puerto Rican Studies and some researchers who were part of the conference, I was asked what my dissertation was about. In the thick of library research and interviews at that moment, I explained, as I usually would, that it was an interrogation of the radical democratic potential of the Young Lords. Then, I received a rather odd response from one of the researchers, who said that the Young Lords could not possibly be "radical democratic" because they were "nationalist." Although I have since abandoned this radical democratic read of the Young Lords—persuaded, once and for all, by Janet Conway and Jakeet Signh's argument that radical democratic theory problematically and unreflexively reproduces coloniality[13]—I remain troubled by this anonymous scholar's reaction, which I can only understand as rooted in dehistoricized conceptualizations of both democracy and nationalism. The mere presence of this label "nationalism" leads to a misunderstanding about the Young Lords and a tendency among U.S. academics who do not embrace the colonial difference to reinforce binaries (in this case, nationalist versus democratic) in theorizing Latin@ activism.[14] A related misrecognition, one also rooted in a dehistoricized engagement of sorts, creeps into Ogbar's analysis of the Young Lords.

In circling back to Ogbar's argument in his essay "Puerto Rico en Mi Corazón," I want to make clear that I am not trying to get into some kind of academic dustup. Rather, I start with Ogbar because his is truly the only essay so far to devote exclusive attention to the Young Lords' nationalist politics (Thomas's chapter is about a generation of Nuyorican radicals more broadly), and it is a good foundation for future work. Ogbar begins his engagement of the Young Lords with a return to the conventional, Western scholarship on nationalism and nation. In doing so, he elucidates a common framework for understanding nationalism, one that sees it focused on "self-determination, unity, and territorial separatism," and traces out a brief history of nationalism in Puerto Rico and within the pre-Panthers Black Left.[15] Ogbar continues, however, by suggesting that the conventional framework for understanding nationalism does not work once we start dealing with nationalists like the Panthers and the Young Lords. As an alternative, he culls Jyoti Puri's sociological work on nationalism to advance the claim that the Panthers and other Black Power advocates exemplified a kind of radical ethnic nationalism.[16] "Unlike typical ethnic nationalism," Ogbar writes, "this form does not limit its nationalist agenda exclusively to its own group. Indeed, its national consciousness is central to its politics"; but it exceeds national limitations to work with other ethnic groups in common cause.[17] Ogbar argues that riding in on the coattails of Black Power's radical ethnic nationalism, Puerto Rican nationalism in Chicago shifted from a conventionally understood political nationalism to a radical ethnic strain—something that was taken up by the Chicago street gang-turned-political (the original Young Lords) and spread to New York when they chartered the new Young Lords branch. Organizing around what Ogbar calls the "the cardinal 'three evils' of revolutionary nationalists . . . capitalism, racism, and imperialism," the Young Lords challenged racisms on the island and in the mainland, fought sexism within the group and across society, and advocated for socialist redistribution of wealth.[18]

As strong as Ogbar's argument is in relation to the Black Panthers,[19] I fear he may not be attentive enough to the actual discourse of the Young Lords, which has a couple of consequences. On the one hand, it means he overgeneralizes from a narrow data set. For example, he presumes a certain ideological and rhetorical unity between Chicago and the East Coast, which glosses over significant differences—differences that quickly led to the 1970 split between the two main branches—and leads him to treat the discourse of one branch (usually Chicago) as representative of the whole. Additionally, in not looking at the most significant primary texts (those published in the Young Lords' newspapers and pamphlets), Ogbar's engagement does not dig deep enough into the rhetorical and ideological structures of their articulation of nationalism.

For example, he never engages what the Young Lords actually meant by the term "revolutionary nationalism" because it is never explained in the texts he examines. It is, however, explained in New York Young Lords' articles like "On Revolutionary Nationalism" and in their book *Palante: Young Lords Party*. It is further marked as a significant term in places like their radio program, the inaugural broadcast for which includes an instance of chairman Felipe Luciano accidentally uttering "nationalism" and quickly correcting himself with the term "*revolutionary* nationalism."[20]

On the other hand, because he did not access key primary texts (perhaps this is an archive issue and he did not have access to those texts) and because he operates from an epistemic location apart from the Young Lords, Ogbar runs into another problem of perspective: he cannot sense the ghostly traces of coloniality woven throughout the New York Young Lords' rhetoric of revolutionary nationalism. He acknowledges that they position themselves against imperialism and draw conceptually from diverse historical resources. But he wants to see this as something new (his "new brand of nationalism") rather than the re-*re*-emergent product of decolonial struggle, traces of which appear through the Haitian slave revolt, the work of José Martí, the struggles of Ramón Emeterio Betances in El Grito de Lares, the writings of Frantz Fanon, and in everyday acts of local resistance to modern/colonial homogenization of embodied thought and action. Operating in response to the lived experiences of coloniality and struggling for the liberation of all people, the Young Lords' revolutionary nationalism ought to be examined from within the broader context of their discourse and critical-theoretical heuristics cognizant of the colonial difference.

Rethinking Revolutionary Nationalism in Historical and Theoretical Context

Nationalism often functions through a foundational logic that naturalizes the links between people and nation—one in which, Agustín Laó-Montes argues, "peoplehood is defined in terms of an essentialist search for origins, fixed cultural traits, and a common destiny, a logic that promotes homogenization of difference and the exclusion of selected others (racial, sexual, etc.)."[21] We can see, most clearly, such a logic at work in various reactionary nationalisms (e.g., Germany's National Socialists) and even in anticolonial political nationalisms. Ana Y. Ramos-Zayas, for example, points to the way political nationalism in the Puerto Rican diaspora and on the island is focused on national recognition and guided by a politics of recognition—one that operates within modernist accounts of reason and state sovereignty. In contrast to political nationalism, Ramos-Zayas points to a cultural nationalism that eschews embracing the state for a focus on cultural recovery and production.[22] As

Ramos-Zayas shows in her study, this binary marking out political national-ism and cultural nationalism, however, may be too simplistic for understand-ing nationalism in Puerto Rican diasporic contexts.

The Young Lords' revolutionary nationalism materialized out of a long, somewhat contradictory history in which competing versions of nationalism from throughout the Americas came into contact. In the 1960s, U.S. radicals (including, but not limited to, the Panthers) were indebted to broader currents of thought. Thomas, for example, argues that "the long history of radical nationalism and anti-imperialism in twentieth-century Latin America, which formed the ideological roots of both Puerto Rican and Chicano nationalists, was also essential in shaping black nationalists' ideas by the mid-sixties."[23] Ramón Gutiérrez similarly demonstrates the international roots of "internal colonialism," which developed through both African and Latin American cri-tiques of developmentalism. In its transfer to the U.S. context, he argues, "internal colonialism represented a radical break in thinking about race in the United States after the Second World War."[24] Such a "radical break" is evidence of an initial delinking impulse that divested "race" from modern/colonial constraints.

In the black freedom struggles, the emergence of a concept of internal colonialism provided a specific symbolic and material means for linking the problems of racism and colonialism. "Racism was deeply historical," Gutiérrez explains, "rooted in the legacies of conquest and colonialism, and in personal and systemic effects of poverty, segregation, and White skin privilege."[25] Within this context, Herman J. Blake argued in 1969, "black people became more aware that their situation in this country was very similar to that of colonized peoples throughout the world."[26] The link to Third World liberation and decolonization spread precipitously throughout the 1960s. In one of the earliest and widest circulated statements on black "revolutionary national-ism," Harold Cruse tied this turn to the Third World to the inadequacy of U.S.-based Marxists to account for the uniqueness of situations faced by peo-ples of color. Writing in 1962, Cruse argued, "The failure of American Marx-ists to understand the bond between the Negro and the colonial peoples of the world has led to their failure to develop theories that would be of value to Negroes in the United States."[27]

Within this context, radical black revolutionary nationalism developed as a particular heuristic for engaging questions of the relationship between race, history, space, and capitalism. Huey P. Newton, a leader in the Black Panther Party, described revolutionary nationalism as "nationalism plus socialism" to underscore the commitment to redistributive justice in contexts marked by coloniality.[28] In practice, it meant a shift to an "emphasis upon self-determination for black communities" because, Blake argues, "coloniza-tion, land, self-determination, and accountability are the basic elements in recent developments in black nationalism."[29] Black revolutionary nationalism was also an explicit response to the prevalent cultural nationalism of the time. According to William J. Wilson, revolutionary nationalists challenged the cultural nationalists when they "observed that the inordinate emphasis on the virtues and roots of black culture tends to conceal the fact that black people constitute an oppressed colony in American society, and have empha- sized that it is not the revival of African cultural roots or the wearing of dashi- kis but revolutionary action that will enable black people to gain their true dignity."[30] This view of black space as colonial, and radical action as necessary, was central to Black Power articulations of revolutionary nationalism. "A shift from cultural nationalism to revolutionary nationalism," argues James A. Tyner, "was therefore predicated on a literal, not a metaphorical, view of the black ghetto as a colonized territory. Social justice, self-liberation, and self- determination of all oppressed peoples were to be achieved through a process of decolonization."[31] The Black Panthers would, by 1970, abandon revolutionary nationalism in preference for a concept of "revolutionary intercommunalism" based on the demise of the nation-state.[32] According to Nikhil Pal Singh, this concept describes "an imperialism no longer reliant upon territorial posses- sions, as well as a deterritorialized conception of liberation, in which small groups like the Panthers could participate with other oppressed 'communi- ties,' like the Cubans or the Vietnamese."[33] Despite the Panthers' shift, however, revolutionary nationalism remained a useful concept for the Young Lords—no doubt due partly, at least, to their complicated relationship to calls for Puerto Rican independence and desired alliances with island nationalists.

Like with Black Power advocates, Puerto Ricans in New York advanced an interpretation of their community as an internal colony. In fact, Thomas argues, activists advanced such analyses even earlier than black radicals. The island-based Movimiento Pro-Independencia was pointing in 1962—well before the Black Panthers theorized internal colonialism and the same year that Cruse first articulated revolutionary nationalism—to "the victimization of African Americans and US Puerto Ricans at the hands of 'the empire that oppresses us.' "[34] However, at that early point, and even into the late 1960s, U.S.- based Puerto Ricans lagged behind their African American counterparts. Writ- ing from the island, Manuel Maldonado-Denis argued that, notwithstanding "Puerto Rican participation in the Poor People's March on Washington, and some sporadic outbursts of rebellion, it can hardly be said that Puerto Ricans in the United States—as a group that faces the prejudices and hardships of a nonwhite group in a racist society—have achieved, in their struggle for libera- tion, a level of consciousness and of militancy similar to that of Afro-Americans."[35] Perhaps contemporary with Maldonado-Denis's moment of argument, how- ever, radical Puerto Ricans in the metropolis were making a shift.

Just prior to the formation of the Young Lords in 1969, the East Harlem branch of the Real Great Society argued forcefully that Puerto Ricans in New York were a colony:

East Harlem is an underdeveloped country. Most of it is owned and controlled by private and governmental interests outside the community. In the past, the development of East Harlem has served these outside interests at the expense of an essentially powerless community, but this will not continue to be so. East Harlem is awakening to its rights and abilities for self control and self determination, and the balance of power has begun to shift towards the people. The people have become aware, as part of a nationwide movement, that they must control their own environment in order to determine their own future, and that control begins at the planning level through the utilization of the community's own environmentalists.[36]

RGS's East Harlem branch was, then, at the forefront of crafting a Nuyorican analysis of coloniality. Unlike MPI, this was not a "true nationalist orthodoxy," Thomas argues, because Nuyorican radicals "interpreted issues of independence and sovereignty in general terms, often as *symbols* for local power relations and the oppression of Puerto Ricans in New York" rather than a simple extension of Puerto Rican nationalism.[37] Borrowing language that was common to the Puerto Rican struggle for independence, RGS redeployed that language in the East Harlem context to imagine the kinds of resistance in which they were engaged in terms of a global struggle against domination that shared linkages to other radicals of color in the United States. The Young Lords' articulation of revolutionary nationalism emerged from within this context.

In addition to being attentive to the historical context of emergence, it is important to approach the Young Lords' rhetoric of revolutionary nationalism in a manner that is attuned to the uniqueness of their articulation, which requires being open to revolutionary nationalism's performativity. Ramos-Zayas, for example, advances an understanding of nationalism that revels in the interstitial space and dialectical tension between political nationalism and cultural nationalism.[38] As an alternative to both, she posits a "performative nationalism" that avoids the conceptual simplicity of the political/cultural binary and is attentive to the complex ways in which "nationalism creates both the spaces to illuminate internal boundaries and the possibility of addressing the basic material and social needs of [Chicago] barrio residents."[39] Thus, I read Ramos-Zayas's formulation as pointing us to the ways in which nationalism performatively and discursively functions to negotiate a set of tensions and social problematics produced by the lived experience of coloniality.

Coloniality, as I addressed in the Introduction, does not rely on the existence of functioning colonial political relations, although *de jure* colonialism existed in Puerto Rico in the Young Lords' era as well as today. Instead, and especially in the context of this chapter, I want to posit an understanding of coloniality as something more in line with what Juan Flores calls the "lite colonial," which "is eminently discursive colonialism, a thickly symbolic form of transnational domination which emphasizes both a consensual identity ('we are all Puerto Ricans, across all lines') and at the same time multiple identities of a nonmonolithic, fragmented kind, including the diasporic."[40] Scarred by coloniality, then, Nuyoricans can resist dominant nationalist logics and discourses through a hybridized rhetoric that transcends and transgresses the nation while simultaneously advancing claims for independence and liberation.

Operating within a terrain marked by what Aníbal Quijano calls the "colonization of the imagination of the dominated,"[41] the Young Lords' revolutionary nationalism functioned as an ambiguous nationalism: one that rhetorically exploited the common label of "nationalism" through an enactment of *jaibería*, which Ramón Grosfoguel describes as a "subversive complicity" and I would consider a mode of "border thinking" born of the in-between space that remains in contact with modernity/coloniality but ever so conscious of that contact.[42] Contrary to the conventional nationalist discourses on the island, which risk unreflexively reproducing a Euro-American-centric imaginary, "revolutionary nationalism" functions rhetorically. Karlyn Kohrs Campbell points to the importance of the *term*, which functions as "a symbolic agency"[43] enabling the rearticulation of peoplehood delinked from the modern/colonial imaginary. The movement, Mignolo might suggest, is from a "politics based on identity" to "an identity based on politics."[44] So what does that look like?

For the Young Lords, "revolutionary nationalism" was a complex, rhetorically powerful term signifying unique normative commitments and functioning as a kind of nodal point through which a host of political and historical elements could be articulated.[45] Following Mariana Ortega and Linda Martín Alcoff, who suggest that "if we want to analyze nationalism as a norm governing individual practices . . . we must analyze it in the discrete and specific particularity of its (ever-shifting) context,"[46] I turn now to texts published in the Young Lords' newspaper (*Palante*), their book (*Palante: Young Lords Party*), and their pamphlet on ideology (*The Ideology of the Young Lords Party*) between 1970 and 1972—a key period of ideological development for the New York group. In engaging the Young Lords' revolutionary nationalism, I approach it from two angles. First, I examine how they frame the emergence of the concept by exploring the ways in which they rhetorically craft an exigence for which revolutionary nationalism is a fitting response.[47] This exigence is what I'm calling coloniality—the legacy and traces of colonialism that function psychically, physically, and structurally to oppress Puerto Ricans specifically and Third World people generally, particularly with regard to issues of race and gender. Second, I analyze what revolutionary nationalism is—how the Young Lords define, explain, and deploy the term in their discourse—and how it functions as a corrective to the problems of coloniality. In the end, I argue that revolutionary nationalism functions as a symbolic agency that figures the Young Lords' political and cultural space, enabling differential moves between Puerto Rican national identity and a rejection of identity and class categories. Such differential movement between seemingly paradoxical commitments marks the uniqueness of the Young Lords' ideology and sets the backdrop for their engagements of bigger topics like gender equality as well as specific instances of direct action explored in the remaining chapters.

Coloniality as Exigency in the Young Lords' Revolutionary Nationalism

Analyzing the Young Lords' rhetoric of revolutionary nationalism must begin with recognition of the nuanced ways in which they crafted their colonial past and present. Early in the group's clearest statement on the subject, "On Revolutionary Nationalism" (see Figure 2.1)—which was published in May 1970, just prior to the Young Lords' announcement of a split from Chicago—Felipe Luciano argued:

> Puerto Rico is oppressed as a nation. It is a colony of the united states and the colonial status of Puerto Ricans follows them from the countryside to New York City. Form changes, substance doesn't. In Puerto Rico the whole damned island, composed of Ricans, is oppressed. In the u.s. Borinquenos are one of the many colonized peoples living in a colony within the intestines of the snake.[48]

Linking the colonial status of Puerto Ricans on the island with those in the United States, and linking both to other Third World peoples, Luciano mapped a geography of colonial wounds and wounding coloniality that marks all aspects of colonized lives. Colonialism, the Young Lords argued, is felt, literally, on the body through various oppressive mechanisms: genocide, slavery, police brutality, denial of sanitation services, poisoning from lead, forced sterilizations of women, malnutrition, and more. In the United States, the Young Lords argued in their pamphlet *The Ideology of the Young Lords Party*, "hunger and oppression expose quickly the lies of the amerikkkan dream."[49]

Colonialism, however, is not an isolated process. The Young Lords advanced an intersectional analysis that articulated a link between capitalism and colonialism, which directed them to understand the two as fundamentally inseparable. Colonialism and capitalism operate synergistically to divide the Puerto Rican people and turn them against one another. Being attentive to hierarchical relations, they described capitalism as "a system that forces us to climb over our brothers and sisters' backs to get to the top." Such a system of

Figure 2.1   Felipe Luciano's "On Revolutionary Nationalism," *Palante* 2, no. 2 (May 8, 1970).

relations is internalized as a struggle for survival that creates divisions within the Puerto Rican nation. The Young Lords continued, "We fight against each other to live, and we are divided into groups that fight against each other. These groups are formed out of artificial divisions of race and sex, and social groupings." Rather than read these divisions as a product of capitalism alone, however, the Young Lords argued that they "are a result of colonization.

Puerto Ricans are a colonized people. . . . The colonizers divide us up, teach us to think we are inferior, and teach us to fight against each other, because as long as we fight against each other we won't deal with our real problems— slavery, hunger, and misery."[50] In the Young Lords' analysis, colonialism, capitalism, racism, and sexism all function together—in ways that are mutually constitutive, though stressing roots in the relationship between capitalism and colonialism—to generate oppressive conditions that are regenerative. In other words, it is not simply the case that capitalism/colonialism oppress people from above, but they also carry a productive capacity that encourages the Puerto Rican people to participate actively in their own oppression both on the island and in the diaspora.[51]

Understood in this way—as recursive power relations from above and below—the Young Lords hit on a key dimension of the coloniality of power, namely, the way in which coloniality functions to craft subjects whose agency is constrained in a manner that compels practiced relations of inequality. For the Young Lords, this speaks to the psychological dimension of coloniality, which they explained through attention to the development of a "colonized mentality" and the erasure of history. For decolonial scholar Quijano, coloniality's "repression fell, above all, over the modes of knowing, of producing knowledge, of producing perspectives, images and systems of images, symbols, modes of signification, over the resources, patterns, and instruments of formalized and objectivised expression, intellectual or visual."[52] The Young Lords seemed to concur.

Pointing to the ways in with the minds of Puerto Ricans have been colonized, Denise Oliver argued passionately:

We are [so] brainwashed by the newspapers we read, the books they write for us, the television, the radio, the schools, and the church, that *we don't know what our real thoughts are anymore*. We are afraid to be leaders, because we are taught to be followers. We have been told that we are *docile* so long, that we have forgotten that we have always been fighters. We are afraid to speak in public because we have been taught not to speak out. We are told that we cannot exist without amerikkkans in Puerto Rico, and we believe it, even though we know that our nation existed for hundreds of years without them. *All of this brainwashing, this "colonized mentality" holds us back from our liberation.*[53]

For Oliver, writing in the official statement of Young Lords ideology, coloniality generated practices of docility and instilled a fear that inhibited counteraction. Similarly, Luciano addressed how colonialism had "messed our minds so badly"[54] and "taken the chains off our hands and put them on our minds."[55] "Amerikkka," he continued, "makes sure that though we have eyes, we don't see; and though we have ears, we don't hear; and though we have tongues and minds, we don't think or speak about the cruelties and injustices we go through every day."[56] The sensory dimension of Luciano's rhetoric is significant. Although he, Oliver, and others pointed to coloniality's psychic dimension, its impact was felt on the body and experienced in their everyday lives. Such everyday "cruelties and injustices" are too numerous to list; but two that the Young Lords paid special attention to were racism and machismo.

Racism

In "On Revolutionary Nationalism," Luciano addressed how the colonized mentality directed Puerto Ricans to "reject our cultural values and basic human values by imitating that which is not natural to us and by stomping on our own reflections. We've been systematically taught to hate ourselves while being reminded constantly by racist america that we ain't her kind of people either. . . . Puerto Ricans have suffered as a group, racially and culturally."[57] Underscoring the cultural and racial dimension of the oppression Puerto Ricans faced, Luciano helped articulate one of the key motivations and issues for the Young Lords: to confront racism, especially as it is rooted in and exacerbated by relations of coloniality. That this was linked to decolonial politics, however, is hardly a surprise to anyone familiar with the Young Lords or late 1960s and early 1970s radicalism in general. The era saw a host of groups—from the Young Lords to the Black Panthers, Movimiento Estudiantil Chicano de Aztlán (MEChA), the Brown Berets, the American Indian Movement, and others—who advanced a set of demands intent on dismantling colonial powers and challenging imperialisms.[58]

Connecting their nationalism with a Third World consciousness, the Young Lords broke with previous generations of Puerto Rican nationalists by tapping into a specific kind of decolonial discourse that rejected whiteness, which was inherently counterhegemonic within Puerto Rican political discourse. As Miriam Jimenez Román argues, a "widely accepted belief in the superiority of 'whiteness'—and its corollary, the inferiority of 'blackness,'" was "popularly expressed in the notion of *mejoramiento de la raza* [improvement of the race]";[59] and the Young Lords challenged this dominant notion. Indeed, as Iris Morales shows, "The organization opposed white supremacy and cultural genocide—the devaluation and destruction of our culture. Instead, we celebrated our African ancestry and culture; members wore large Afros, and some assumed African names."[60]

Beyond such cultural nationalist performances, however, the Young Lords advanced a critique of racism that posited its roots in some specific social, historical, and material way in Puerto Rican coloniality and even the broader colonial experience of the Third World. "Colonization," wrote Oliver, "is responsible for the racism that exists in our nation."[61] Racism, in the context of coloniality, works on two related and reinforcing levels. First, racism is directed to colonized peoples by the colonizer. For example, in an article entitled "Puerto Rican Racism" (see Figure 2.2), Morales documented the ways in which the Spanish racialized people in order to justify "slavery and rape, saying that [they] are inferior, uncivilized, and of an alien race."[62] Morales deepened her analysis by drawing a link between such racialization and the development and spread of capitalist exploitation through colonization. "The spanish colonizer," she said, "had certain economic interests in Puerto Rico and Latin America: that's why they used racism as a justification for exploiting labor to get economic profit."[63] The United States, of course, fared no better. The "amerikkkans did make it worse," Morales continued. "The u.s. took advantage of the racial and class divisions within our country to better control by playing one group against the other."[64] Thus, under colonialism and extended coloniality, racism became mapped onto the subconscious of Puerto Ricans.

This second gesture of racism creates an internalization of inferiority endemic to the colonial mentality. "Amerikkkan racist influence has really succeeded in dividing Puerto Rico along color lines," wrote Morales. Internalizing those divisions and their concomitant hierarchies, "both Black and light skinned Puerto Ricans adopt racist attitudes towards Afro-American brothers and sisters" and reject notions that they are anything but "Spanish."[65] In this way, argued Oliver, racism "is so deep that we just don't see it anymore. . . . We believe that Black is bad and ugly and dirty, that kinky hair is 'pelo malo [bad hair],' we call Black Puerto Ricans names like prieto, moulleto, and cocolo [dark-skinned, mulatto, and black, respectively]."[66] Racism and colonialism become intertwined in a complex recursive process. So while colonialism is responsible for racism, racism plays a central, rather than merely epiphenomenal, role in securing coloniality's ideological hold. "We are all racists," Oliver wrote, "not because we want to be, but because we are taught to be that way, to keep us divided, because it benefits the capitalist system."[67] Such self-loathing undergirds a kind of psychic ethnocide: it salts the fertile ground of the mind, destroying roots to Taíno and African culture and eradicating non-Western, local knowledge.

Machismo

Sexism and machismo, which are the primary foci of the next chapter, function similarly to racism: they are the product of coloniality and applied both externally and internally. Freya Schiwy argues that while scholars interested in coloniality have done well to theorize the link between race, capitalism, and coloniality, "how gender imaginaries themselves have entered colonial constructs and their aftermath . . . has not received the same attention."[68] The Young Lords, however, were largely cognizant of the connections, as their

RACISMO BORINQUEÑO

Los indios Tainos fueron los primeros habitantes de Borinquen, el nombre Taino para la isla que todavía se usa hoy. Los españoles vinieron a Borinquen en el 1493, le cambiaron el nombre a San Juan Bautista y forzaron los Tainos a la esclavitud, explotando su labor en las minas de oro y las plantaciones. Los esclavizadores se dividieron la tierra y la gente aprovechándose del beneficio y ganancias del trabajo del indio. De vuelta se le daba tan poco que casi ni tenían para comer. La mujer Taina también fue explotada, no solo su trabajo sino también su cuerpo. En el principio de la colonización, los españoles no trayeron con ellos mujeres españolas y así pues, abusaron o ultrajaron a nuestras hermanas indias. Justificaron estos actos de inhumanidad y asesinato diciendo que los indios eran salvaje, no cristiano, y de otra raza.

Rapidamente, el colonizador, asesino, y esclavó a nuestros primeros compatriotas y fue a Africa para una nueva fuente de esclavos. En 1518, el primer contrato para importar un cien numero de esclavos Africanos fue firmado. El opresor aceptó la esclavitud como normal; la iglesia nunca condenó esto y el gobierno nunca enforsó las leyes en contra de esto. Nuestras hermanas Africanas también fueron ultrajadas y usadas para "procidir" más esclavos. El numero de esclavos era importante para las plantaciónes de caña, diremos que hacían mucho dinero de la azucar donde hacían el esclavo Africano. De nuevo los españoles justificaban la esclavitud y el ultrajamiento diciendo que los Africanos eran inferiores y de una raza estrangera.

Desde el siglo 16 hasta la mitad del siglo 19, los Africanos y los Tainos se rebelaron contra los colonizadores españoles, muchas veces, unidos luchaban contra el opresor en común. Ya para el 1868 Puerto Rico como nación, se levantó para peliar contra los españoles en "El Grito de Lares" pero Puertorriqueños Negros permanecían esclavos; la esclavitud Negra no fue eliminada hasta 1873. Al Puertorriqueño no le gusta hablar sobre el racismo ni tan siquiera admitir que existe entre los Puertorriqueños. Los Boricuas hablan de una isla libre de racismo o dicen que los amerikkkanos fueron los que introdujeron el racismo en Puerto Rico. Aunque es cierto que los amerikkkanos hicieron el problema peor, racismo en Puerto Rico comenzó con los españoles. Segun ellos una gota de sangre "blanca" significaba que era blanco y mejor que su compatriota Negro. La persona era aceptada de acuerdo al grado de "blanquesa". La clase alta era blanca, decendientes de los españoles creoles. El colonizador español tenía ciertos intereses económicos en Puerto Rico y toda latina america; por eso usaron racismo como justificación para explotar labor para conseguir ganancias económicas.

Cuando los e.e.u.u. invadió a Puerto Rico en 1898 el racismo fue reenforzado y intensificado por ellos. La clase alta blanca puesta en poder por los españoles anteriormente, ahora hace tratos y recibe dinero de industrias norteamerikkkana y en cambio apoya la posición colonizadora de norteamerikkka. Los e.e.u.u. se agarraron del racismo y división de clase entre nuestro país para mejor controlar poniendo un grupo en contra del otro. Nosotros tenemos una frase "mejorar la raza." Nosotros nos criamos con estos conceptos y aprendimos a ver piel oscura como fea, labios gruesos como bembu, nariz grande como aplastada y pelo

grifo como malo. Referendose al perfil de una persona se dice "perfil o perfilado" describiendo a la persona blanca. El Puertorriqueño cree que para "mejorar la raza" uno se tiene que casar con un Puertorriqueño más claro de piel que él. Un resultado es que toda familia Puertorriqueña tiene Puertorriqueños claros y oscuros. Por esto decimos: "El que no tiene dinga, tiene mandinga. Por esto te pregunto, ¿y tu abuela donde esta?"

Durante el 1940 los Puertorriqueños fueron obligados a imigrar a los e.e.u.u. Aquí la formula racista es una gota de sangre "negra" te hace Negro. Como una raza mezclada somos considerados Negros y todo Puertorriqueño es victima del racismo en e.e.u.u. Los amerikkkanos no nos aceptan porque ellos creen que la mezcla racial nos a causado un decayo en nuestra capacidad física y mental. Por eso los amerikkkanos nos paternalisan o son racista a la clara vista; puercos canallas. No ha sido hasta reciente que hasta los blancos radicales han estado cambiando este

racismo de base honda.

El racismo amerikkkano ha tenido gran influencia y ha triunfado en dividir al Puertorriqueño en lineas de color especialmente en los ultimos 10 años. De acuerdo a los estudios, 96% de la clase media es blanca y 60% de la clase pobre es Negra en nuestra isla de Puerto Rico.

Ensima de todo esto el capitalismo amerikkkano hace un paqueton de chavos, juntos con los capitalistas Puertorriqueños (gente como luis a. ferre, vendepatria gobernador canalla).

Mientras tanto en los e.e.u.u., Puertorriqueños y Negros son puestos en las mismas comunidades. Son victimas los dos pueblos del racismo, drogas, desempleo, el servicio militar obligatorio, servicios medicos inferiores, viviendas malas y educación inferior.

Uno al otro aprende a odiarse, a creerse superior al otro. Para el Puertorriqueño claro quiere decir que comienza a verse como blanco y sus compatriotas como negro, reflejo de la

sociedad amerikkkana. El Negro Puertorriqueño se agarra de que es Puertorriqueño claro dice say "Puertorriqueño hispano" o "trigeño" en orden de evitar indentificarse como Negro. Tanto el Puertorriqueño Negro como el blanco adaptan atitudes racistas contra nuestros hermanos Afro-Americanos.

Nosotros, el Partido de los Young Lords, somos nacidnalistas revolucionarios y nos oponemos al racismo. Realizamos que el capitalismo ha usado racismo para mantener los pueblos oprimidos, oprimido divididos peleando uno con el otro para los pendejos hacerse del dinero.

Tenemos que poner fin al racismo contra nuestros hermanos y hermanas Afro-Americanos. Nos criamos juntos, somos victimes del capitalismo juntos y así pues tenemos que levantar armas juntas y juntos luchar contra el puerco capitalista juntos!

¡UNIDAD ENTRE LOS PUERTORRIQUEÑOS Y TODA GENTE OPRIMIDA!
¡NACIONALISMO REVOLUCIONARIO NO RACISMO!
¡LIBERTAD PARA PUERTO RICO AHORA!

Iris Morales Luciano
Ministerio de Educación
PARTIDO DE LOS YOUNG LORDS
El Barrio

PUERTO RICAN RACISM

The Taino Indians were the first people of Borinquen, the Indian name for the island that is still used today. The spaniards came to Borinquen in 1493, changed the name to San Juan Bautista, and forced the Tainos into slavery, exploiting their labor in the gold mines and on plantations. The enslavers divided the land and people among themselves getting all the benefit and profit from the work of the Indian. In return the Taino was given barely enough to keep him alive. The Taino women were also exploited, not only their labor, but their bodies as well. In the early days the spanish did not bring any of their women, so they took, abused or raped our Indian sisters. They justified this inhumanity and murder, saying the Indians were savage, unchristian, and of another race.

Quickly, the colonizer killed, enslaved, or chased into the mountains our first ancestors. The spaniards then had to look to Africa for a new source of slave labor. In 1598, the first contract to bring in large numbers of Africans was signed. The oppressor accepted slavery as normal; the church never condemned it; and the government never enforced the laws against it. Our African sisters were also raped and used as breeders of more slaves. The number of African slaves was important to the sugar plantation owners who made a lot of money off the sugar cane fields where they put the African to slave. Again, the spanish justified slavery and rape, saying that the African was inferior, uncivilized, and of an alien race. **CONT. TO P. 7**

Figure 2.2 "Racismo Borinqueño"/"Puerto Rican Racism," *Palante* 2, no. 7 (July 17, 1970).

collectively authored "Position Paper on Women" illustrates. Externally, coloniality imposed sexism and misogyny through practices of colonial administration, including rape, other controls over reproduction (including forced
sterilization and forced abortions), and the feminization and infantilization
of the nation.[69] Furthermore, coloniality enunciates a complex politics of sex
that subjugates and objectifies all Third World people and doubly subjugates
Third World women.

Since the next chapter is dedicated to a more complete analysis of the
Young Lords' engagement with and critique of machismo, here I want only to
point briefly to a connection with coloniality. Like with racism, the Young
Lords posited that sexism was a primary mechanism for the division of the
Puerto Rican people. "We have realized that the division of the sexes between
male and female have existed for such a long time, that all societies have
accepted the 'fact' that there is a difference between men and women."[70] The
facticity of sexual difference, its naturalization and dehistoricization, allowed
it to function unconsciously and unreflexively in the minds of Puerto Ricans.
Furthermore, "Because Puerto Rican society is structured in a sexist way, it
is very difficult to fight against things that we are not aware of."[71] Coupled
with an analysis of the social construction of gender, revolutionary nationalism functioned as a retort to sexism, racism, and racist sexism from without
and within.

Revolutionary Nationalism: The Young Lords' Decolonial Alternative

In response to the horrendous conditions established through coloniality's
various modes of functionality, the Young Lords offered "revolutionary
nationalism" as a theoretically distinctive and organically developed concept
that enacted, through its usage and utterance, a unique rhetorical function. In
"On Revolutionary Nationalism," Luciano argued that nationalism is key to
addressing their problems. "To combat psychological imperialism we could
begin by teaching our people pride in being Borinquenos."[72] Nationalism
must go further, however, than merely cultivating cultural pride. "But would
this nationalism by itself resolve the question of liberation for our people on
the island and self-determination for Puerto Ricans in amerikkka?" he asked
rhetorically. The answer is, of course, in the negative: "Culture without revolutionary politics is like a sword wrapped in foam rubber."[73] Cultural pride
and education about their past—an education that included general historical
lessons, recovering "equipment for living"[74] from prior activists, and a broad-
based political education engaging Western and Third World figures (e.g.,
Marx and Fanon)—were important; but this was not a simple Third World
fundamentalism. Pablo Guzmán concurred, suggesting, "We've seen how the

Black colony in America has been divided in terms of culture versus politics. We don't want to see the Puerto Rican colony divided that way. We don't want to create divisions where there need not be any."[75] Like Ramos-Zayas's heuristic concept of performative nationalism, then, revolutionary nationalism functions as a bridge between cultural and political nationalisms that is simultaneously both and neither—it is, borrowing from Chela Sandoval, a *differential* alternative that rejects binary thinking in preference for an organic alternative that can rework hegemonic articulations.[76]

Along these lines, the Young Lords refused to embrace a pure/orthodox version of the nationalism practiced on the island. Sure, they supported independence and the liberation of the Puerto Rican nation from U.S. political and legal control; but they clashed with the organizations on the island that failed to transcend or productively engage the colonial difference. As Grosfoguel argues, "Nationalist discourses in Puerto Rico fall into the trap of a colonialist underestimation of Puerto Rican agency and subalternity. . . . Similarly to colonialist/Eurocentric positions, nationalist ideologues do not recognize the cultural and political strategies deployed by Puerto Rican subaltern subjects as valid forms of knowledge and politics."[77] Island nationalists the Young Lords encountered often embraced an essentialist nationalism that tightly patrolled who counted as Puerto Rican and what counted as Puerto Rican culture (young folks from New York, sporting Afros, and speaking Spanglish did not). Additionally, according to Oliver's report after the Young Lords visited the island to explore coalitions, many nationalist ideologues were unreflexive of their machismo, propped up internal racism, and were fairly classist.[78]

Counter to and subsuming cultural and political nationalisms, Luciano first defined revolutionary nationalism thusly: "Revolutionary nationalism is the coming together of Puerto Ricans because of a similar culture, life style [*sic*], and a similar political reality, oppression, for the purposes of forming a masses-oriented organization to implement a common ideology which will struggle for liberation of our people through armed struggle."[79] Despite this turn to armed struggle, however, the Young Lords were not quick to jump the gun. "The first phase of any revolution," Luciano clarified two months later, "is political struggle. It is this phase that the YOUNG LORDS PARTY is presently involved in. We must first educate our people to struggle before we begin to take up arms by the thousands."[80] By teaching people about their Afro-Taíno history, to "think politically," to address "self-hatred" endemic to the colonized mentality, to break free from liberal individualism, and to challenge the modern/colonial system, the core of revolutionary nationalism sought to change the way people thought and acted. They articulated what Mignolo calls an "other thinking" that was in constant contact with their recovered history, local and embodied knowledge, and the stinging touch of coloniality.[81]

Rhetorically, the usage of the term "revolutionary nationalism" is significant for multiple reasons. First, as I mentioned previously, the term functions as "a symbolic agency through which" the Young Lords "change[d] its notion of itself as a preface to and prerequisite for commencing the struggle" for liberation.[82] The term is an agency in the sense that it enables certain kinds of activities and authorizes particular forms of activism—actions, activities, and ideologies that would not be possible operating solely under the sign of "nationalism" or "revolution." Linking revolution to nationalism taps into the amor patriae, the love of country that Puerto Ricans feel, the sense of *roots* that harken to an origin; but revolution tempers such romantic and potentially chauvinistic attachments by demanding an *up*rooting. "Revolution," argued Juan Gonzalez in May 1970, "is a complete change, an overturning of dead soil, a new way of life, with new government, new laws."[83] Tapping into a vast history of revolutions for liberation and the rhetoric of liberation already established in the immediate context by Black Power, other Third World Left advocates in the United States, decolonization in Africa, and nascent liberation theory in Latin America, "revolutionary nationalism" signified a kind of "repetition with a difference"[84]—a both/and plus neither/nor approach operating at the interstices of the local and global, present and past, modern/Western and Third World.

Such a theoretical and rhetorical move placed the Young Lords within the terrain of a kind of differential consciousness. Sandoval describes differential consciousness as "a strategy of oppositional ideology that functions on an altogether different register."[85] Rather than reinforce strict distinctions between different forms of social movement activism (Sandoval identifies "equal rights," "revolutionary," "supremacist," and "separatist" as four modes in women's movement contexts), differential consciousness functions simultaneously as an alternative to distinct modes of political engagement and a connection between them all. "The differential mode of social movement and consciousness," she argues, "depends on the practitioner's ability to read the current situation of power and self-consciously choosing and adopting the ideological stand best suited to push against its configurations."[86] To borrow from José Esteban Muñoz, differential consciousness operates as a form of "disidentification"[87] that negates the forced choice of ideological orthodoxy and seeks a paradoxical perspective where, in the Young Lords' formulation, things can be made "compatible."[88]

Within such differential compatibility, the Young Lords never sought to resolve the inconsistencies between their internationalist Third World perspective and island-based nationalist politics. Rejecting implicit nationalist demands to repatriate, for example, Guzmán mapped out a new "American Revolution" lead by the Young Lords in the Nuyorican context.

When we talk about our role in terms of creating the American Revolution, we are not saying we are going to take Puerto Rican people and ship them back to Puerto Rico. We are saying that we have been here in this country for two generations—in some cases, maybe three generations—we've been here for so long, right, that it would be too convenient for us to move back now, and just create a revolution there. We're saying that we want pay back for the years that we have suffered, the years that we have put up with the cockroaches and rats. We had to put up with snow, we had to put up with English, we had to put up with racism, with the general abuse of America. And we are gonna hook up with everybody else in this country who's fighting for their liberation—and that's a whole lot of people.[89]

Revolutionary nationalism afforded the Young Lords the flexibility to claim *both* (the liberation of Puerto Rico and internationalist Third World affiliation) and in doing so opened up a third space where "nationalism" tapped into deep structures of feeling and resistance significant to the Puerto Rican nation. But the connections are not limited to those between Puerto Ricans on the island and Puerto Ricans in the United States. The Young Lords linked the struggle to a history of resistance and revolution *within* the United States, positing a new "American Revolution" that complicated their intellectual and practical genealogy and added layers of "compatibility" that resisted ideological oversimplification.

At the same time, however, revolutionary nationalism was built on certain exclusions. It seems cliché, though perhaps no less apt, to reference Benedict Anderson's conceptualization of the nation as an "imagined community," which is a product of communicative and technological flows that demarcate a national inside and concomitant outside.[90] While not rooted principally in an essentialist concept of the nation-state, the Young Lords' crafting of a revolutionary community, even while reclaiming a label like "American Revolution," was exclusionary. Their invocation of "amerikkka" is a good example. Cotemporaneous with Black Power advocates,[91] the Young Lords consistently deployed the term "amerikkka" to rhetorically craft a nation imbued with racist and fascist politics. The term was deployed, as one can see throughout this chapter, to demarcate both a uniquely problematic/dangerous nation-state and its agents/supporters, particularly as they all enacted a set of colonial/capitalist/racist/sexist practices and reinforced a colonized mentality. It is important to note, though, that "amerikkka" did not work as a simple replacement for "white." As Guzmán once underscored, "it's not white *folk* . . . but a system created by white people" that was the target of their revolutionary nationalism.[92] In this context, "amerikkka" functioned oftentimes as the condensation symbol of that "system," the constitutive outside to which revolutionary nationalism was a response—even when particular U.S. Americans (e.g., the Weather Underground and the Young Patriots) were welcomed as allies and core agents in the global struggle for liberation.

Although nationalism has the potential to signify reactionary politics, the Young Lords' revolutionary nationalism guarded against such tendencies by stressing creativity, mobility, and equality and rejecting oppression in all of its forms. "Contrary to cultural nationalism," Luciano argued, "revolutionary nationalism work[s] with either groups and/or individuals from different nationalities and races provided these groups are revolutionary in theory and practice."[93] Viewing revolutionary nationalism as an appropriate and creative response to racist coloniality, Guzmán concurred:

> In this country, for example, racism is like a stick that the pigs are clubbing you on the head with. Now you got to grab the other end and hit them back with it—and the other end of the stick is nationalism. And if you do it righteously, if you do it with the interest of the people and with the backing of the people, then it becomes revolutionary. Now that's revolutionary nationalism—that is the kind of nationalism that says, "Yes, we are proud to be Puerto Rican, we are proud to be number one—but we want everybody else to be number one too, and we're gonna help everyone else be number one." See, cause the other kind of nationalism is reactionary nationalism—where you say, "Well, I'm number one. Fuck everybody else."[94]

Through their inventive approach and vocabulary, revolutionary nationalism functioned as the Other of racist coloniality. The turn against racism, then, is not merely a reversal that results in the subjugation of a group different than themselves, which would be a form of colonial mimicry that Fanon warned against;[95] rather, the Young Lords' commitment to the "liberation of all oppressed people" and concomitant rejection of the racist/sexist/capitalist "system" advanced by modernity/coloniality compelled them to, in the words of Fanon, "shake off the heavy darkness in which we were plunged, and leave it behind."[96]

Delinking from coloniality also meant a rejection of the sexism the Young Lords so aptly diagnosed and critically engaged. Remember that for the Young Lords, sexism was not an isolated problem. Rather, they took an integrated approach that recognized a recursive relationship between racist/sexist/capitalist oppression and coloniality. This is significant because, as Schiwy argues, gender and race become intertwined to secure coloniality. "Both concepts interact," she says, "coalescing into gender specific forms of oppression and meshing longstanding imaginaries in order to justify hierarchies of subjectivity, economical and political as well as epistemic orders associated with these subjectivities."[97] Oliver argued similarly, "If we want to change this society and develop a new one that no longer oppresses anyone we must try to eliminate the sexism that we 'non-consciously' retain in our minds. We must become instead of men and women—new humans, revolutionary people."[98] This transition from identity politics to a political identity is what opens up the space for a reconceptualization and other-enactment of politics delinked from coloniality.[99]

The Young Lords explained that this other-enactment of politics was guided by the desire to "develop people into good revolutionaries."[100] In the essay titled "The Party and the Individual," within their pamphlet on ideology, they underscored this emphasis on politicization. "A person becomes political, then they join the Party, then, after a period of time, they become a leader of the people. But it isn't as simple as that. There is a big change in the whole life of the individual."[101] Two processes that are intimately connected guided that change. First, the Young Lords pointed to a process of "de-classizing," which is not just about class in a Marxian analysis; rather, they described this as the process of "losing the bad traits from the class they originated from, like individualism, machismo, sexism, racism, intellectualism, superiorities and inferiorities."[102] Along with this move away from the categories of division endemic to capitalism was a rejection of coloniality. "Second, is the big change that the individual has in getting rid of the scars that capitalism has left in the person's mind, like liberalism (not doing something you know is right), pessimism, and the biggest of all, colonized mentality. Colonized mentality is the effects of oppression. . . . We call this change, 'de-colonizing.'"[103]

Through revolutionary nationalism, then, the Young Lords aimed to "unchain [their] minds from this colonized mentality"[104] and challenge the limitations imposed by a modern/colonial rationality that split identity according to race, gender, class, and all of their permutations. "We will never be free," Oliver argued, "until we have broken all the chains of our 'non-conscious ideology' and our colonized mentalities."[105] Breaking those chains in a differential mode, however, does not dissolve all of the links; rather, it reconfigures them in less problematic ways and vacates their epistemic privilege. Toward the end of his piece on revolutionary nationalism, Luciano drew a fine line in the following way: "Revolutionary nationalism is not chauvinistic. It should not make distinctions between cultures, but function so that Puerto Ricans feel pride in their uniqueness and understand and love the common cultural-political ties with Blacks, Indians, Asians, and other Latin people."[106] Such a rhetorical move preserves a certain level of uniqueness in Puerto Ricanness and allows for a re-cognition of "men," "women," "classes," and so on, but it also marks out broader connections between all who struggle against coloniality in their lived contexts. In this light, delinking through revolutionary nationalism does not rely on a complete and clean break with modernity/coloniality. Operating at the interstices of "the colonial wounds and imperial subordination,"[107] a space in between and in simultaneous contact with Western power knowledge and pluriversal alternatives,[108] the Young Lords' revolutionary nationalism enacts a form of border thinking and differential consciousness. In doing so, border thinking becomes "the connector between the diversity of subaltern histories . . . and corresponding subjectivities."[109] From this space—the space of the trickster, coyote, and jaibería—the Young Lords articulated affiliative linkages and appropriated from multiple ideologies in order to generate new possibilities for lived political thought and action.

This third space of differential consciousness and border thinking generates an alternative way to negotiate the problematic of nationalist political rhetoric. The Young Lords show that nationalist politics are not necessarily exclusionary or even focused on one particular nation. They certainly can be, and in so doing they can fall into a trap of purification whereby the nation comes to be defined in further exclusionary ways—for example, as Grosfoguel notes, the ways in which a "nationalist definition of Puerto Rican-ness as a 'national identity' privileges the Spanish over the African heritage."[110] But nationalism need not be so problematic. The Young Lords' configuration of revolutionary nationalism charts an alternative path on which a complex "national" identity can be crafted that is simultaneously nation-based and international, inclusive of heterogeneous constructions of the nation and broader "cultural" linkages between all who are affected by the long reach of coloniality. This *figural* revolutionary nationalism is more than a "radical ethnic nationalism" that makes connections between multiple ethnicities in political cooperation. Instead, it is a *transcendent* and *transgressive* rhetorical agency that draws from and recovers the embodied histories of coloniality and resistance, simultaneously reclaiming the symbolic power of national connection and charting a Third World figural "nation" that can unite a host of people under pluriversal commitments to liberation.

In the next chapter, I continue exploring the ways in which the Young Lords extended and translated their revolutionary nationalist commitments and demands for broad-based liberation. Focusing sustained attention on the elevation of women within the organization, I engage oral history, archival, and textual evidence to show how the Young Lords transformed from an organization demanding that "machismo must be revolutionary" to an organization that offered one of the earliest and most nuanced critiques of the intersectionality of oppression in that era. Exemplifying the Young Lords' rejection of the politics of recognition, women and men in the organization rooted their liberation politics (enabled partially by the symbolic agency of revolutionary nationalism) in a critique of intersectional oppression. The Young Lords' Third World feminist liberation politics fortified the affiliation-based coalitional connections and helped to solidify an ethic of decolonial love.

II

Decolonial Praxis

3

"We Refused to Cave In"

Gender, Race, Class, and Decolonial Intersectionality in the Young Lords' Liberation Politics

Culture and communication are nourished by stories, not only in order to conserve piously the great moments of a time past, nor in the vain hope of compiling a complete catalogue of a sacred patrimony, but in order to engender the future by reinscribing the present within the past.

—MICHEL DE CERTEAU, *The Capture of Speech and Other Political Writings*

When sisters have to go, like, cooking to cleaning the house to taking care of children, right, washing their clothes and ironing—all that has to be done in the house. Right? That is, like, a lot of work; right? But, like, when a man looks at that—because of the way he thinks, right—like, he always has to consider that, like, shit. Right? 'Cause who's doin' it? A woman.

—ANONYMOUS, *El Pueblo se Levanta* (Newsreel)

One of the fundamental paradoxes of "new social movements" arising in the late 1960s and early 1970s was the disjuncture between their theoretical and practical stances on equality. Despite organizing some of their goals explicitly around demands for equality, these movements were not always exemplary at practicing their theoretical commitments. This was true notably in different race-conscious organizations that arose in partnership with and in response to the mainstream civil rights movement. While sometimes (though not always) featuring demands for the equality of all people, groups like the Black Panthers, Nation of Islam, MEChA, and the early Young Lords frequently paid only lip service to the equality of a large portion of their membership: women.[1] Despite their active participation in the daily functioning of these organizations, women often were relegated to subservient positions and denied an equal voice in communal governance as such performances of leadership did not fit expectations of hegemonic femininity.[2] But in the New York Young Lords, women banded together and demanded more than the theoretical equality announced by the organization.

When the New York Young Lords were founded in the summer of 1969, as I discussed in Chapter 1, they filled a need for radical Puerto Rican activism created when McCarthyism drove the first generation of militants underground in the 1950s. In the beginning, however, some of their eventual goals with respect to gender equality were not yet being enacted. Women's labor was devalued, treated like "shit," as the second epigraph to this chapter shows. Indeed, as Jennifer Nelson suggests, "At first, gender was not a matter of great importance for the [Young Lords]. Women joined the party for many of the same reasons men did,"[3] but a group of men handled the organizational and leadership aspects. Women quickly became involved, but they were not invited into the leadership. The disjuncture between theoretical demands for gender equity and practical failures to actuate those demands made present, to some in the organization, the need for immediate change—especially in the context of an evolving sense of revolutionary nationalism and its attendant critique of coloniality, which I explored in Chapter 2. "Within months of [their] founding," Nelson writes, "gender conflict emerged as women pursued a greater role in determining the direction of the movement."[4] More specifically, women in the Young Lords confronted their male leaders with a simple demand: start promoting women's equal agency in the revolutionary struggle.

Initially, this ultimatum fell on deaf ears and hurtful fists; but the women persisted in their demand and resisted through their actions. Although their mandates were finally met and the Young Lords women were elevated to equal roles in the organization, their public story of resistance has been largely lost.[5] This absence of a markedly *gendered* struggle from our collective memory, however, should probably not be surprising. As Marianne Hirsch and Valerie Smith argue, "gender is an inescapable dimension of differential power relations, and cultural memory is always about the distribution of and contested claims to power. What a culture remembers and what it chooses to forget are intricately bound up with issues of power and hegemony, and thus with gender."[6] Accordingly, when the history of an organization is baptized in a sexist revolutionary politics and recounted officially from within a cultural frame marked by machismo, that frame shapes what is remembered and forgotten. Those memories, then, have an extended impact on our contemporary public discourse. As Kristen Hoerl argues, "Consistent patterns of discourse that ignore significant events in the history of social and political struggle create an impoverished discursive landscape by depleting rhetorical resources for shared reasoning about public policy, national identity, and social justice."[7]

Gradually, women and men in the organization worked together to find innovative ways to resist machismo (in their analysis, a virulent form of sexism rooted in the intersections of colonial racism/classism/sexism) and eventually transform the structure and culture of the organization to support gender and sex equality. The transformation was not easy. Once women in the

Young Lords asserted a voice, however, they set their sights on using it for further productive purposes. The initial victory—gaining representation of women on the organization's Central Committee, structural equality in the operations and activities of the organization, and embodied public evidence that women could lead alongside men—set a background in front of which a new rhetorical offensive would be waged. When the women performed an intelligible public voice on behalf of the Young Lords, they set out to advance a decolonial Third World protofeminist critique rooted in an analysis of the intersectionality of oppression along gendered/raced/classed axes.[8]

In this chapter, I assemble a story of women in the Young Lords. Keeping in mind that histories are always partial and perspectival, I choose to privilege the voices of women in the organization so that their stories of struggle can recalibrate the male-centered tales that are most often told. In the first part of this chapter, then, I draw principally from oral histories that I conducted so that I might operate in the interstices of the archive and the repertoire. Oral histories, according to Maylei Blackwell, function as "a hybrid that fits somewhere in between the archive and the repertoire, depending on how the narrator narrates, how the listener listens, and how the researcher wields the apparatus of objectivity that records or captures this performance."[9] In drawing from these oral performances of embodied memory, I rely heavily on the women's own words and act as much as possible as a facilitator bringing their story of change over time to the reader. As a listener of their stories, my praxis is undergirded by a decolonial ethic of love and grants an epistemic priority to the voices of these women.

In being a loving listener, however, my role is suspect. *I am suspect.* I am a man trying to give voice to women in the organization about things that men—in their histories of the organization and in their interviews with me—refuse generally to discuss. I am fundamentally torn between wanting to let the women's voices speak for themselves and knowing (a) that such a disinterested research position is never possible and (b) that such a standing aside is the very strategy used by men to excuse their own culpability in machismo's structures of domination (and to marginalize the already marginal voices of women). Although this should not be about me or about my guilt, I need to take ownership of my own voice in recording and assembling these testimonios.[10] Taking a cue from Aimee Carrillo Rowe, my engagement of these conversations can never transparently reflect what happened.[11] The interviews were always-already performances of embodied memories. As a Latino rhetorician, I aim to analyze them as a particular story and collected testimonio of what happened; but also I aim to interpret them in a way that can tease out theoretical lessons. This is, in part, a work of recovery and an attempt to build decolonial theory in ways that make such theory bound intimately to intersectional questions of gender, sex, sexuality, and race. In that vein, and following the admonition of Linda Martín Alcoff, I aim to avoid speaking *for* these women and try my best to speak *with* them.[12]

In the remainder of the chapter, I draw principally from archival materials—engaging in textual exegesis and critical analysis of visual and verbal discourses produced after the initial period of women's struggle within the Young Lords. Examining documents like their "Position Paper on Women" and writings about gender, sex, and sexuality in their book *Palante: Young Lords Party*, I demonstrate the ways in which their decolonial enactment of revolutionary nationalism is translated into a rhetoric of liberation rooted in a critique of the intersectionality of oppression. I conclude this chapter by exploring the implications of such a liberation politics, reading it as an alternative to the politics of recognition inherent to liberal democracy.

Testimonios de Transgresión: A Story of Women in the Young Lords

A story of women in the Young Lords ought to begin prior to the actual formation of the organization. As mentioned in Chapter 1, people who were drawn to the Young Lords came from myriad backgrounds: some were students with experience in late 1960s radicalism; others had been community activists in New York City; still others had little political experience outside their homes and/or jobs. This diversity of backgrounds and experiences is important when considering the politicization of women within the Young Lords because it serves as a reminder that women's concerns emerged out of a multiplicity of motivations, impulses, and theoretical foundations. Due to the histories of women and men alike in the Young Lords, the problem implied by a phrase like "the subjugation of women" was not entirely legible in their earliest stage of development. Given that the Young Lords were officially founded by a group of radical and charismatic men, equality with women was initially only a partial concern, examined primarily on the theoretical level. So when the Young Lords created their first "13 Point Program and Platform" in July 1969, the question of the role of women was dealt with as follows, in point number ten:

WE WANT EQUALITY FOR WOMEN. MACHISMO MUST BE REVOLUTIONARY . . . NOT OPPRESSIVE. Under capitalism, our women have been oppressed by both the society and our own men. The doctrine of machismo has been used by our own men to take out their frustrations against their wives, sisters, mothers, and children. Our men must support their women in their fight for economic and social equality, and must recognize that our women are equals in every way within the revolutionary ranks. FORWARD SISTERS IN THE STRUGGLE!

While such a statement on women and equality seems progressive on first glance, and it was progressive for a group of macho men to have any sense of gender consciousness, there were latent problems with the Young Lords' formulation of equality.[13] Deferring for a moment the question of whether machismo could ever be revolutionary, the grammatical structure of the program point suggests a less-than-equal affiliation between men and women. Note, in particular, the pronoun usage in the statement: women belong to the authors of the Program and Platform ("our women") and, more specifically, they belong to the men in the organization ("their women"). Read within the context of a macho male leadership, the language is paternalistic and sexist at worst and unreflexive at best. This practical relationship between men and women, along with the suggestion that machismo could be revolutionary, would eventually become one of the focal points of the women's "revolution within the revolution," but not before the women met and formed a protofeminist consciousness and ideology.

In 1970, the Young Lords' newspaper, *Y.L.O.*, ceased being published in Chicago and moved to New York as *Palante*. Not having a printing press of their own, the Young Lords sought the help of local organizations already publishing their own papers.[14] Linking up with the women's editorial collective of *The Rat*, minister of information Pablo Guzmán and "noncommissioned officer" (read: not part of the Central Committee) Denise Oliver began editing and printing *Palante*. Oliver, who came from politically active family and personal backgrounds, spent a significant amount of time in the office of *The Rat* and began talking with its staff and members about their feminist politics. Dissatisfied with the "ideological underpinnings of radical feminism . . . because they were talking about separatist feminism," Oliver extended discussions of feminist politics to other women within the Young Lords.[15]

As Young Lords women increased their exposure to feminist politics, the sexism of the organization became more legible and pronounced. According to Iris Morales, "The gender thing was problematic from the beginning because the Central Committee was all male." Morales continues:

> Within the Lords it was problematic and it was more problematic because of the articulation, obviously by the guys, of what women's liberation meant: which was "revolutionary machismo. . . ." The women felt like, "revolutionary machismo," hmmm, is there such [a thing] as "revolutionary racism"? How can there be such a thing as revolutionary machismo? That doesn't make sense because part of the ideology that was predominating was this thing and this mythology about women of color all not being strong and the men take the forefront; and also with this other ideology of our culture—this cultural nationalist view, which said that we've lost our culture in this country, this

decadent white European country where the women don't know their place and our culture/our women know their place and that's how we maintain family and they know their roles.[16]

Morales's critique is poignant. So often, it seems, radical critics and activists become focused on one axis of oppression at the expense of others. Indeed, decolonial scholarship is often most focused on race and capitalism, sometimes at the expense of attention that could be paid to gender—a methodological move that scholars like Freya Schiwy and María Lugones have critiqued it for.[17] "Revolutionary machismo" captures this inattention well. Here, Morales analogizes that none of the men who penned the program point would find a similar construction about race to be fruitful. Revolutionary racism is, on face, a ridiculous concept; so why should it be so easy to think about racist sexism (machismo) in this way? Significantly, Morales links her analysis to an implicit critique of simplistic cultural nationalism to highlight the ways in which something that seems resistive (the affirmation of "culture" in the face of racist Americanity) can also be oppressive. She was calling into question the mythologized construction of women in Puerto Rican culture. "What became clear," Oliver adds, "was that we were going to have to bite the bullet and begin to address" the issue of women in the Young Lords, especially "considering that there were more women in the Lords than men."[18] The organizational positions that women held, however, were out of the spotlight and, significantly, beyond the scope of decision making. Olguie Robles, a female cadre, recounts, "We were put into positions to cook. My first position was to sell newspapers and then to cook for the collectives," which was a common story for women in the organization.[19]

At this point, the women of the organization started to meet regularly in, what they called, the "women's caucus." The caucus served multiple purposes. According to Morales, "one was that we said, 'we're talking about human liberation here; but somehow our liberation as women is secondary to the liberation of men.'"[20] Another purpose was that the caucus allowed them to talk about practical issues they had, "concerns," as Oliver puts it, "with the brothers; concerns with the fact that we weren't being acknowledged for the work that we did; for some extremely male chauvinist behavior on the part of some of the brothers, especially in interpersonal relationships; but also just that programmatically we were really upset about the—machismo can't be 'revolutionary,' it's impossible."[21] The caucus also helped women articulate a strong public voice and grow through that voice. According to Robles, "That's where the women's caucus came in as a catalyst for my personal growth. Because I realized, man, you've got a voice, you know? You don't have to be quiet; you don't have to be a victim here. You can be a survivor."[22]

This issue of voice cannot be overemphasized. Women's voices were being systematically and structurally excluded as women were kept outside of leadership positions and pushed into seemingly menial labor that was devalued by men. The caucus became a space, a practiced place, where women's voices could be generated and heard. That women practiced these dual roles, as speakers and as listeners and audiences for their own voices, proved at least to them that their ideas and experiences had real value. The caucus served a constitutive role: it generated the space where gendered subjectivity could become something, where subjectivity could begin to emerge as a set of practices oriented around an ethic of love built on witnessing to one another. "This is to say," argues Kelly Oliver, "that addressability and response-ability are the conditions for subjectivity. The subject is the result of a response to an address from another and the possibility of addressing itself to another. This notion of subjectivity begins to go beyond the categories of subject, other, and object that work within scenarios of dominance and subordination."[23]

The caucus was also a space for education in which participants learned about issues and historical figures relevant to the struggle of Third World women. According to Oliver, "We started reading and doing our own political education about transforming ourselves, because not all of the sisters' opinions were anti-chauvinist either—they had been raised to be passive-servant-Puerto Rican-housewife-doormat types—and undoing a history of accepting oppressive and sexist behavior from men, which required working with some of these sisters."[24] As such, they educated themselves by reading and talking about strong, diversely positioned, revolutionary women, such as Lolita Lebrón, Blanca Canales, Rosa Parks, Sojourner Truth, Angela Davis, and Yuri Kochiyama. Such acts of recovery helped generate countermemories of resistance and served to craft a transhistorical narrative of gendered resistance that would undergird their subjectivity.[25] They also met with other activist women, including Bernadette Devlin, an Irish nationalist who had been given the key to New York City in honor of her struggles for Irish civil rights.[26] Furthermore, they discussed and debated women's issues relevant to Puerto Rican and other Third World women: abortion, birth control, forced sterilization, health care, and the role of women in revolutions (e.g., Vietnam, Puerto Rican nationalism, and the Cuban revolution). Political education in the women's caucus served the dual purpose of educating women and of articulating and reclaiming a history of women-in-struggle.

In the early stages of the women's caucus, sexist attitudes and actions among men, especially the "older" male leaders of the group who were only in their early to mid-twenties, flourished unhindered. A particularly pointed example came in the context of Felipe Luciano seeking out a new partnership with Amiri Baraka, an African nationalist poet who lived in New Jersey. Luciano and several other Central Committee members were asked to meet with Baraka to explore an alliance. Although she was not a member of the Central Committee, Oliver was invited to attend. Arriving at Baraka's headquarters, the Young Lords were greeted outside by a group of men in dashikis performing militant Black nationalism. Oliver recounts the troubling scene upon entering:

> We get into this room and these African American women in African garb come in like this [she is hunched over, head lowered, arms lifted up as if holding something in front of and above her head] bringing bowls of fruit; and then they backed out of the room bowing. And I'm standing there—me, [Juan] Fi [Ortiz], and Pablo [Guzmán] are standing like this [gestures with mouth wide open]. And I'm like "oh shit." Then we go and sit down with Baraka and I start asking questions about "what's the role of women in your organization?" And he ignored me! So Pablo asked the question and he said, "well, women are our goddesses; they're the mother of our children—" all this nationalist shit. I'm fucking flippin.' I couldn't believe . . . I got up and walked out. I started to walk back to New York. [laughing]27

After returning to New York and being disciplined by the leadership for her insolent reaction, Oliver recounted her tale to the members of the women's caucus.28 "I went right back to the women's caucus and gave them a dramatic recreation of the entire event. I said, 'Well, we're all going to have to get on our knees dragging in bowls of fruit and bowing.' You know? 'This is fucking shit.' The women were—they flipped."29 Oliver's retelling draws attention to the way women were cast as primitive, not modern (out of time), which recalls the role of women in the "modern" nation and links to the question of the place of women in nationalism. Such a romanticization and, perhaps, fetishization of a "pure" premodern past sidesteps the constitutive relationship between colonialism, capitalism, racism, and sexism and naturalizes gender subordination.

As women continued meeting in their "free time," usually on Sundays after they had completed all of their assigned tasks for the week, the all-male Central Committee became distressed with the women's rising consciousness. The women were subsequently instructed to put an end to the caucuses. According to Oliver:

> We were trying to hold our meetings, then we were told from above "No meetings." Ordered "No Meetings." You know . . . "You're talking some of that crazy feminist bullshit. What are you a bunch of white women?" No we weren't. No. And in fact, we had already discarded— we had plenty of opportunities to say "Fuck all of you—let's go be the Young Ladies" and quit. We rejected that as being counterrevolutionary. We examined it; we talked about it; we critiqued it.30

Also considered was the option of joining the Third World Women's Alliance (see Figure 3.1), a U.S. women-of-color feminist organization challenging

Figure 3.1 Front cover of the first issue of the Third World Women's Alliance's newspaper, *Triple Jeopardy* 1, no. 1 (September–October 1970).

racism, imperialism, and sexism. The presence of mindful analysis, here, is significant. The women were committed to bringing all members around to their position because it was, in their analysis, key to a successful revolutionary struggle. While they certainly had problems with many white feminist positions—because these were too reformist, too exclusionary of women of color, and/or too separatist—they knew that women needed acceptance as equal partners in the revolution. Accepting commonsense divisions along the axis of gender would only impede their attempts to advance *human* liberation.

Rather than either disband the women's caucus or split from the Young Lords, the women instead sought ways to resist. For example, women who were in intimate relationships with Young Lords men held a special meeting to discuss Aristophanes's *Lysistrata*, a play in which women decide to stop a war by kicking the men out of their beds. In that meeting, they decided that they would no longer have sexual relations with their male partners until the Central Committee and organization were reformed. Oliver recalls, "We knew we couldn't go on strike because that would mean all of the programs for the people would collapse. That would be counterrevolutionary—we were not going to not do our work. And we were certainly going to not have anything to do with them that we were related to at all. 'Hello. The revolution stops right here at the bedside.'"[31] The *Lysistrata*-style sexual strike did not go over well with some of the male leaders of the organization, and it became clear that "revolutionary discipline" would result. One day, a number of the leading women reported to martial arts class, which was a regular part of the Young Lords' training program. "We get into a situation where we've been told not to meet and we go to dojo training and the men had obviously met," remembers Oliver. "And there were these brothers who were there to give us discipline. We had been listening to 'crazy feminists' and doing all of this and won't give up these meetings and we've gone against, we're violating whatever whatever whatever—political justifications; I don't remember the arguments."[32] What it boiled down to was that the women would face harsh, physical discipline that day. It started with two hundred push-ups, followed by one hundred sit-ups.

Retelling what happened next, Oliver notes that the women were ordered to line up on the wall to practice katas (an exercise to practice form—e.g., punching or kicking into the air repeatedly, in the same pattern), and the men began "throwing punches at [our] stomach[s] and connecting," which she demonstrated by punching her own stomach a few times. Oliver continues, "I, to this day, have the hardest stomach muscles on the planet [punches stomach repeatedly and rapidly about fifteen times]. We took it. And they *thought* we were going to do the 'girly' thing and cry."[33] The embodied dimension of this story (something Oliver repeated every time she recounted it to me) is important because it underscores the connection between memory, knowledge, resistance, and the body—the stuff that forms a repertoire of resistance central to decolonial ways of knowing-in-being. The difficulty of this situation was magnified by the fact that some of the men handing out "discipline" were in intimate relationships with the women they were now assaulting. "And we had eyes straight forward; we didn't flinch; we didn't change expression; we took the discipline; we took more discipline,"[34] says Oliver. "We took everything they could throw at us and kept having our meetings. We refused to cave in."[35]

It is important to note that this is one part of the Young Lords women's story that is rarely retold in public forums—and is missing from all published accounts. Oliver verbally stumbles, "But these are very rarely has . . . I guess . . . I don't know. You know? We don't talk about this stuff much."[36] Nevertheless, it was an important moment in consciousness raising and the transition to a more egalitarian organization. As I listened to her tell this story and, years later, I put pen to page to write about it, I am struck by conflicting feeling of grief for what she reencountered as I asked her to relive the experience and doubt about whether I should even retell the tale for fear that some people will read it as "airing dirty laundry." Such stories must be retold, however, lest we risk romanticizing some revolutionary past and never correcting mistakes in our activist presents and futures. The discipline continued—"and not one sister broke; not one gave up and fell on the floor saying 'I can't do another pushup'"—and the women watched as "a number of the brothers began to get disgusted with what they were ordered to enforce."[37] As machismo started to play a role in its own undoing and women started gaining more support from, especially, the younger men in the organization, tensions peaked and the final door was opened for a structural and cultural transformation in the Young Lords.

But after weeks of discipline ordered by the Central Committee, something odd happened: the Central Committee disappeared. At a time when the Young Lords had reason to believe that the Italian American Mafia had murder "contracts" out on their leaders who had disrupted the Mafia drug trade, and when they were coming under the watchful eyes of the New York City Police's "Red Squad," the Central Intelligence Agency (CIA), and the FBI's COINTELPRO, the Central Committee was under strict security rules, imposed by themselves and security personnel, that required hourly check-ins. According to Oliver, they "were supposedly off doing the Lords' business and they weren't. When challenged about it, not only did they lie about their whereabouts, but so did their security (who were supposed to know where they are at all times). . . . They all covered up."[38] In Oliver's words, "this was the straw that broke the camel's back."[39]

Upon discovering the cover-up, the Young Lords women were livid. From their perspective, they felt that the male Central Committee members, their brothers in struggle, had been lying to them, too. "And the shit hit the fan when the word came out and it was like 'enough is enough.' So the initial confrontation came around disciplining those people who are at the top of the totem pole that should have been exemplary in their behavior and weren't," Oliver remembers. Young Lords members, especially the women but also some men, believed that "they wouldn't have been able to get away with a conspiracy of silence had there been a woman who knew what was what." According to Oliver, "it was a great opening for [. . .] the women's demands to come to the fore."[40]

Contrary to other accounts of the transformation toward gender equality within the organization,[41] what happened next demonstrated a genuinely democratic moment in the Young Lords. As Oliver explains:

> Remember that the structure was about "democratic centralism." Now it was more central than democratic; but that was on the books. That was what cadre had been trained about. And they decided to put it in to practice. And a massive meeting of cadres was pulled together in the main office. The central committee members were brought up on charges. And people testified about what they knew. A decision was ultimately voted on by the body to discipline all of the central committee members. . . . They were all demoted from their positions, which they could resume at the point that they accepted culpability for their actions, took responsibility, and transformed their mistaken ideas. And as a collective, so that it never happened again, there needed to be a female presence to—obviously they'd gone on a wrong track in bad thinking because there were [im]balances. And it just so happened that at that point in time, the only woman who had a certain level of information and authority to hand out discipline . . . at the time was me. So I was the first woman to be put on the central committee; and then later after that they put Gloria Fontañez. . . . And then women [including Morales] went on to central staff too.[42]

This is an incredibly important point: it was not just the women or the Central Committee itself that bravely solidified the place of women in the Young Lords. Rather, the structural reformulation of the Young Lords was a direct result of the cadre asserting their rights to democratic participation and holding all members accountable to the same rules. Morales offers a similar assessment:

> I've come to analyze it from a slightly different perspective, which was really a struggle to democratize the organization because all of the decisions were being made by men, basically, and with very little—we were supposed to be a democratic centralist structure, but basically it was centralist with very little democracy. . . . This also represented a way to open up the organization to more voices.[43]

"More voices," not just mere ideas, are critical to decolonial democratics. Just as the women had earlier generated space for their voices in the women's caucus and a critical terrain for the emergence of response-ability and human subjectivity, so too did they expand the spatial terrain for their voices into the organization at large. These were embodied voices that brought with them situated knowledge and experience that would transform the organization through their embodied presence and lasting interests.

In August 1970—once the cadre disciplined the Central Committee, moved women into the higher ranks of the organization, and opened up Central Staff positions to the women—other changes started being implemented. For example, from this point on, all Young Lords activities (rallies, political education sessions, group newspaper sales, etc.) required the participation of both men and women; Defense Ministry positions were opened up to women; and women asserted a stronger public voice in the Young Lords more generally. Additionally, the women's caucus (which became an officially recognized part of the Young Lords and eventually became the Women's Union) formulated a couple of key documents: a position paper on women that was published in *Palante* and a revision to the broader group's program and platform. The revised program point (moved up to the fifth spot in November 1970) read:

> WE WANT EQUALITY FOR WOMEN. DOWN WITH MACHISMO AND MALE CHAUVANISM [*sic*]. Under capitalism, women have been oppressed by both society and our men. The doctrine of machismo has been used by men to take out their frustrations on wives, sisters, mothers, and children. Men must fight along with sisters in the struggle for economic and social equality and must recognize that sisters make up over half of the revolutionary army; sisters and brothers are equals fighting for our people. FORWARD SISTERS IN THE STRUGGLE!

The first change was in the slogan. No longer calling for revolutionary machismo, point five now denounced machismo and male chauvinism in their totality. Within the text of the point, the only possessive pronoun refers to men ("our men"), a pointed rebuke of "our women" and "their women" (belonging to men) in the earlier text. Women are also placed rhetorically on equal footing with men through a rhetoric of kinship ("sisters and brothers"). Furthermore, the tone of the point shifted to create a demand, not that men must "support" women in "their fight," but that men must "fight along with sisters," who "make up over half of the revolutionary army." This change reinforced several important things: (a) that women were entitled to at least an equal position in the governance of the organization due to their numerical status; (b) that women were not lower in a hierarchy but sisters in the parentless revolutionary family; and (c) that men and women were equal participants in a historical, material, and ideological struggle against oppression. With this doctrinal change, the first movement of "revolution within the revolution" was well on its way.

While Lords women experienced a significant theoretical victory, acceptance of their equality was less than immediate, especially among the men (mostly from the Defense Ministry) who voted against the new measures of inclusion and decisions to discipline the Central Committee. According to Oliver, "Some of the brothers had a problem with it and I don't blame them—it's hard to undo twenty-some years of oppressive thinking and acting overnight and we were attempting to transform people almost instantly."[44] Although Mickey Melendez asserted in an interview that "there wasn't much resistance around the women's stuff," women in the organization would beg to differ.[45] According to Robles, "Some of [the men] were very open to the ideas because they were sincere. And some of them were very shut down to it because they were not sincere—because it was more about their egos than about true qualitative change. . . . It took a long while. It took a long while."[46]

The Position Paper on Women: Figuring Gender, Nation, Race, and Class

As women began challenging the lived experience of machismo within the organization and its structures, they also began enunciating a stronger public voice. Part of this public voice, as I demonstrated in the last chapter, was an integration of their critique of machismo with the broader organizational ideology surrounding revolutionary nationalism and internal colonialism. Jumping right into these ideological shifts, women's voices were front and center in the second issue of the Young Lords' *Palante* newspaper after their internal struggle, in September 1970. Featuring the organization's "Position Paper on Women," volume two, issue twelve (dated Friday, September 25, 1970) of *Palante* begins on its cover with a subversive visual element. A popular icon of the postcommonwealth status of the Puerto Rican government in 1952 was the image of a racial triad that signified the Puerto Rican nation composed of Spanish, African, and Taíno heritage, which is a rhetorical construction I discussed in Chapter 1. Semiotically, the different government-sponsored images were similar in that they represented the three "faces" of the nation in a way that depicted an idealized racial/national harmony. Often, the image illustrated the races in passive poses. As such, the viewer would have no reason to be threatened unless they were racist and sought to repress and/or suppress the very idea of the racial triad.[47] Furthermore, the representation of races/faces was always male, thus authorizing men as the symbolic faces of the respective political parties.[48] The image drawn by Denise Oliver on the cover of *Palante*, however, offers a stark contrast (see Figure 3.2).

Figure 3.2   Front cover of *Palante* 2, no. 12 (September 25, 1970), announcing the issue's publication of the "Position Paper on Women."

In this image, the setting is rural and mountainous, which places the figures in a geographical region similar to Lares, the site of the founding nationalist rebellion in Puerto Rico in 1868 (El Grito de Lares). Visually, then, this
links the Young Lords with a continued struggle for Puerto Rican national
independence, a link continued later in the issue through articles about Ramón
Emeterio Betances and El Grito de Lares, the anniversary of which was being
commemorated in the issue. Furthermore, the sky is dark and the land is
untouched by industrialization, allowing a visual reminder of the island's pre-
capitalist state. On this background, there are three figures, each of whom
represents one of the three races. The first is an androgynous figure of African
descent, hair "natural," clothing dark, rifle in hand, with a defiant gaze looking directly at the reader. The positioning of the African first and in an inter-
pellative role calls on the reader to identify with this often-repressed element
of Puerto Rican nationality. Also significant is the figure's androgyny—perhaps
emblematic of the Young Lords' broadening stance on gender identity and performativity or a refusal to visually represent men or women as the majority.[49]
The second person is a white man, of Spanish descent, performing jíbaro—a
word, as discussed in Chapter 1, that translates into something like "hillbilly"
but had been appropriated by the island independentistas to have a positive
connotation, in large part because of the jíbaro's role in the Lares revolt. The
jíbaro is also defiant, with one fist raised in a uniquely U.S. "power to the people"
manner; he holds a machete in the other hand, ready for combat.[50]

The third figure, anchoring the other two under the Nationalist Party flag,
is a Taíno woman. While the two figures in the front obscure part of her body,
possibly representing the emergence of women as the face of resistance, she
holds in her hand the master signifier of the nation. Without her, there is no
need for the other two because they would have nothing for which to fight; she
is the nodal point connecting the others and therefore the nation. Furthermore, the Taíno woman is also active and defiant. She may not be interpellat-
ing us as the objects or subjects of her gaze or calling out with fist raised; but
she *is* calling out—over the heads of the foregrounded figures as if her voice
covers the entire nation. She is the embodiment of the *grito*/cry of Lares. Such
a cry (both the woman's in the picture and Lares's) is important because it
makes a demand for action and constitutes a disruptive subject that challenges dominant ideologies. "The cry is," Nelson Maldonado-Torres argues,

> a sound uttered as a call for attention, as a demand for immediate
> action or remedy, or as an expression of pain that points to an injustice
> committed or to something that is lacking. The cry is the revelation of
> someone who has been forgotten or wronged. Before the word reaches
> the horizons of meaning, where the world is unveiled and the meaning
> of reality becomes clear, the cry becomes a call for the recognition of
> the singularity of the subject as such. The cry indicates the "return of

a living subject" who impertinently announces his [or her] presence and who by doing so unsettles the established formulations of meaning and challenges dominant ideological expressions.[51]

She looks away from the men, though, marking her as simultaneously part of the nation and separate from it with a unique and important voice. As a woman holding the Nationalist Party flag, she conjures the voice of Lolita Lebrón: "¡Que viva Puerto Rico libre!"[52] Although her placement in the background risks visually making her one with the land, such visual analogizing was not a tropic convention of the Young Lords' discourse, unlike Chicano filmic discourse from the same era.[53]

As problematic as we might view this feminine gendering of the nation, the significance of the cover image rests in two places. First, all three figures are engaged actively in poses of defiance and resistance. Figured against the background of El Grito de Lares, the people are linked to a history of demand, resistance, protest, and rebellion against racist/colonialist capitalism. Second, the rich inclusion of a Taíno woman, separated from the men by her placement above and between, subverts gendered hierarchies of the nation in which women had been placed into subservient roles.[54] We are left, then, with the impression that women (a) are a unique and integral part of the nation and (b) have (and have had) what may be the most important role to play in leading those decolonial struggles to reclaim the nation for the people.

Within the pages of this issue of *Palante*, we can see a rich collection of essays and articles that sets it apart from other issues of the newspaper. While all issues of *Palante* were thematically revolutionary, this one is particularly so. The back cover includes an image of new women leaders in the organization. Commemorating El Grito de Lares, it begins with an essay on Betances, followed by an advertisement and schedule for the Puerto Rican Student Conference to be held at Columbia University. The fourth and fifth pages of this twenty-four-page issue contain an article written by Iris Morales, the new Education Captain, on El Grito de Lares. The article ends with the call, echoing the visual citation of Lebrón on the cover, "THE DUTY OF EVERY PUERTO RICAN IS TO MAKE THE REVOLUTION! QUE VIVE PUERTO RICO LIBRE!" After some news articles about police repression and Young Lords expansion, there is an interview with Blanca Canales, a key figure from the 1950 Nationalist rebellion in Jayuya, Puerto Rico. Two pages later, in this context of revolutionary advancement and female-centered reporting, we have the "Young Lords Party Position Paper on Women" (hereafter referred to as the PPW), which is the first and most programmatic critique of machismo ideology produced by the Young Lords (see Figure 3.3).[55]

Spanning four pages, the PPW is divided into five topical sections and includes seven images. The first section is entitled "Historical," and offers an overview of Puerto Rican women's oppression, focusing principally on familial

YOUNG LORDS PARTY POSITION PAPER ON WOMEN

Puerto Rican, Black, and other Third World (colonized) women are becoming more aware of their oppression in the past and today. They are suffering three different types of oppression under capitalism. First, they are oppressed as Puerto Ricans or Blacks. Second, they are oppressed as women. Third, they are oppressed by their own men. The Third World woman becomes the most oppressed person in the world today.

Economically, Third World women have always been used as a cheap source of labor and as sexual objects. Puerto Rican and Black women are used to fill working class positions in factories, mass assembly lines, hospitals and all other institutions. Puerto Rican and black women are paid lower wages than whites and kept in the lowest positions within the society. At the same time, giving Puerto Rican and Black women jobs means the Puerto Rican and Black man is kept from gaining economic independence, and the family unit is broken down. Capitalism defines manhood according to money and status; the Puerto Rican and Black man's manhood is taken away by making the Puerto Rican and Black woman the breadwinner. This situation keeps the Third World man divided from his woman. The Puerto Rican and Black man either leaves the household or he stays and becomes economically dependent on the woman, undergoing psychological damage. He takes out all of his frustrations on

his women, beating her, repressing and limiting her freedom. Because this society produces these conditions, our major enemy is capitalism rather than our own oppressed men.

Third World Women have an integral role to play in the liberation of all oppressed people as well as in the struggle for the liberation of women. Puerto Rican and Black women make up over half of the revolutionary army, and in the struggle for national liberation they must press for the equality of women; the woman's struggle is the revolution within the revolution. Puerto Rican women will be neither behind nor in front of their brothers but always alongside them in mutual respect and love.

Historical

In the past women were oppressed by several institutions, one of which was marriage. When a woman married a man she became his property and lost her last name. A man could have several wives in order to show other men what wealth he had and enhance his position in society. In Eastern societies, men always had several wives and a number of women who were almost prostitutes, called concubines, purely sexual objects. Women had no right to own anything, not even their children; they were owned by her husband. This was true in places all over the world.

In many societies, women had no right to be divorced, and in India it was the custom of most of the people that when the husband died, all his wives became the property of his brother.

In Latin America and Puerto Rico, the man had a wife and another woman called la corteja. This condition still exists today. The wife was there to be a homemaker, to have children and to maintain the family name and honor. She had to be sure to be a virgin and remain pure for the rest of her life, meaning she could never experience sexual pleasure. The wife had to have children in order to enhance the man's concept of virility and his position within the Puerto Rican society. La corteja became his sexual instrument. The man could have set her up in another household, paid her rent, bought her food, and paid her bills. He could have children with this woman, but they are looked upon as by-products of a sexual relationship. Both women had to be loyal to the man. Both sets of children grew up very confused and insecure and developed negative attitudes about the role

Women have always been expected to be wives and mothers only. They are respected by the rest of the community for being good cooks, good housewives, good mothers, but never for being intelligent, strong, educated, or militant. In the past, women were not educated, only the sons got an education, and mothers were respected for the number of sons they had, not daughters. Daughters were worthless and the only thing they could do was marry early to get away from home. At home the role of the daughter was to be a nursemaid for the other children and kitchen help for her mother.

The daughter was guarded like a hawk by her father, brothers, and uncles to keep her a virgin. In Latin America, the people used "duenas" or old lady watchdogs to guard the purity of the daughters. The husband must be sure that his new wife has never been touched by another man because

Cuban militia member

Figure 3.3 "Young Lords Party Position Paper on Women," *Palante* 2, no. 12 (September 25, 1970).

relations and the institution of marriage. The second section, "The Double Standard, Machismo, and Sexual Fascism," examines the links between the capitalist system, machismo, masculinity, and "sexual fascism" (someone who "thinks of the opposite sex solely as sexual objects to be used for sexual grat- ification and then discarded" [12]). The third section, "Prostitution," examines the systemic causes of sexual and economic prostitution and demands repro- ductive freedoms for Third World women.[56] The fourth section, "Day Care Centers," identifies briefly the need for adequate day care facilities. The final section, entitled "Revolutionary Women," crafts a genealogy of women in decolonial and anti-imperial struggles, identifying a tradition of activism and revolutionary leadership to which the Young Lords and their contempo- raries could look for guidance, hope, and inspiration.[57] The images of revo- lutionary women, in order, are a black Cuban militia member, a Vietnamese guerrilla, Lolita Lebrón being escorted by police, a women's protest centered on a black woman holding a Third World Women's Alliance sign, Leila Khaled (a Palestinian revolutionary), a large and unidentified multiracial women's rally (possibly set in front of a courthouse), and a lithograph of an ambigu- ously ethnically marked woman (she could be African, Caribbean, or other- wise Latin American) with what looks like a baby on her back and a rifle in her hand.

The PPW begins with a proposition of fact: "Puerto Rican, Black, and other Third World (colonized) women are becoming more aware of their oppression in the past and today" (11). As such, the PPW frames itself as serv- ing the dual purposes of identifying the problems of Third World women (their historical and material oppression and the implications of that oppres- sion) and an attitude of resistance adopted by the Young Lords to combat those problems. The main demand of the PPW is best represented in its third paragraph and underscores the representational force of the Taíno woman on the front cover:

> Third World Women have an integral role to play in the liberation
> of all oppressed people as well as in the struggle for the liberation of
> women. Puerto Rican and Black women make up over half of the rev-
> olutionary army, and in the struggle for national liberation they must
> press for the equality of women; the woman's struggle is the revolution
> within the revolution. Puerto Rican women will be neither behind nor
> in front of their brothers but always alongside them in mutual respect
> and love. (11)

Here we see textual evidence of the Young Lords' resistance to an either/ or mentality that marked some variants of radical feminism, as well as other ethnic nationalist groups, at the time.[58] More important, perhaps, is their invocation of love, which is rendered as "alongside"—a becoming-with that functions differentially to traverse and transgress sedimented power relations in the global struggle for liberation.

In advancing a strong position on the equality of women, the Young Lords were careful not to alienate the men—separatism was not what they were after; rather, this initial statement bound the interests of women and men in revolutionary struggle. This is one key difference in how the Young Lords dealt with feminism(s) as compared with their Chicano counterparts. Where the Young Lords saw the interests of revolutionary women and men inextricably tied together in a manner that required gender equity, groups like MEChA and Latino Unidos Party failed to be inclusive, and Chicana feminists often had to articulate their voice outside those organizations until years after their initial demands for equality.[59] Simultaneously, the PPW enunciates recognition that women's equality represents a unique challenge that cannot be explained or solved by a simple Marxist critique. To balance this tension, the PPW names a "revolution within the revolution" that marks out the layers of domination and resistance and maintains the centrality of *human* revolution to the struggle.

A good example of this dual-pronged move of challenging inequality in the party and advancing equality outside the party is found in the PPW section called "The Double Standard, Machismo, and Sexual Fascism" (12). The section begins with a systemic analysis of the contradictions of capitalism: "Capitalism sets up standards that are applied differently to Puerto Rican and Black men from the way they are applied to Puerto Rican and Black women. These standards are also applied differently to Third World peoples than they are applied to whites." Consistent with other radical discourses of the time period and with the Young Lords' own rhetoric of revolutionary nationalism discussed in Chapter 2, the Central Committee laid blame on a racist and sexist system of oppression that ought to be the target of analysis, critique, and revolution.[60] In this particular instance, "the system" was identified as an authorizing force that erects a double standard allowing the advancement of whites, especially white men. Where whites are understood as capable of advancement, Third World men "are looked upon as rough and sexual, but not as intellectuals." Similarly, women are "not expected to know anything except about the home, kitchen, and bedroom. All they are expected to do is look pretty and add a little humor"—perhaps like the women dragging bowls of fruit encountered earlier. Such expectations are the product of coloniality's denigration/devaluation of embodiment, concomitant elevation of the mind, and its alignment with, primarily, Western men.

In both instances, "the system" defines Third World people outside of modernity as uncivilized brutes who are fully embodied but incapable of reason. Such a take on embodiment has strong roots in Cartesianism, which, Maldonado-Torres argues, "introduces a highly abstract conception of subjectivity that renders embodiment unimportant or problematic."[61] Mignolo takes this a step further, pointing to a disembodied and dislocated "zero point epistemology" as the ungrounded grounding of modern/Western knowledge "in the mind and not in the brain and in the heart."[62] Within this already inequitable set of relations, men are placed (they are also objects, after all) into positions of superiority over women, which gives them "license to do many things— curse, drink, use drugs, beat women, and run around with many women." Furthermore, this positioning of men over women is naturalized, thereby reifying essential differences between Third World men and Third World women. "As a matter of fact," the PPW argues, "these things are considered natural for a man to do, and he must do them to be considered a man. A woman who curses, drinks, and runs around with a lot of men is considered dirty scum, crazy, and a whore." "The system," then, creates two sets of double standards: one between whites and Third World men and a second between Third World men and Third World women. The consequence is, at worst, hostility toward Third World women and, at best, an indifference that, Lugones argues, "is insidious since it places tremendous barriers in the path of the struggles of women of color for our own freedom, integrity, and well-being and in the path of the correlative struggles toward communal integrity."[63]

Perhaps more significant are the ways in which "the system's" authorizing force is discursively aligned by the Young Lords, in part as a double standard but also as essentialist in its treatment of race and gender more broadly. As a result of the double standard, the PPW argues, a fundamentally unequal and counterrevolutionary system of gender relations between Third World men and women (machismo) is propagated:

> Today Puerto Rican men are involved in a political movement. Yet the majority of their women are home taking care of the children. The Puerto Rican sister that involves herself is considered aggressive, castrating, hard and unwomanly. She is viewed by the brothers as sexually accessible because what else is she doing outside of the home. The Puerto Rican man tries to limit the woman's role because they feel the double standard is threatened; they feel insecure without it as a crutch. (12)

In this rich passage, we can identify the ideological force of the double standard and the damaging effects of an essentialist gender politics. The very same system that keeps Third World men in a position of subjugation becomes an enabling force, the highest source of agency, in the men's relations of domination over women. As such, the performance of revolutionary agency by women threatens the little agency that men feel they have; it calls into question the order imposed by capitalism's double standard. Through its critique, the PPW calls into question the fixity of "the system" at all levels and invokes a demand to rethink gender as denaturalized because that would be the most *revolutionary* way to think and perform gender.

My analysis up to this point demonstrates that, when confronted by a system of oppression that forced Third World people generally into a subjugated position and Third World women particularly into a kind of doubled subjugation resulting from racist sexism, the women of the Young Lords articulated a revolutionary consciousness that could not be separated from demands for equality and critiques of naturalized gender roles. On its own, this is a significant achievement because it represented the strength of decolonial politics and authorized the agency of women in the struggle for broader social transformation. If my analysis stopped there, however, we would miss a second constitutive gesture of this "revolution within the revolution"—namely, the way in which it extended an antiessentialist identity politics beyond gender in order to problematize naturalized conceptions of sex and sexuality. Their Third World feminist critique exposed the antagonism inherent to identity/difference in a manner that called into question essential foundations of the self and, I argue, underscored a performative and decolonial understanding of subjectivity and agency.

The "Revolution within the Revolution": Gender and Sex in Public Culture

"Revolution within the Revolution," a section in the Young Lords' 1971 book *Palante: Young Lords Party*, begins with a quotation from Ernesto "Che" Guevara: "Let me say at the risk of seeming ridiculous that a true revolutionary is guided by great feelings of love." As I argued in the Introduction and earlier in this chapter, love is central to a decolonial ethic that challenges dehumanization in its many lived forms. I believe love, here, marks the narratives that follow in fundamentally *open* ways—that is, they are orienting the reader toward what Oliver calls "a responsibility to response-ability. . . . To serve subjectivity, and therefore humanity, we must be vigilant in our attempts to continually open and reopen the possibility of response."[64] Such openness to response-ability underwrites decolonial ethical relationships and subjectivity in ways, for the Young Lords, that would no longer be exclusionary toward women and those who identify as lesbian, gay, bisexual, trans*, or queer (LGBTQ), as becomes evident in the four brief narratives that follow the introductory Che quotation. First, Pablo Guzmán writes about gender norms. Second, Denise Oliver writes about the role of women within the organization and in society at large. Third, Richie Perez writes about the dangers of machismo and the importance of equality in the struggle. Finally, Guzmán ties the

Young Lords' evolution on the gender issue into their broader decolonial socialist politics. Rather than deal with all of these narratives in order, I focus attention on Perez's and Guzmán's first contributions, as these two essays both speak most directly to their progressive stance on gender without repeating the PPW and demonstrate uptake of the ideas first publicly laid out in the PPW a year earlier.

In his only entry in *Palante: Young Lords Party*, Perez demonstrates a key critical sensibility that was emblematic of the organization's praxis in what I call the second movement of the "revolution within the revolution." Perez begins his contribution with a critique of machismo, not masculinity, writing, "In our community *machismo* is something that is a particular problem. It's one of the trademarks of Latin culture. It is that exaggerated sense of manhood that constantly must be proven in a number of different ways."[65] Like the women in the Young Lords, what he calls attention to is not masculinity generally—some might argue, in fact, that even the women in the Young Lords embraced a particular performance of masculinity in order to resist male oppression and get their demands met (e.g., seeing crying as a form of weakness and avoiding it when they were being beaten by men in martial arts training)—but the specific problem of racist/sexist/classist machismo for Latin@s. As something to be proven, machismo is a performance that works itself out in the most insidious ways: through acts of physical aggression against men and women, through the *erection* of strict gender roles, and through certain forms of aggressive verbal discourse. Furthermore, machismo's aggressions were normalized, explained by men as "a natural thing."[66]

Like others, Perez critiqued machismo for being counterrevolutionary and a hindrance to the Young Lords' struggle for social justice and multiple equalities. One particularly pointed example of his critique is worth quoting at length. In the context of confronting machismo's normalization, Perez writes:

We've talked about all kinds of things, like the fact that brothers don't know how to talk about sisters. Words like "broad" and "chick" are negative terms—again, they *take away the humanness* of the people that you're applying them to and *make them into objects*. Of course, no brother would like to be referred to as, "That's my stud," or something like that. Instead of saying "manpower," we're trying now to use the word "peoplepower," 'cause we're not only talking about men—we're talking about brothers and sisters. This isn't an organization of just men. At first people said, "well, it's just words. Terminology doesn't mean anything, you know, it's how you really feel." We had to break that down. *Words do show an attitude, and if you want to change that attitude, you have to begin by changing the words that you're using to describe people.*[67]

Framed in terms of dealing with problems of interpersonal communication the
men were having among themselves, Perez advanced some profound points
regarding the importance of language. First, he rehearsed the now familiar
critique of sexist language as propping up objectifying relations. Second, he
underscored the practical political move of desexing terms like "manpower"
because they discursively excluded women from the ranks. Equality, through
Perez's perspective, is a position that must be advanced in all aspects of the
Young Lords' activism, including the specific language that they used.

Perez continued by making a key, perhaps banal, point: language matters.
Sounding a bit like a rhetorical critic, Perez called attention to the need to
break down a dominant view within the group that words do not matter, that
it is what is *inside* that "counts." Perez's stance seems to be a practical example
of delinking, which posits a "need to change the terms of the conversation,"
Mignolo suggests. "Changing the terms, and not just the content, of the conversation means to think and act decolonially."[68] In this sense, Perez drew
attention to the formation of political subjectivities by the language of the
Young Lords' membership. "As far as controversies and interpretations remain
within the same rules of the game (terms of the conversation)," Mignolo elab-
orates, "the control of knowledge is not called into question."[69] Perez seems to
concur. "Words do show an attitude," he wrote, and changing those words is
key to both changing attitudes and changing the positionality of various rhetorical agents—key to moving people from a colonized mentality, as was discussed in Chapter 2, toward decoloniality. Shifting attention to the "knower,
rather than the known" and "to the very assumptions that sustain locus of
enunciations,"[70] Perez's critique exhibits sensibilities central to delinking from
modernity/coloniality. Dominant sexist terms, in Perez and the Young Lords'
assessment, were constitutive of a problematic, dehumanizing agency that was
counterproductive to the Young Lords' revolutionary aims.

For Perez, rhetoric has real, practical consequences for the potential of
social movement among the Young Lords and in society at large. If machismo were allowed to continue, the Young Lords' rhetoric would authorize or
stabilize agency in an inherently inequitable manner. Concluding his contribution to *Palante: Young Lords Party*, Perez wrote, "It's no use making revolution if after we make it and take state power we're as fucked-up as the people
we replace. We not only have to change the political structure of this country,
we've also got to change everything else. Revolution means change from the
top to the bottom, and that includes the way we deal with each other as human
beings."[71] It is this nonsexist fraternal, relational aspect of everyday practices
(including embodied, verbal, and other forms of symbolic action) that Perez
demands must be challenged in the Young Lords' articulation of "revolution,"
which requires envisioning and enacting new forms of humanity. Consistent
with Frantz Fanon's critique of colonial anti-black dehumanization and concomitant articulation of a decolonial humanist politics, Perez's call seems

rooted in what Maldonado-Torres identifies as "the humanizing task of building a world in which genuine ethical relations become the norm and not the
exception."[72] In this ideological and rhetorical context, "liberation" and "revolution" are "not so much a struggle for freedom and equality as a struggle for
human fraternity . . . the formation of a human community where subjects are
not only recognized as possessors but as givers as well."[73]

Perhaps the most telling example of the effect of such decolonial fraternal
politics is Pablo "Yoruba" Guzmán's first essay in the "Revolution within the
Revolution" section of the *Palante* book. In this rich but short piece (taking up
less than two pages in the book), Guzmán addresses explicitly at least two
issues relevant to this argument. On the relationship between race, class, and
gender oppression, Guzmán challenged what Judith Butler has called "the
insistence upon the coherence and unity of the category of women"[74] characteristic of public perceptions of feminisms at the time. Furthermore, Guzmán
embraced the performativity of gender and sexuality, which ends up being a
key step in the Young Lords' progression toward a broader decolonial politics.

Guzmán begins his piece by admitting frankly the prevalent attitude of
men in the Young Lords at the time when women began strengthening their
calls for equality. "The first time we heard about Women's Liberation our
machismo and our male chauvinism said, 'Well, these chicks are all
frustrated—that's their main problem. What they really need is a good—you
know.' That was the thing that we were coming from."[75] Motivating this attitude, Guzmán suggested in the spirit of the PPW, was a complex interweaving
of race, class, and gender analyses. Careful to recognize that women's oppression cannot be totalized through the discursive field of Marxism or anticapi-
talism ("No, we can't blame this totally on capitalism, it is a thing that goes
way back to the tribes"), Guzmán pointed out the difference between the
oppression of white, middle-class women and Third World women. "The
thing with the white women is that they have been put on a pedestal, right;
however, with Third World women the problem has been that the white man
has put the white woman on a pedestal, and then messed around with Third
World women."[76] While this quotation belies a bias toward compulsory het-
erosexuality, both in the actions of white men and in the epistemology that
informs Guzmán's critique of colonial, white, capitalist masculinity, it also
indicates an attention to the intersectionality of oppressions absent from what
he calls "Women's Liberation";[77] that is, Guzmán's statement demonstrates a
practical consciousness of the ways race, class, and gender intersect to produce
oppressive conditions greater than the sum of their parts.[78] This oppression
has further implications for his own masculinity, Guzmán acknowledged,
because the "white cat has also helped turn around the brothers into a thing
where to prove their manhood, to prove that they are like that white person,
they go around oppressing sisters."[79] What we see here is an internalization
of the argument from the PPW; or, more accurately, we see evidence of the

internalization of the PPW's critique through the outward manifestation of Guzmán's discourse.

If this critique of the intersectionality of oppression sets a background for Guzmán's acts, what is most interesting is the direction in which Guzmán's argument goes. Following the formation and success of the women's caucus in the Young Lords, a "gay and lesbian caucus" started meeting with the aim of getting their voices heard. These discussions had a tremendous impact on Guzmán and the outlook of the Young Lords. "Since I'm talking about sexism," Guzmán wrote, "the second thing that made perhaps a greater impact on us was when we first heard about Gay Liberation." As one can imagine, the same machismo that reinforced boundary-defining discourses about women (calling them "whores," etc., if they acted "out of place") also informed discourses about gays and lesbians. "There's this whole thing about faggots, you know, and queers, and this and that. From the time you were a kid your folks told you the worst thing you could be was gay."[80] Guzmán and the Young Lords confronted this attitude rooted in heteronormativity and began to rethink the implications of *being* gay or lesbian.

Such an inquisitive attitude led Guzmán to make one of the most striking statements in *Palante: Young Lords Party*:

> *Now, I'm not gay, but maybe I should be. It would probably give me a better outlook on a whole lot of things.* At this point, I am talking from a theoretical point of view where I feel like I understand the problem. *Being gay is not a problem; the problem is that people do not understand what gay means.* See, there is a biological division in sex, right—however, this society has created a false division based on a thing called gender. *Gender is a false idea,* because gender is merely traits that have been attributed through the years to a man or a woman. Like, the man is supposed to be strong, noble, hearty, hairy, rough, and the woman is supposed to be light, tender, pretty, fragile, crying, and weak. And what happens when you find a guy that's light, pretty and tender? The guy is obviously a "queer," right. And if you find a woman who has the gender traits of the man, then that woman is obviously a "lesbian." And both words are said very negatively—they're both supposed to be very fucked up, right. In other words, a man trying to be a woman and a woman trying to be a man. Well, that's not true, you see, because in our analysis of the Gay struggle—and I like to put it in those terms, the Gay struggle for liberation—it's been clear to us that *what this means is really rounding out of the person.*

The time I spent in the academic world there was always talk about how you could get an education that would round out the individual. The Gay struggle really rounds out the individual, you know. *Because certain traits have been assigned to people historically by society, we've actually developed as half-people, as half-real.* We're saying that to be totally real, it would also be healthy for a man, if he wanted to cry, to go ahead and cry. It would also be healthy for a woman to pick up the gun, to use the gun.[81]

The quotation begins with a radical admission rooted in a fundamental problematization of the gendered subject. Gender, Guzmán posited, is a lie, a "false idea" that limits human potential through a sociohistorical bifurcation. Although he speaks as if "sex" is a real, material difference, gender is a construction for Guzmán. In the suggestion that maybe he "should be" gay, Guzmán draws attention to the fluidity and performativity of gender and sexuality.

More important, though, his statement indicates the adoption of a broader antiessentialist identity politics. If the boundaries of the "Gay Liberation" struggle are articulated as permeable, allowing Guzmán to enter its fray, then the boundaries of identity generally are also permeable. You do not need to "be gay" to enact "Gay Liberation" because "gay" is performative; it is a contingent, contextually bound, discursive articulation. "The problem is that people do not understand what gay means," Guzmán said. The rest of what follows, then, is an attempt to (re)articulate "gay" through this antiessentialist, decolonizing lens. In today's critical lexicon, such an articulatory moment appears thoroughly "queer" insofar as it rejects the naturalization of gender and sexual binaries. While this queering may be undercut somewhat by Guzmán's apparent claims to authenticity (being "totally real" humans), those claims should be read within their context as responses to a naturalized order imposed on gender/sex by a sexist/racist/capitalist system. Although "real" persons may occupy an important signifying role for Guzmán, its reality is empty and without specificity: realness is roundedness and multiplicity marked by the play of difference.[82] Simultaneously, the realness to which Guzmán alludes is full of the kind of positive content that Fanon sees as essential to escape the "zone of nonbeing" definitive of the colonial anti-black and sexist world.[83]

Liberation as an Alternative to Recognition

The Young Lords' stance on gender became so flexible that, within a very short period of time, they were welcoming not only to women but to gays, lesbians, and others who were queer.[84] For example, Stonewall combatant, STAR (Street Transvestites Action Revolutionaries) cofounder, and Gay Liberation Front member Sylvia Rivera was welcomed into the Young Lords' revolutionary fold. Speaking about a mass demonstration in East Harlem in the fall of 1970, Rivera recounted her first and subsequent experiences with the Young Lords:

Later on, when the Young Lords [. . .] came about in New York City, I was already in GLF [Gay Liberation Front]. There was a mass demonstration that started in East Harlem in the fall of 1970. The protest was against police repression and we decided to join the demonstration with our STAR banner.

That was one of first times the STAR banner was shown in public, where STAR was present as a group.

I ended up meeting some of the Young Lords that day. I became one of them. Any time they needed any help, I was always there for the Young Lords. It was just the respect they gave us as human beings. They gave us a lot of respect.

It was a fabulous feeling for me to be myself—being part of the Young Lords as a drag queen—and my organization [STAR] being part of the Young Lords.[85]

The point of recounting Rivera's experience is not to applaud the Young Lords for something they should have done all along. Rather, the point is to make note of how far they came in a short period of time. The transformation—from assaulting men's masculinity by calling them "punks" (read: fags) if they were not macho and physically assaulting women who did not conform to their notions of what women should do, to openly embracing trans* activists in the revolutionary struggle—was almost instantaneous.

The Young Lords represent an early example of both revolutionary gender politics and decolonial politics made possible through the opening of difference. In our conversations, members who stuck through the organization's transformation from revolutionary machismo to protofeminist revolutionaries admitted that there was always work to be done. Struggles for nonsexist fraternity are never complete; they are always processual and must be propelled through continued practices of social critique and self-criticism. The critical edge of the Young Lords' praxis, exemplified in the instances of how they addressed issues of gender and machismo, speaks to larger issues about how we conceptualize what the organization did and what their politics were about.

In her compelling account of Puerto Rican identity and politics in twentieth-century New York City, Lorrin Thomas offers an interpretation of the Young Lords and their cohort that fits them within a broader narrative of struggling for "recognition." For Thomas, young Puerto Ricans like the Young Lords "began to challenge the moderate, liberal approach of the older second generation and embrace a more radical agenda." As I noted in Chapter 2, she continues that rather than operating within an understanding of "recognition in a liberal discourse of inclusion-as-equals, militant youth . . . framed their demands for recognition in American society in more challenging terms."[86] As I have been showing over the course of the present and previous chapters, however, the Young Lords might have been up to something different than a politics of recognition, as is evident by their choice of terms (revolutionary nationalism, liberation, human, etc.) and their avoidance or rejection of more dominant rhetorics of recognition. Indeed, locking ourselves into a set of theoretical perspectives located firmly within the colonial matrix of power, as rhetorics of recognition risk, is a mistake. Argues Mignolo, "It is no longer possible, or at least it is not unproblematic, to 'think' from the canon of Western philosophy, even when part of the canon is critical of modernity. To do so means to reproduce the blind epistemic ethnocentrism that makes difficult, if not impossible, any political philosophy of inclusion."[87] This is not *mere* semiotics or theoretical nitpicking because, as Perez exhorts, "words do show an attitude"; and the language of human liberation shows a radically different attitude compared with the language of recognition.

Even if not reliant explicitly on the "liberal discourse of inclusion-as-equals," as Thomas frames the logic to which the Young Lords responded, the politics of recognition is inherently problematic. According to Maldonado-Torres:

> The problem with the politics of recognition . . . resides in self-centered claims for redistribution. In other words, the danger is when the struggle for recognition is reduced to questions about the respect, freedom, and equality of subjects who aim to overturn the system of lordship and bondage by coming finally to possess something of their own and to be recognized as proprietors. This conception of the struggle for recognition is fated to leave untouched the basic structure of the oppressive system that creates pathological modes of recognition and to hinder the chances for the formation of what has been aptly called "a coalition politics of receptive generosity."[88]

In my reading of the Young Lords' activism and rhetoric, they advanced a multivalent systemic critique that, beyond challenging the system that dominated at the time, sought to articulate new terms and perspectives aimed at a fundamental reorganization of human relations. That said, I think that some people at the time *read* them—that is, sought to *understand* them vis-à-vis their zero-point epistemology—by translating their discourse and activism into the language of recognition. We have been witness to the same rhetorical move by establishment power structures in the recent Occupy Wall Street protests, when protesters were asked, "What do you want?" Such a simple question forces its target into a mode of legibility and a logic of recognition that cuts short the process of political imagination necessary to challenge the deeply sedimented logics and rhetorics of modernity/coloniality. While we *could* read the Young Lords' rhetoric, then, through a logic of recognition, such a hermeneutic practice risks reinforcing the dominant monotopical orientation (which demands, in a sense, operation within a politics of recognition in order to be intelligible) and missing the uniqueness of their revolutionary liberation politics.[89]

Within the context of decoloniality, liberation is a crucial alternative to recognition. Liberation does not necessarily presume a Western notion of freedom; rather, according to Maldonado-Torres in his reading of Enrique Dussel, "liberation refers to the many attempts, especially by former colonized subjects, to affirm their own selves and to create a world *in which many worlds can fit*. Liberation claims liberty, equality, and fraternity, but also solidarity and the embrace of alterity, including epistemic diversity."[90] We will see another example of this orientation toward liberation in Chapter 4, when I examine the Young Lords' "garbage offensive"—their first activist campaign in East Harlem through which they modeled crucial practices of alterity and decolonial love by listening to the residents of El Barrio and addressing the issue those residents saw as most urgent. In this chapter, we have seen the enactment of liberation politics in the context of struggles for gender equality and their relationship to other questions of race and class. Through a decolonial perspective that linked sexism, racism, and classism, the Young Lords advanced an intersectional critique of machismo in a manner that would become central to their broader ideological positions related to the "colonized mentality" and "revolutionary nationalism."

The *ways* the Young Lords advanced this intersectional critique, however, are vitally important to a politics of liberation and decoloniality more broadly. Women within the organization had to *speak from* their embodied, located positions and make such body- and geo-politics relevant to the evolution of the organization. While male founders had an abstracted conception of justice rooted in their theoretical commitments, which authorized a problematic conception of "revolutionary machismo," women were able to draw from their lived experiences of oppression to both (a) generate insightful knowledge about the status of women within the movement and (b) generate modes of activism (like the *Lysistrata* strike) that relied more on embodied performances of resistance than formal argument. With spaces opened to generate broader support for women's voices by both women and men within the organization, the Young Lords were better able to craft liberatory rhetorics that addressed the destructive processes of dehumanization at work in commitments to machismo. Through their "Position Paper on Women," a visually reimagined gran familia puertorriqueña, and the extension of their intersectional critiques, the Young Lords practiced ways of delinking from modernity/coloniality that cultivated forms of nonsexist fraternity and underscored their commitments to human liberation.

Rather than continue a linear temporal narrative, the next chapter takes us back in time to the Young Lords' initial emergence on the scene in New York City. As the organization began formalizing their structure and mission, they tried to identify an issue around which they could mobilize and generate community awareness and support. Listening to the residents of El Barrio—the quintessential practice of decolonial love—the Young Lords decided to organize around the issue of garbage. Through various physical and otherwise discursive practices of delinking, the organization negated the racist and colonialist practices of "the system" and affirmed ethical orientations and human subjectivities in significant ways. The garbage offensive was a crucial moment for the Young Lords that carries the potential to teach us, today, a lot about how delinking and decoloniality can work on the ground.

4

Dirty Love

Collective Agency and Decolonial Tropicalization in the Garbage Offensive

Space must be normed and raced at the *macro*level (entire countries and continents), the *local* level (city neighborhoods), and ultimately even the *micro*level of the body itself (the contaminated and contaminating carnal halo of the non-white body).
—CHARLES W. MILLS, *The Racial Contract*

Without love, our efforts to liberate ourselves and our world community from oppression and exploitation are doomed. As long as we refuse to address fully the place of love in struggles for liberation we will not be able to create a culture of conversion where there is a mass turning away from an ethic of domination.
—BELL HOOKS, "Love as the Practice of Freedom"

When the New York Young Lords began to emerge in the summer of 1969, they sought creative avenues through which to enter public consciousness within their immediate community in El Barrio and beyond. As I detailed in Chapter 1, the Young Lords at this point were led primarily by academic revolutionaries—a small group of college-educated young men who were well read in revolutionary theory, but many of whom had little practical organizing experience. Faced with the dilemma of how to begin reaching the people, and guided by Chicago Young Lords leader Cha Cha Jiménez's insistence on connecting ideas to community action, they approached members of the community to begin figuring out what problems most urgently needed attention. "We must go to them . . . to the masses. . . . They may know something we don't. So first, we must go to the people of El Barrio," said Juan Gonzalez—who was the only Young Lords founding leader with any sustained organizing experience, which was gained in his time as a community organizer in the neighborhood surrounding Columbia University and as a leader in SDS.[1] Out of these conversations emerged the need to address garbage in El Barrio.

The garbage offensive surfaced in late June and early July 1969, when El Barrio was dirty and the city's Sanitation Department was ignoring the needs of the neighborhood. To address the problem, the Young Lords began, quite simply, by arriving every Sunday to clean up the garbage. On July 27, one day after officially becoming the New York chapter of the Young Lords Organization, and two weeks after starting to clean the neighborhood streets, the first point of social discord surfaced when some members attempted unsuccessfully to procure new supplies (brooms, cans, etc.) from the local sanitation department. Together with a variety of community members who had been helping them clean up the neighborhood, the Young Lords took heaping trash collections and placed them in several busy intersections, blocking significantly the traffic coming into and going out of Manhattan. The tactical placement of garbage peaked on August 17 when hundreds of Barrio Boricuas expanded their rebellion to include overturning cars, lighting fire to the trash, and assaulting police property. The Sunday garbage offensives continued until September 2, with Young Lords and other community members engaged actively in ongoing and growing dissent. Minister of information Pablo "Yorúba" Guzmán recounted, "We would hit and run, block to block, talking and spreading politics as we went, dodging the slow-moving pigs sent to crush any beginning Boricua movement for freedom. The garbage offensive united us through struggle."[2]

That the garbage offensive had such a political effect, uniting the Young Lords and the community, is undeniable. The long-standing constraint on agency to which they were responding—the exigence creating a need to be "united . . . through struggle"—demanded an inventive rhetoric that was decolonial both in its aim and in its form. In terms of aim or function, the Young Lords asserted a kind of independence; they demanded, through their words and actions, freedom from an oppressive system that had subjugated Puerto Ricans for half of a millennium. With regard to form, the Young Lords resisted impulses to mimic the oppressor's rhetoric and reforms (e.g., leader-centered rhetorics, public speeches, or legal changes). They engaged, instead, in an intersectional rhetoric that, I have argued elsewhere, refused to privilege or be disciplined by a single rhetorical form (e.g., verbal, visual, or embodied forms).[3] If, as John Louis Lucaites has argued, "every rhetorical performance enacts and contains a theory of its own agency—of its own possibilities—as it structures and enacts relationships between speaker and audience, self and other, action and structure," then we would be wise to attend to the *form* of the Young Lords' rhetoric as it is a critical component for addressing this broader problematic of agency.[4] By encouraging the intersectionality of diverse discursive forms to produce a rhetoric of social movement, the Young Lords constructed a collective agency challenging the status quo and, in some ways, foreshadowing subsequent movement discourses.[5] Examining the

Young Lords' garbage offensive, then, poses both a challenge and an opportunity to revise our collective and growing understanding of how marginalized groups might exercise power through rhetoric. But more specifically, engaging the garbage offensive as an exemplar of decolonial thought and action, as a touchstone of delinking in praxis, alters and strengthens the theoretical terrain within which the decoloniality of power/knowledge/being can operate.

Using the Young Lords' garbage offensive as a focal point, this chapter demonstrates the need to explore more fully the relationship between agency and rhetorical form by illustrating the ways in which the Young Lords constituted a space for social movement in El Barrio through delinking rhetorics and other forms of decoloniality. I interpret the garbage offensive as an action by the Young Lords that laid bare the internal inconsistencies of the system and established a decolonial sense of agency for the people of El Barrio, partially through use of the popular Puerto Rican tradition of *jaibería*, which is a form of subversive complicity. Importantly, this agency was established scenically through a transformation and tropicalization of the space of El Barrio. Most often, tropicalization takes a more hegemonic form as an appropriation of Latin@ culture and a reworking of it to suit white, neoliberal capitalism. With the Young Lords, tropicalization was a spatial accent; it was a way of symbolically restructuring El Barrio by imbuing it with new attitudes toward politics and social life. Although the garbage offensive ultimately failed in keeping El Barrio clean, it successfully constituted the people and space of El Barrio as potential agents of change—it accented both the people and the space as colonized and crafted that colonial accent as an exigence to be addressed through decolonial forms of agency that the Young Lords both modeled and discussed.

In the pages that follow, my argument develops over three sections, over the course of which I craft a narrative for the garbage offensive. In the first section, I explore the ways in which the garbage offensive emerged within and helped to craft an ethic of decolonial love. Building off of my formulation of decolonial love from previous chapters, I examine how the Young Lords engaged in practices of listening that generated the potential for responseability. In the second section, I focus attention on what the Young Lords *did* with the garbage in El Barrio. Analyzing both their literal and figurative interactions with the trash, I interpret the meaning of "trashing the system" anchored in a rhetoric of presence that helped to constitute a different world in El Barrio. In the final section, I consider the implications for being attentive to the ways in which the Young Lords transformed the space of El Barrio. Arguing that the garbage offensive can be understood as a kind of tropicalization, I return to the importance of rhetorical accents for interrogating decolonial agency and practices of delinking.

Loving Beginnings: The Garbage Offensive's Ethical Roots

On August 19, 1969, two days after the climactic moment of the garbage offensive, the *New York Times* offered a somewhat sanitized account of the scene in El Barrio:

> Against a backdrop of decaying tenements, a low-income housing project, and the Penn Central tracks that carry commuters to the suburbs, a purple-bereted youth told yesterday why his group, the Young Lords Organization, had sparked a garbage-dumping protest in East Harlem on Sunday.
>
> During the protest, residents of the area around Park Avenue and 110th Street joined in heaping and burning garbage at several intersections. . . .
>
> In claiming credit for the protests, a group of Young Lords said yesterday that they had acted to show the people of El Barrio, East Harlem's Puerto Rican Slum, that such activity was necessary to get city action to meet community needs.[6]

In an article that originally appeared in the *Village Voice* over twenty-five years after the garbage offensive introduced New York City to the Young Lords, Guzmán recounted, with exhilaration and a more personal tone, the climax of the scene on August 17, 1969:

> I had never done anything like this before. Twelve other guys, one woman, myself, and a small handful of people who, until moments before had been spectators, were about to set a barricade of garbage on fire. Garbage in the ghetto sense: rusted refrigerators from empty lots, the untowed carcasses of abandoned vehicles, mattresses, furniture, and appliances off the sidewalk as well as the stuff normally found in what few trash cans the city saw fit to place in El Barrio.[7]

This was an important (even critical) moment for the burgeoning Boricuas leading the Young Lords in their first protest, which represented a turning point for the organization and signaled their dramatic entrance into the New York political landscape. Their emergence was significant, too, for the community members who had been living in squalor largely because of the city's unwillingness to provide services to them equal to those offered to the affluent white citizens down the street. Having been principally a study group, the Young Lords had to first figure out exactly what it was that the people of El Barrio needed.

Donning their grassroots activist hats, members of the Young Lords began venturing out into El Barrio.[8] Coming across some men playing dominoes (a common pastime for Nuyoricans at the time), the young radicals inquired as to what these men thought was the biggest problem facing their community. Said one older man of El Barrio, "Don't you see the garbage all throughout the streets? It is overflowing the entire area with smelly odor . . . everywhere! Don't you smell it? It's horrible!"[9] This opinion was reaffirmed later in the day when they came across a group of doñas (older, presumably married women): ' "Look at the garbage!' said one of the doñas. 'It smells! For how long do we have to take this . . . ?' the vehemence of their outrage was surprising to us only because we failed to recognize the obvious."[10] In the first airing of their WBAI/Pacifica radio program, *Palante*, on March 27, 1970, chairman Felipe Luciano recounted coming to the issue:

> We looked at the situation in El Barrio, the Young Lords did, and we decided that rather than attack the jobs, and the racism, and the . . . educational system in El Barrio (which were problems, but which had been attacked by so many antipoverty organizations—by so many poverty pimps—who had raised the people's hopes to a higher level without ever achieving any kind of concrete solutions to these problems), we decided to take something that nobody had really tackled before. So that the first offensive was the garbage that was there—we live with it, we smell it, we eat it, and we die by it. But no one had really attempted to solve the problem.[11]

Standing amid the stench, they realized promptly that the all-pervading garbage indeed was an important, if not the most important, issue that they had to address.[12]

But the *process of coming to* the issue of garbage is perhaps as important as the fact that it became their first issue at all. Realizing that they were facing a theory/practice gap of sorts—due, in part, to some of their relatively privileged positions as current or former college students—the act of *listening* to the people of El Barrio represented an exemplary act of decolonial love and is itself a key mode of delinking. According to Nelson Maldonado-Torres, many "philosophers and critics have not realized that the first and most basic gesture of the critique of Eurocentrism lies in listening to what the people of the periphery have to say about truth, justice, love, critique, community life, and so forth."[13] Cognizant (a) that they had no clear idea of what the community needed or wanted and (b) that they wanted to avoid reproducing problematic power relations by forcing their position on an unwilling community, the Young Lords' simple act of asking the people about their lives was transformative. They seemed to grasp what Maldonado-Torres insists: that they had "to hear the people on the periphery, learn from them, and fight with them for the attainment of a condition in which such people are able to reproduce their lives and contribute fully in discussions about the future of humanity."[14]

Hearing and listening, however, are not easy. "Whichever way it is glossed—as rhetoric, dialogue, language, or argumentation," argues Lisbeth Lipari, "the Western conception of logos emphasizes speech at the expense of listening" and "obscures how listening makes the ethical response possible."[15] Such an ethical response—what I call in the Introduction (following Maldonado-Torres, Chela Sandoval, Junot Díaz, Kelly Oliver, and others) an ethic of decolonial love—is rooted in a Fanonian ethics of critique that privileges positivity over exclusive negativity.[16] "Man is a *yes* that vibrates to cosmic harmonies," writes Fanon.[17] And that "yes," argues Maldonado-Torres, functions as "a radical affirmation of sociality and interhuman contact" that can be "expressed as *non-indifference* toward the Other" and "leads to a conception of ethical struggle against the dehumanization of the sub-alter." That *yes*, which Maldonado-Torres also renders as "altericity," is "simultaneously affirmative of generosity and critical of damnation."[18]

Such affirmative generosity is related to Oliver's "responsibility to response-ability" that I discussed in the last chapter; it is a commitment to finding ways to listen to others' literal and metaphorical voices and to allow such listening to have its full, transformative effects on subjectivity.[19] Adding to this conception, Oliver posits, "this means that love is an ethical and social responsibility to open personal and public space in which otherness and difference can be articulated."[20] Following Fanon, she further insists that "love is a means to overcome the objectification of the oppressed and restore a sense of subjective agency. Love operates on both the psychic and social levels by restoring the agency necessary to imagine oneself as an ethical and political actor."[21]

By talking to community members in El Barrio, the Young Lords practiced a loving listening that engaged in a generous *yes* toward the people and invented a space within which they could begin to craft their own agency and subjectivity. According to Luciano:

First the older people began to come out on 110th street; and then the younger children began to come out. And we began to notice that people began to respond to the kinds of things we were doing in the streets. Now, we didn't go out with a whole bunch of rhetoric, because one of the first things we realized is that our people are sick of rhetoric. Our people are sick of words—words that have no action behind them. So we said nothing. We just swept the streets; and we were laughed at and we were called madmen.[22]

Bracketing his rejection of rhetoric, what is key in this passage from their radio program is that the Young Lords were self-reflective about the importance of listening to what the people wanted—they acted on those expressed desires and (at least for a brief period of time) remained silent so that the people could find their own voices. Born out of the loving desires and voices of El Barrio's subalterns, the garbage offensive emerged as a radical act of love that simultaneously affirmed and generated the space for decolonial subjectivity and agency to emerge and rejected the filthy conditions of wretchedness generated by a racist system against the (internal) colony.

The Rhetorical and Literal Presence of Garbage

The apparent target of the Young Lords' garbage offensive—the filthy trash littering their streets—cannot be easily textualized. Garbage lacks the cleanliness and permanence of the archive; it is, instead, fleeting, ephemeral, lost in time, and constantly changing. As the winds shift, so do the lingering smells of rotting and rusting trash. Garbage belongs, in Diana Taylor's terms, to the repertoire, and as such, it escapes our grasp.[23] Of course, this may be one of the lessons of the Young Lords, especially (though not exclusively) in the context of the garbage offensive: decolonial methods are most at home outside of the archive, outside of those political and intellectual spaces that tend toward stability, fixity, and intelligibility. Centered on embodied acts and experiences, decolonial methods will privilege those things most fleeting and hardest to textualize. In fact, the whole garbage offensive event presents significant difficulties in terms of textualization and rhetorical critique. Unlike the speeches delivered in the mainstream civil rights movement or the discrete "image events" for contemporary radical environmentalists and Tea Party protesters, there is no single static "text" to which we can turn to critique. Even in their newspaper and their book, the Young Lords declined the opportunity to offer up a sustained text of the event.[24] As Dwight Conquergood suggests, "Subordinate people do not have the privilege of explicitness, the luxury of transparency, the presumptive norm of clear and direct communication, free and open debate on a level playing field that the privileged classes take for granted."[25] This creates a methodological problem because we are now forced to make sense of the event by stringing together the various discourses of different members of the Young Lords into a more or less coherent accounting of events. The critic must be a bricoleur, assembling "texts" and defining the bounds of a fragmented rhetoric.[26] Once we do this, we have a very moving and powerful, though always evolving, social drama about the material and symbolic conditions under which the Young Lords lived and operated.

Their situation, environmentally, politically, and economically, was one marked by filth and decay. The images of these decrepit conditions were represented in part through words drawing attention to the physical (omni)presence of the garbage. Seeing garbage as a key issue began to structure the narratives and experiences of the Young Lords. For example, one early issue of their newspaper, *Palante*, states, "East Harlem is known as El Barrio—New York's worst Puerto Rican slum. . . . There is glass sprinkled everywhere, vacant lots filled with rubble, burnt out buildings on nearly every block, and people packed together in the polluted summer heat. . . . There is also the smell of garbage, coming in an incredible variety of flavors and strengths."[27] Furthermore, in another early issue of *Palante*, Luciano wrote:

> They've treated us like dogs for too long. When our people came here in the 1940's, they told us New York was a land of milk and honey. And what happened? Our men can't find work. . . . Our women are forced to become prostitutes. Our young people get hooked on drugs. And they won't even give us brooms to sweep up the rubbish in our streets.[28]

This return to the centrality of garbage is indicative of the broader dialogues occurring at the time.

The sight, the smell, the feel of this trash—real, *felt* garbage, not just a statistic or some other abstraction—was crafted as a central material problem in its own right. It was the proverbial slap in the face in light of all the other conditions faced by the people of El Barrio. Garbage represented both evidence of the state's disrespectful and malicious attitude toward the community and proof of "the system's" incapability to deal with its own intemperance. The Young Lords and members of the community experienced the rotting and rusting garbage of El Barrio on a daily basis, which is a factor important to consider when reading the offensive critically. This relatively unmediated, multisensory, and affective experience provided a physical manifestation of the frustrations the people felt about the system and its failure to take into account its own excesses, especially where poor Latin@s were concerned. Why would the garbage trucks drive through El Barrio to pick up trash in Manhattan but rarely stop to pick up the same trash in the Nuyorican neighborhood? Such a question became an impetus to movement.

Reflecting back one year after the Young Lords organized, Guzmán recounted the decision to act: "We decided that the first issue we could organize people around was the filth in the streets and lots, since it was clearly visible. . . . For the two Sundays before the Tompkins Square rally, we cleaned 110th Street in El Barrio, rapping while we went."[29] Although the practice of cleaning may not seem all that radical—indeed, Luciano acknowledged on their radio program that it sounded "reformist"—the Young Lords' actions early in the garbage offensive are important rhetorically in several ways. In contrast to the way in which Puerto Ricans had been defined by scholars and government officials as "docile," inactive, and dirty, Guzmán's sweeping (an embodied symbolic act, as much as a form of labor) is instructive of an active life in opposition to racist docility. An act like sweeping participates in, what Taylor calls, "the transfer and continuity of knowledge," especially in the context of the verbal messages and lore surrounding the event.[30] Young Lords like Guzmán, David Perez, and Juan Gonzalez were not from El Barrio but rather were college-educated, working- to middle-class Puerto Ricans and looked the part: they regularly dressed in working- to middle-class clothing, sometimes wearing button-up oxfords, and occasionally looked more like the kind of people Barrio residents would work for than have working for them. When they were seen sweeping up the street, their bodies served as a critique of labor hierarchies and inequality through their presence-in-action in El Barrio. Just by being there—on and with the streets—the Young Lords performed resistance by reclaiming and redrawing their own public space by performing a sense of ownership and, even, separatism. "This brought the college people and the street people together, 'cause when street people saw college people pushing brooms and getting dirty, that blew their minds."[31] Exploding such a "mind bomb" was a critical step in jarring fundamentally the consciousness of Barrio people to get them to imagine a world beyond inaction.[32]

On Saturday, July 26, 1969, after sweeping the streets for two weeks, the group received their official charter to become the New York chapter of the Young Lords Organization and held a rally at Tompkins Square to announce their existence and state their agenda. The next day, they went about cleaning the streets; this time, however, they reached another turning point. Recalls Guzmán, "On Sunday, July 27, we needed more brooms for all the community people who were with us. We went to a garbage (sanitation) office nearby and were given a racist run-around."[33] The precise details of what happened at this point are unclear. Some stories claim that Guzmán punched a sanitation official and stole some supplies. Other stories portray a scene wherein they were sent to another office and denied supplies there, too. Regardless of details, Melendez's assessment seems to hold consistent: "The only choice we had was confrontational politics";[34] and by "confrontational politics," Melendez means direct-action protests, which were repeated nearly every Sunday (and at least one Friday) up to and after August 17—the biggest protest of them all.

Fed up with the perceived contradictory and inherently racist actions of the system, the Young Lords and the people of El Barrio sought to rectify the situation. According to Luciano, on the *Palante* radio program, the specific ideas for action came from community members in El Barrio:

After three weeks of sweeping the streets with the people in the streets, the people came up to us and said, "You know, we're sweeping the streets but nothing is happening." So political lesson number one: when you try to do something for yourself, the city just ignores you. What do we do? So rather than the so-called vanguard (and that's a word I don't like to use because it gives some bad connotations of an elitist group), rather we discussed it with them and they offered their own solution: let's go into the streets with the garbage. Why? Because every time we did put the garbage on the sides of the streets, the garbage men first of all would never pick it up and when they did, they would throw fifty percent of the garbage on the street and the other half in the truck then fling the garbage can across the street. Now these may seem like very very *simple* little things, but to the minds of our people they *are* very important—the fact that their streets are not clean, the fact that their babies in the summertime (and many Puerto Ricans go around without shoes) are cut and suffer tetanus as a result of it.[35]

"With that," Luciano recounted, "we took to the streets and we blockaded all of the major thoroughfares" with the trash they had been collecting. Lexington, Madison, and Third Avenues were blocked at 110th, 111th, 115th, 118th, and 120th Streets. After they noticed people in cars and buses moving the trash out of the way, they got a little more insistent and began lighting fire to the trash. "Fires were set to cars, bottles were thrown, and the people proved for all time that the spirit of the people is always greater than the man's pigs."[36] The Young Lords' activism, cast as "guerrilla-like, lightening-like raids" by Luciano,[37] served as a moment of radical possibility opening up the available means of persuasion and action so as to make meaningful social movement probable; as such, the people had challenged the system and made clear that the prevailing bureaucracy was neither invincible nor contained. In the end, Luciano triumphantly asserted, "We're building our own community. Don't fuck with us. It's as simple as that."[38]

Echoing Luciano, Guzmán detailed similarly the ways in which this guerrilla offensive was part of both short- and long-term struggles: "The handful of us who were there employed basic techniques of urban guerrilla warfare: flexibility, mobility, surprise, and escape. By involving our people directly in revolution and participation (Thousands of spics blocked streets and fought cops that summer), we made many LORDS and won friends to the struggle."[39] Note that for Guzmán, the garbage offensive was not principally about cleaning up the streets, although that was important; the garbage offensive was always about more than just trash—it was about *guerrillismo*, constituting political subjects, building a community, and constructing a place and space for decolonization in El Barrio.[40]

It may be tempting, in line with a history of similar social movement scholarship, to read the garbage offensive as a political tool. This is the interpretation preferred by historian Johanna Fernandez in one of the few sustained analyses of the garbage offensive.[41] Declining to acknowledge the interpretive move she makes in analyzing the garbage offensive, Fernandez presents a matter-of-fact appraisal of the offensive from a social services perspective. Fernandez advances a causal argument about the effect and success of the garbage offensive based on a reading of sources from the time period. In her assessment, the value of the garbage offensive was in the act of picking up the trash; the garbage offensive was a success in her estimation because the city Sanitation Department began regularly picking up trash in El Barrio.

Missing the fact that the Sanitation Department quickly went back to irregu-
lar trash collection (which can be verified by looking at subsequent issues of
the *Palante* newspaper and Luciano's reporting on *Palante* radio when he said
"we didn't solve the garbage problem and we have to admit that to ourselves"),[42] Fernandez overlooks the political implications of the garbage offensive. One of her sources would agree. Writing for the *Guardian* in 1970, Carl
Davidson observed, "City sanitation officials were forced to meet with the
community three times and promise to remedy the situation, but with few
results so far. . . . However, the actions had the effect of establishing the presence of the Young Lords in the community."[43]

Mickey Melendez offers a similarly instrumental read of the garbage
offensive but directs his attention instead to politics. He argues, "An 'offensive'
has no value in itself; it is a political tool. It is a resource in the political education of the masses. What we intended to do was to show the people a path
toward a high level of political consciousness, to understand the power that
lies in the hands and the souls of the working people."[44] We can imagine
Melendez's position as, in a sense, a standard rhetorical account of what the
Young Lords were attempting in their resistance. Likewise, while Melendez's
account goes beyond the idea that the offensive was merely about getting the
trash picked up, the offensive retains a kind of instrumental quality. The offensive, in Melendez's reading, was a tool—an instrument like a compass helping
people get their bearings straight. Like the way that a compass directs people
toward their destination, the offensive pointed people to an awareness of politics. It showed people that their political voice could be acknowledged in an
era where quite the contrary seemed the case.

The political consciousness of which Melendez speaks, though, does not
suggest a fundamental shift in the way the people of El Barrio saw the role of
the political or themselves within a political system. Rather, the offensive
swept people up in the fervor of the moment, helping them to understand
that politics and resistance were possible. Yet this perspective does not seem
to go far enough. While it is certainly the case that there is a pragmatic element in any offensive, reducing the garbage offensive to instrumentality
misses the possibility that the act of protest itself has a constitutive effect on
the people involved and those who bear witness to it.

One feasible way to move beyond this instrumental focus on the garbage
offensive is to interpret it as an embodied act of decolonization. This attitude
is best exhibited by Agustín Laó, who argues that the garbage offensive
engaged in a "Spatial Politics of recasting the colonized streets through direct
action [that] is grounded in the common sense of cleanliness ('we are poor but
clean'), and the performative power and polyvalence of the symbolism of
cleansing."[45] Furthermore, Laó suggests, "This great sweeping-out became an
act of decolonization, a form of humanizing the living space, a way of giving
back dignity to our place, by taking it back."[46] Notice that Laó does not really

reduce the offensive to pure instrumentality; rather, he seems to be cognizant of the ways in which the form of the protest has significant implications. His attentiveness to the spatial politics of the offensive is particularly significant because it makes the focal point the performance of cleansing and/in protest, suggesting that the act itself has important political and identity-constituting implications that come prior to any benefits accrued as a result of the protest (i.e., as a result of the offensive's instrumentality). Laó's interpretation is incisive.

Taking a cue from Laó and radicalizing Melendez's point about political consciousness, a differently productive engagement of the garbage offensive would understand it as a delinking rhetorical performance of trashing the system. To begin unpacking this metaphor, we might return once more to retrospective remarks made by Guzmán:

> We hoped to show that our object as a nation should not merely be to petition a foreign government (amerikkka) to clean the streets, but also to move on that government for allowing garbage to pile up in the first place. By *questioning this system's basic level of sanitation,* our people would then begin to question drug traffic, urban renewal, sterilization, etc., until the whole corrupt machine could be exposed for the greedy monster it is.[47]

One of the central devil figures for the Young Lords (as it was for many radical groups of the era) was the system.[48] Drawing primarily from Herbert Marcuse's *One Dimensional Man*, I would argue that the system represents the (more or less) monolithic, assimilating machine that is able to keep the dominant group dominant and ensure that resistance can never be truly successful.[49] The system keeps the rich rich, the poor poor, and maintains that inequality without critical reflection. Engagements of "the system" from the Third World Left took on post-Marcusean qualities that were unique to a broader critique of colonialism and position of anti-imperialism. As I demonstrated in previous chapters, the Young Lords and others in common cause advanced an analysis that went beyond one-dimensionality and pointed to the uniquely problematic ways in which racism and capitalism intersected to produce devastating results.

The italicized portion of Guzmán's quotation seems particularly perceptive because it offers a triple meaning that could be overlooked easily but demonstrates nicely the performative aspect argued by Laó. First, there is a literal and material read of the fragment: literally, the activities of the garbage offensive served the purpose of questioning the cleanliness of their material environment. This was certainly part of the offensive's effect, given the immediate concerns they had about the "squalor of the barrio."[50] Second, there is an initial symbolic reading of the fragment: through the garbage offensive, they were questioning the cleanliness of the system, suggesting that "this system" is dirty, corrupt, and drenched in the garbage water of inequality. The system is part of the exigence of coloniality that must be addressed, struggled against, and, if necessary, burned to the ground. Finally, there is another, more Marcusean symbolic read of the fragment: through the offensive, they were questioning the sanitizing force of the system; that is, they questioned critically the system's capacity to clean or whitewash politics and eradicate opposition. Reading the "the system's" apostrophe, then, as possessing the tools and agency to clean demonstrates a different performative critique underdeveloped in both Melendez's and Laó's interpretations.

All of this is helpful analysis, but to realize its fuller impact and glean more out of the garbage offensive (rhetorically, materially, and politically), we must be attentive not only to the instrumental and performative nature of the events but also to the material resources and the contingently universal moves the Young Lords were proffering vis-à-vis the system. It is to this end that we ought to look at how different elements of the situation fit together to form a remarkable rhetoric about how the people of El Barrio should act politically, that is, a rhetoric about the decolonial ethos and ethics of their agency. Here we could understand garbage to be functioning as a synecdoche for the excesses of coloniality (capitalism, racism, sexism, etc., functioning intersectionally), while the Sanitation Department's refusal to assist functions as a sign of coloniality's failure to cope with those excesses. Through a mobilization of verbal, visual, performed, and other material discourses, the garbage offensive incited a moment of rupture and delinking in which the literal and symbolic excesses of the liberal capitalist system were called into question, opening up a space for the Young Lords to advance decoloniality more broadly (through future activism) within El Barrio.

Thought of in this manner, we have to take into account the ways that the raw, stinky materiality of the garbage functioned as a part of a larger whole (the system) that is made to show the people the excesses of modernity/coloniality. This is painfully obvious in the descriptions of the garbage offered by the Young Lords and made even more poignant in circulated images of children playing atop seas of garbage (see Figure 4.1). Published after the fact in *Palante*, the images served to reactivate and remind people of the conditions in which many Nuyoricans were forced to live. Such images served to *make present*, through a remembering and re-visioning of trash, the material scope of the problem.[51] Borrowing from Phaedra C. Pezzullo, we could understand such "presence" as a "*structure of feeling* or one's *affective* experience when certain elements . . . in space and time appear more immediate to us, such that we can imagine their 'realness' or 'feasibility' in palpable and significant ways."[52] Whether through images, news articles, their radio program, or whatever format they chose to represent it, the Young Lords' rhetoric of presence served to interpellate those who may not have been in that particular

Figure 4.1   Two images from "Why the Young Lords Party," *Palante* 2, no. 17 (December 11, 1970). (Photographer unknown.)

time and place—it positioned audiences as witnesses to the ephemeral materiality of trash in El Barrio and activated that embodied repertoire I mentioned earlier. Additionally, in the stories about their exchanges with the Sanitation Department, the Young Lords made the department's refusal to assist another sign of the system's failure to cope with its own immoderation.

When we combine this symbolic-materialist reading with the kind of performative interpretation Laó offers, we end up with the point that the Young Lords were able to call into question the logic of the system (coloniality) in such a way as to open up a discursive space. Within this space, a kind of social movement is advanced. Through this complex, multimodal rhetoric, the Young Lords fundamentally altered peoples' consciousness about their relationship to the system and the possibilities for their futures. Understood in this way, it is not simply the case that the Young Lords directly changed people's minds; rather, they generated the opportunity and possibility for people to be better able to articulate their problem and envision different solutions.

The space made possible new significations and practices of decolonial agency that were tied intimately to both the Young Lords' message and the form that message took. As such, it is in the intersectional rhetorical act of making the garbage do something and its twin of doing something with the garbage (and the words, images, and performances invoking garbage) that we more fully understand the greatest strengths of the offensive. The ways in which bodies were positioned vis-à-vis the colonial system in the garbage offensive are a critical component of this intersectional rhetoric. Just as words and images seem to advance an argument about the relationship between the people, the system, and the environment, so too did bodies enact a similar message of dissent. Focusing on one discursive form, however, elides the way in which the rhetoric of the garbage offensive was inherently intersectional. By enacting this significant critique of the system, the Young Lords articulated a fundamentally political and decolonial social imaginary that altered the Latin@ political landscape in New York for years to come.

Despite the apparent constitutive benefits of the garbage offensive, there remains a looming question: Why does any of this matter given that the garbage offensive failed to achieve its instrumental goal of getting El Barrio cleaned up? This is certainly a noteworthy question, and one that raises another question: How can we interpret the Young Lords as challenging the system when their explicit demand for the Sanitation Department to pick up the trash (a clear reliance on a component of the very system they were critiquing) was reformist in nature? These are both important challenges for which reasonable answers can be offered. While the practical goal of any rhetoric may be to persuade people to act in one way or another, instrumental success is but one rather shortsighted criterion on which to base our critical judgments.[53]

Rather, we would do well to remember that rhetorics serve constitutive functions that craft a people and imbue them with certain qualities, capacities, and ideals.[54] Thought of as a moment of constitution, the garbage offensive should be understood as a success because the performance of an intersectional rhetoric of resistance challenged the constraints of the modern/colonial system on sociopolitical agency. Specifically, the Young Lords were able both to translate a language of revolutionary consciousness into the language of the people (the residents of El Barrio) and to provide a set of practical resources for enacting that consciousness. By enlisting the people of El Barrio in this initial struggle, the Young Lords both created a revolutionary, decolonial discursive space and defined a radical ethos that escaped the tentacles of the system. José Esteban Muñoz makes a similar point vis-à-vis the constitutive potential of Latin@ performances today, writing, "The performance praxis of U.S. Latina/os assists the minoritarian citizen-subject in the process of denaturalizing the United States' universalizing 'national affect' fiction as it asserts ontological validity and affective difference."[55] The uptake of this ethos is found in the widespread community support for this and other public actions (e.g., the church offensive, discussed in Chapter 5, and the 10,000-person march on the United Nations).

Furthermore, the fact that the Young Lords sought ultimately to use the system does not undercut this constitutive success. While it may seem paradoxical for them to make such a move, the Young Lords' demands on the system were performed in the spirit of jaibería. Ramón Grosfoguel, Frances Negrón-Muntaner, and Chloé S. Georas turn to "the popular tradition of *jaibería*" to articulate a space for oppositional agency among Puerto Ricans struggling for sociopolitical agency. Defined, in Puerto Rican usage, as "collective practices of nonconfrontation and evasion . . . of taking dominant discourse literally in order to subvert it for one's purpose, of doing whatever one sees fit not as a head-on collision . . . but a bit under the table,"[56] jaibería is "a form of complicitous critique or subversive complicity"[57] that can result in the extreme adoption of dominant and ruling ideologies, beliefs, or actions in order to demonstrate their shortcomings and instigate movement. Put differently, jaibería is a kind of border thinking/acting that exploits the interstitial space between colonial inside and outside, which enables and exhibits a particular technique for delinking, partially through disidentification.

Although they did not always adopt such an attitude, it is exactly this strategy that the Young Lords deployed in advancing their demands in the garbage offensive. Reflecting on the lessons learned in this instance of activism, Luciano found significance in this point about playing along (with a nod and a wink) with reformist modes:

> And the people began to understand that through unity there is strength. Through Puerto Ricans coming together under a common banner, struggling *politically*—because the thing was done politically, the garbage offensive, because we did meet with some garbage department officials and they offered us and they promised us and we let the people listen to those promises because *we knew that they would never be fulfilled.* And the people's hopes were gradually diminished as they began to understand that New York City offers no solution for spics, or niggers, or anyone else who's oppressed.[58]

They could have rejected the system outright. Instead, they adopted a differential relation to the system by demanding a leveling equality (the literal promise of liberalism) with respect to garbage collection. Rather than simply continuing to pick up all of the garbage themselves, the Young Lords demanded that the Sanitation Department assist in various ways—mainly that they do their job. The subversion, however, lies in their knowing full well that New York City's sanitation officials were unwilling to meet their demands. In making demands that could not be fulfilled, the Young Lords' apparent complicity functioned as a critique and rupturing of the system's racist, classist, colonialist underpinnings.

This reliance on the system points also to a key difference between the Young Lords and other anticolonial groups in the United States at the time. Seen from a postcolonial vantage with an emphasis on national independence, such reliance on the state would be read merely as complicity with oppression—as the further perpetuation of a "colonial mentality."[59] The Young Lords' case, though, problematizes that analysis by challenging one of the lines between "us" and "them" in a Manichean struggle. As such, their ultimate reliance and insistence on the system served as a "complicitous critique" undermining the system's legitimacy when it could not meet the Young Lords' demands. In this sense, the Young Lords' failure in getting the Sanitation Department to pick up trash regularly was a success for the organization because it both furthered their critique and demonstrated another way in which resistance could occur; it constituted an attitude toward decolonial politics that would become central to the Young Lords and El Barrio in the years to come.

Tropicalizing El Barrio: Garbage, Space, and Delinking

Although we cannot deny the possibility of a primarily instrumental political offensive, the desirability of interpreting this instance only (or even predominantly) through such a lens is challenged when we begin to recognize what it ignores. As Kenneth Burke argues, while symbols may be used as tools, instrumentality is not their principle purpose (they are a form of action, he says); similarly, my argument in this chapter suggests that the complex, formally intersectional rhetoric of the Young Lords' garbage offensive represents a way of acting in the world and, in the process, serves to constitute that world by delineating a material place (East Harlem) and discursive space (political Nuyoricans in El Barrio) for this altered public consciousness.[60] Taylor writes, in a manner reminiscent of Burke's theorization of the relationship between dramatistic scenes and acts, that "the place allows us to think about the possibilities of the action. But action also defines place. If, as Certeau suggests, 'space is practiced place,' then there is no such thing as place, for no place is free of history and social practice."[61]

The rhetorical constitution of such a space afforded the Young Lords the opportunity to challenge prior constructions of Barrio Boricuas and invent a new, decolonial political consciousness that played in the hybrid space between U.S. American and Puerto Rican, domestic and foreign, and so on. In her engagement of Chicana feminist writing, Lisa Flores suggests that "creating space means rejecting the dichotomy of *either* at the margins *or* in the center and replacing that perspective with one that allows for Chicana feminists to be at their own center intellectually, spiritually, emotionally, and ultimately physically. The desire for space is the need for both a physical location and an intellectual one."[62] Raka Shome echoes Flores's connection of space/place and identity, arguing, "instead of treating identities as though they occur on the head of a pin, we have to recognize that identities occur not just anywhere, but *somewhere*; social agency is derived not just anywhere but *somewhere*."[63] In this manner, the Young Lords invented a *somewhere*—an intellectual, political, and physical space in which decolonial agency through "community control" could be envisioned and, in some cases, realized.

Animated by jaibería, the Young Lords' space was a kind of tropicalized border zone at the interstices of "the colonial wounds and imperial subordination"[64]—a space in between and in simultaneous contact with Western power-knowledge and pluriversal alternatives. As I mentioned (drawing from Frances R. Aparicio and Susana Chávez-Silverman) in the Introduction, tropicalization is a kind of troping that imbues a rhetorical scene with an indelibly Latin@ ethos; it is "a way of mapping Latinidad onto the rhetorical scene."[65] As I have summarized elsewhere:

> Certainly, tropicalization can be hegemonic in the sense that it can reproduce marginalizing constructions of Latinidad or marginalizing social practices, like the commodification of Latina/o culture. In its more tactical, even radical, forms, though, tropicalization "emerges from the cultural productions, political struggles, and oppositional strategies deployed by some U.S. Latinos/as. The margins that bell hooks evokes as 'sites of radical possibilities' are the locations from which these re-tropicalizing tendencies are surfacing."[66]

In tropicalizing El Barrio, the Young Lords' garbage offensive accented the space with the markers of latinidad—both in terms of the aspirational and revolutionary agency they were attempting to cultivate and in terms of the ways they demystified multiple lived systemic excesses.

The "excesses" I tied the trash to earlier weren't simply systemic; they were raced and classed (and, though outside the Young Lords' rhetorical scope in mid-1969, gendered); they were the product of *colonial* excesses that followed Puerto Ricans from the island into the mainland and functioned as a defining feature of their lived space. Garbage helped constitute "Amerikkka the Beautiful" (see Figure 4.2). Assaulting all of the senses, however, garbage was exemplary of the colonial wound in another way: it symbolized their own complicity in an unjust system. As Lisa Flores and Mark Lawrence McPhail note:

> While self reflection is an important step in the process of liberation, of asserting and affirming one's own identity, it is insufficient in-and-of-itself for moving from the deconstruction of domination and oppression to the reconstruction of social intercourse and interaction. The next step, which is profoundly more difficult, entails the recognition of one's implication in oppression.[67]

Others did not produce the trash outside of their community; rather, it was *their own* excess, made visible and magnified by racist governmental indifference,

Figure 4.2   Back cover of *Palante* 2, no. 13 (October 16, 1970).

rooted in the knowledge that Puerto Ricans had accepted their interpellation as docile (and dirty) subjects.[68] Drawing attention to these things, the Young Lords' rhetoric of presence accented the community and its residents as colonized and tropicalized (through hegemonic caricatures) and crafted that colonial accent as an exigence to be addressed.

This initial rhetorical gesture was, itself, a decolonial move. Modernity/coloniality, Mignolo argues, is underwritten by a kind of "grounding without grounding"; knowledge becomes "hidden in the transparency and universality of the zero point" and regional, geopolitical specificity is lost.[69] Now, with rare exceptions, I do not think that nominalist rhetorics are enough to solve problems;[70] however, understood as a nominalist move of sorts, *accenting* El Barrio as a colonial space and its people as colonial subjects was a crucial first step to unveiling and delinking from the colonial matrix of power. Not merely descriptive, geopolitical attentiveness (what I describe in the Introduction as decolonial critical regionalism) functions as a corrective that wrenches loose modernity/coloniality's epistemic stranglehold—one possible form of delinking that generates short circuits in the colonial matrix of power. By *naming* El Barrio "colonized" and anchoring the presence of said coloniality in the materiality of their discourse and sensory experiences of the garbage, the Young Lords practiced a form of epistemic disobedience that they modeled for/with the people of El Barrio.

Furthermore, the Young Lords' taking over, cleaning up, and reframing of El Barrio as a decolonized space fundamentally altered the scene in a manner that allowed for different agents and agencies to emerge. Their tropicalization of El Barrio, then, generated unique opportunities for rhetorical agency delinked from modernity/coloniality. The Young Lords' delinking rhetoric transformed El Barrio into something Other—a re-tropicalized space resistant to modernity/coloniality. If regions are, as Ronald Walter Greene and Kevin Douglas Kuswa note, "rhetorically drawn into maps of power as actors, objects, and techniques of governance,"[71] then the Young Lords' decolonial accent redrew those maps in important ways. It marked El Barrio as an internal colony, but it also marked it as a space of resistance in a manner that activated political subjectivities and practices delinked from procedural democratic politics, transcending both liberal individualism and narrow identity politics.

Finally, delinking in the garbage offensive also takes place on a formal level vis-à-vis their discourse. The Young Lords refused to comply with the formal norms of (the) Anglo rhetorical tradition(s). In the sense I used the term in this chapter, "intersectional rhetoric" can be a descriptive label for a style of delinking that appeared in the Young Lords' rhetoric of social movement challenging a *formally* one-dimensional (colonial) system. Intersectional rhetoric is a *kind* of rhetoric wherein one form of discourse is not privileged over another; rather, diverse forms intersect organically to create something challenging to rhetorical norms. Intersectional rhetoric is more than words + bodies + materials, because those different forms can be present without intersecting and challenging norms of textual boundedness. Instead, intersectional rhetoric is better represented as three intersecting lines. In their intersection, one is not privileged over another; they are not ordered hierarchically. In so challenging rhetorical norms, intersectional rhetoric functions also in a hybrid political space, exhibiting a kind of incredulity toward the political traditions (e.g., U.S. liberal democracy) with which rhetorical traditions are bound. Incredulity does not necessarily mean that they simply rejected those traditions; instead, intersectional rhetoric pushes the boundaries of traditions and encourages a hybridization, mixing, or creolization of ideas. It is, fundamentally, a form of border thinking. Furthermore, this difference in form represents a distinctive stylization of power compared with what we find in the speeches of Malcolm X or the writings of the New Left, for example. The intersection of materiality, words, and actions from an entire community of individuals formally mimics an articulation of collective agency that finds strength in the articulation of a people rather than any particular person. Such a people-centered rhetoric and mode of agency is the focus of the next chapter, where I examine the Young Lords' church offensive.

Recognizing the ways in which the Young Lords engaged the dialectical tensions between coloniality and decoloniality provides for a rich analysis of what their rhetoric accomplished in El Barrio. From the very beginning of the garbage offensive, the Young Lords exhibited the ability and desire to listen to the residents of El Barrio and tackle the problem of garbage; and in doing so, they enacted a key practice of decolonial love. While scholars like Maldonado-Torres and Oliver underscore the importance of listening to an ethic of decolonial love and response-ability/responsibility, their arguments are more normative than descriptive. With the Young Lords, however, we can understand better what listening means in practice (on the ground) and how it can be further translated into forms of resistance against lived coloniality. Face to face with others, the Young Lords, after their own practices of self-reflection, became an embodied argument against modern/colonial constructions of Puerto Ricans as docile, dirty, and so forth. Giving the gift of self, they opened up the discursive space for others to reflect on their place within the colonial matrix of power. Furthermore, the Young Lords mobilized the very materiality of garbage as a rhetoric of presence that accented the community and its residents as colonized, thus crafting such a colonial accent as an exigence to address. Their decolonial alternatives—found both in their diagnosis of a colonial condition and in their complex, discursively intersectional responses to it—modeled forms of epistemic disobedience and critical border praxis that are central to delinking.

Following the garbage offensive in the fall of 1969, the Young Lords focused their efforts on community service programs rather than direct action resistance. Programs dealing with other environmental justice issues (like lead poisoning, tuberculosis, and food security), general outreach, and political education occupied their day-to-day operations. Faced with expanding membership and increased demand for their programs and resources, the Young Lords began partnering with churches and others in the community who had unused space and were willing to share the space with them. When negotiations with one prominent community church, the First Spanish Methodist Church, failed, the Young Lords forcibly "took" the space, renamed it "the People's Church," and made it a vibrant center of community activity until the police arrested all of its occupants eleven days later. More than a simple takeover, however, the church offensive showed additional ways in which the Young Lords delinked from modernity/coloniality. Oriented around a rhetoric of "the people," the Young Lords' church offensive demonstrated that decoloniality does not have to reject terms central to liberal democracy; instead, one technique of delinking can be rooted in the rearticulation of key terms, called ideographs, that are central to social imaginaries. Like their problematization of "reformism" in the context of the garbage offensive, the Young Lords again demonstrated ways to delink while resisting the temptations of either/or thinking.

5

Decolonial Imaginaries

Rethinking "the People" in the Church Offensive

God is not dead.
God is bread.
The bread is rising!
Bread means revolution.
Organize for a new world.
Make the church a people's church.
Wash off your brother's blood.
The streets belong to the people.
And the church belongs to the streets.
In the midst of occupied territory,
The liberated zone is here.

—New York Young Lords,
   "Celebration for a People's Church"

This nomadic "morphing" is not performed only for survival's sake,
as in earlier, modernist times. It is a set of principled conversions that
requires (guided) movement, a directed but also a diasporic migration
in both consciousness and politics, performed to ensure that ethical
commitment to egalitarian social relations be enacted in the everyday,
political sphere of culture.

—Chela Sandoval, *Methodology of the Oppressed*

After initiating the process of articulating a space for revolutionary activism in El Barrio through their garbage offensive, the Young Lords turned their attention to expanding activities in the community and concretizing what they envisioned in their "13 Point Program and Platform" by terms such as "community control," "self-determination," and "liberation." Faced with a long history of outsiders controlling nearly all aspects of their daily lives, the Young Lords instituted practical programs to challenge the exercise of power by the state and outsider-run institutions—an exercise of power that had profound effects on both their material and mental conditions. In so doing, they featured and redefined "the people" as a key term structuring their experiences, their social imaginary, and ultimately their decolonial politics. In this chapter, I examine one key instance of popular rhetoric by the Young Lords: the church offensive. Late in 1969, about three months following the start of their garbage offensive and their official formation as an organization in New York, the Young Lords began implementing their community control program after examining how local institutions were serving the people of El Barrio. In addition to testing community members for lead poisoning and tuberculosis with the assistance of medical student volunteers, as I detailed in the Introduction, they addressed hunger by serving breakfast to poor children.[1] They also looked at how churches, one of the most dominant institutions in the community, were serving (or failing to serve) the people in the community of which they were supposed to be a part. When a prominent church, the First Spanish Methodist Church on 111th Street and Lexington Avenue, failed to respond to the community's needs, the Young Lords overtook the church, occupied it, claimed it in the name of community control, renamed it "the People's Church," and declared a "liberated zone" "in the midst of occupied territory."[2]

This chapter is an attempt to come to terms with the Young Lords' popular liberation rhetoric spawned during the church offensive. Building from Michael Calvin McGee's observation that " 'the people' are more *process* than *phenomenon*" and the extension of McGee's research into subaltern contexts by scholars like Maurice Charland and Fernando Delgado, I explore the ways in which the Young Lords crafted "*the people's* repertory of convictions" from diverse rhetorical resources in their verbal, visual, and embodied discourse surrounding the church offensive.[3] In highlighting such a performative repertoire for "the people," I aim in this chapter to craft a link between ideographs and what Charles Taylor and others call the "social imaginary," which is "not a set of ideas; rather it is what enables, through making sense of, the practices of society."[4] Like ideographs, which, according to McGee, "exist in real discourse, functioning clearly and evidently as agents of political consciousness" in "the real lives of the people whose motives they articulate,"[5] the concept of social imaginaries addresses "the way ordinary people 'imagine' their social surroundings" and "is carried in images, stories, and legends."[6] Given that many rhetoricians seem to have a lack of interest in ideology (as suggested by scholars like Kevin Deluca, Joshua Gunn, and Shaun Treat),[7] connecting ideographs with social imaginaries and their attendant concern with stranger relationality can rehabilitate and extend the usefulness of the ideograph, in addition to adding rhetorical specificity to scholarship on social imaginaries.

In making this connection between ideographs and social imaginaries, I read the Young Lords' rhetoric of "the people" as a radical, decolonial challenge to the modern social imaginary. "The imaginary of the modern/colonial world," Walter Mignolo argues, "is not the same when viewed from the history

of ideas of Europe as when looked at from the perspective of colonial difference."[8] For Mignolo and others, the colonial difference is especially relevant
in the context of "the people" because "the people" are the product of sixteenth-
century Occidental expansion and concomitant colonization.[9] As such, argues
Nelson Maldonado-Torres, "Racialized subjects are constituted in different
ways than those that form selves, others, and peoples."[10] While one can infer
from Maldonado-Torres and Mignolo that a rhetoric of "the people" has no
place in a critical decolonial politics, I will demonstrate that such a rejection
is not necessary. In this chapter, I argue that the Young Lords' rearticulation
of "the people" as a pluriversal collective, demanding material and epistemological liberation, delinks and denaturalizes hegemonic constructions of
a liberal/Western "people" that "totalize *A* reality"[11] in the modern social
imaginary.

This chapter develops over three sections. The first section assembles, in
more detail, the theoretical perspective introduced above by connecting relevant scholarship on ideographs and social imaginaries in a manner that
demonstrates synergy between the seemingly disparate concepts. Additionally,
the first section links modern social imaginaries to coloniality and demonstrates how ideographic shifts can function to decolonize the imaginary. While
I have avoided disciplinary terminology as much as possible throughout this
book, I anchor my discussion in the rhetorical concept of the ideograph
because I believe it has much to offer interdisciplinary audiences when coupled with the more commonplace notion of social imaginaries. In the second
section, I begin my critical engagement of the Young Lords' popular rhetoric
in the church offensive, paying particular attention to how their rearticulation
of "the people" enacts a decolonial alternative to the status quo. Finally, I
finish with an extended conclusion that explores some implications that
decolonizing imaginaries might have for how we conceptualize ideographic
research delinked from modernist, neoliberal projects.

Ideographs, (Modern) Social Imaginaries, and Decoloniality

McGee was one of the first to most explicitly posit a link between rhetoric and
ideology, which manifests itself, he argues, in the uses of the "ideograph."[12]
McGee suggests that for one to understand clearly the operation of ideology
in practice, one must look at the different ideographs operative within a particular rhetorical culture. "To participate in a rhetorical culture," Celeste
Michelle Condit and John Louis Lucaites add, "one thus must pay allegiance
to its ideographs, employing them in ways that audiences can judge to be
reasonable."[13] Ideographs do the work of ideology. They are higher-order symbols, similar to God terms, which are single word/phrase encapsulations of a

particular ideology. Ideographs, such as "equality," do the work that cannot be done by rational arguments, in part, because the entire range of the meaning of an ideograph (like "equality" or "the people") cannot be known or wholly expressed.[14]

Given their partial indeterminacy, Condit argues, ideographs "serve as powerful, normative warrants for public behavior" that have "evolved from their historical, discursive interactions with one another and from their standing as 'the moral of the story' in public political narratives."[15] Additionally, ideographs are so ingrained within a culture that their (general) meaning cannot be legitimately questioned or opposed. Ideographs operate not necessarily in theoretical discourse but circulate in real political dialogue, like mass media, popular culture, political debates, and even images.[16] A range of scholars have built on the conceptual foundation offered by McGee to account for the ways in which ideographs do sociopolitical and cultural work, even when the words ("people," "equality," etc.) are not often or ever uttered. Under this revised and modernized framework, ideographs can be understood as the constellation of various discursive forms constituting the verbal, visual, and embodied vocabulary of a public culture. Such a public vocabulary is significant because it materializes normative commitments and equips publics with the discursive and rhetorical resources for stranger relationality.[17]

This need for stranger relationality, Dilip Parameshwar Gaonkar suggests, is a particularly modern one: "modernity in its multiple forms seems to rely on a special form of social imaginary that is based on relations among strangers."[18] Western modernity, he continues, has imagined "the public sphere as a meta-topical place for deliberation and discussion among strangers on issues of mutual concern."[19] By invoking the modern social imaginary, Gaonkar taps into a rich and developing literature, which has roots in (post-) Marxist critics Claude Lefort and Cornelius Castoriadis and is engaged most actively by public culture critics like Charles Taylor.[20] The concept of social imaginary draws attention to the imbrication of social practices and civic habits (like voting and political marches), political doctrines (democracy, liberalism, socialism, etc.), and circulating symbols (metaphors, narratives, myths, images, etc.) to highlight what Gaonkar summarizes as "ways of understanding the social," which "become social entities themselves, mediating collective life."[21] To put it differently, "social imaginary" is one way to talk about the complex hegemonic structuration of "the social" in manners that inform and are informed by political discourse and habitus.

When Taylor discusses social imaginaries, he attempts to name that which in our social world escapes simple definition. Social imaginaries are "the ways in which people imagine their social existence, how they fit together with others, how things go on between them and their fellows, the expectations that are normally met, and the deeper normative notions and images that underlie these expectations."[22] Social imaginaries inform and are informed by factual and normative commitments about "how things usually go" and "how they ought to go." Such norms, by extension, inform understanding of and the ability to identify "ideal cases" that make sense in the context of the background understanding that undergirds the social.[23] The social imaginary, then, drives us to understand, appreciate, and demand a wide set of practices and beliefs that are constitutive of who we are in some meaningful way.

Unlike Castoriadis, who seems focused almost exclusively on the symbolic dimensions of the imaginary, Taylor is concerned with the articulations of symbols, ideologies, and embodied practices. According to Gaonkar, the social imaginary "occupies a fluid middle ground between embodied practices and explicit doctrines. The relation between the three is dynamic. The line of influence is not causative but circular."[24] More to the point, according to Taylor, there is a crucial, recursive relationship between social practices and the understanding produced by imaginaries:

> If the understanding makes the practice possible, it is also true that the practice largely carries the understanding. At any given time, we can speak of the "repertory" of collective actions at the disposal of a given sector of society. These are the common actions that they know how to undertake, all the way from the general election, involving the whole society, to knowing how to strike up a polite but uninvolved conversation with a casual group in the reception hall.[25]

Seeming to echo McGee's aforementioned "repertory of convictions" evident in rhetorical constructions of "the people," the notion of social imaginaries offers a potential alternative justification for studying ideographs.

McGee's ideographs project was, first and foremost, an attempt to elucidate a "link between rhetoric and ideology" (the subtitle of his original essay). The critical thrust of the concept of ideographs, however, comes from their value in explaining the practical rhetorical functionality of social control. McGee extended his attentiveness to social control with arguments on materialist rhetoric,[26] something for which poststructuralists and materialists like Ronald Walter Greene and Dana Cloud have taken him to task.[27] In linking ideographs to social imaginaries, our attention is refocused to the constitutive potential of ideographs—to the ways in which they normalize social relations, construct the background of a society, and enunciate a set of practices that, in turn, inform how ideographs are understood and do their sociopolitical work. Furthermore, bringing ideographs to the social imaginary table adds a well-theorized rhetorical concept to Taylor's, sometimes vague, attention to "symbols" and practices. Ideographs, then, can be understood as (a) the verbal, visual, and embodied symbolic repertoire that (b) is defined by, and in turn defines, the social imaginary, which (c) facilitates ideologically, historically, and doctrinally constrained modes of stranger relationality.

Since the exigence of stranger relationality is a product/productive of modern Western social imaginaries, the Young Lords' rhetorical intervention as a decolonial liberation movement is particularly significant. As Maldonado-Torres argues succinctly, "Modernity as a discourse and as a practice would not be possible without coloniality, and coloniality continues to be an inevitable outcome of modern discourses."[28] While scholars like Maldonado-Torres, Mignolo, and Juan Flores readily acknowledge the virtual disappearance of formal or political colonialism, all are attentive to what Aníbal Quijano calls "a colonization of the imagination of the dominated."[29] For Quijano and others attentive to coloniality, critical scrutiny is directed largely to the "colonization of the imaginary," which is productive of oppressive and repressive epistemologies and master narratives. Since the exigence of stranger relationality is inherent to modern Western social imaginaries, the Young Lords' rhetorical intervention as a decolonial liberation movement is particularly significant. In short, the repression engaged precisely those things that make up the social imaginary. In replacing indigenous knowledge with Western models of thought and rationality organized around a "zero-point epistemology," the modern social imaginaries were born.[30] And while Gaonkar recognizes "multiple modernities" and multiple imaginaries, reference to the racist, classist repression supporting those modernities is lacking, which underscores the ways they are, in Mignolo's words, "blind to the colonial difference."[31]

The fundamental linkage between modernity and coloniality—a linkage that is manifest in the social imaginaries that structure society and recursively inform political identity and practices of citizenship—underwrites the vocabulary of ideographs available to would-be agents. This is particularly true of dominant, Western/liberal articulations of "the people," which, as McGee argues, "produc[e] ontic rhetorics, arguments that promot[e] particular criteria for being or becoming American." McGee continues that both "people" and "public" further "anticipate a homogenous polity and take little or no notice of legitimate ontic or epistemic difference among groups of Americans" even in an era that has supposedly "legitimized heterogeneity."[32] In challenging Western/liberal articulations of "the people" through a rhetoric of liberation, however, the Young Lords' discourse and activism contain "the de-linking seed" that provides "alternatives TO modernity"[33] and the modern social imaginary.

This delinking seed represents a challenge to the conventional wisdom of decolonial theorists, as well. Mignolo argues forcefully and, largely, correctly "that it is not enough to change the content; the terms of the conversation must be changed" because "reversing the terms of the conversation will not work."[34] This is especially true with regard to "the people," where "the expression 'X (national characterization) people' carries, in itself, the silence of the colonial difference and the weapons of the colonial wound: 'people' are supposed to be citizens and citizens are supposed to be of a certain religion and ethnicity."[35] Maldonado-Torres argues similarly that "the condemned . . . cannot be reduced to . . . 'the people' of the modern nation-state"[36] because the wretched of the earth "already live with death and are not even 'people.'"[37] What neither considers explicitly, however, is the possibility that the condemned have the opportunity to speak the language of "the people" without reproducing coloniality. As Chela Sandoval suggests, sometimes the best option is not to speak "*outside* their terms" or to invent "new terms . . . but through the *ideologizing of ideology* itself."[38] In his 1935 speech at the first American Writers' Congress, Kenneth Burke made the case in manner specific to "the people"—arguing that "the people" functions as a more pragmatically useful and persuasive trope than "the worker" or "the masses" because of its history of usage in U.S. American public culture.[39] Operating within a similar symbolic terrain, the Young Lords' rhetoric of "the people" embarks on an "ideologizing of ideology" that reworked the people through a decolonial lens and for a decolonial function.

In the next section, I direct my attention to the Young Lords' church offensive, which offers an exemplary case study as a site at which a fragmented, critical, decolonial imaginary gets articulated through an inventive ideographic rhetoric. In approaching the Young Lords' rhetoric, I heed the call of critical rhetoricians like Kent Ono and John Sloop, who offer an attitude for approaching vernacular/Other rhetorics on their own ground—a call that Fernando Delgado, Bernadette Marie Calafell, Michelle Holling, and others all echo in their own work, similar to what Lisa Flores calls Latin@ "rhetorics of difference."[40] Engaging the Young Lords' church offensive, I try to enact and locate "an other thinking" in their rhetoric—a delinking double critique functioning within both Anglo-American and Latin@ traditions and simultaneously "from neither of them," a critique "located at the border of coloniality" that overcomes the "monotopic epistemology of modernity" and "releases knowledges that have become subalternized" by the coloniality in/of modern social imaginaries.[41]

"The People's Church" and Delinking Imaginaries

Just over a month after the Young Lords formed on July 26, 1969, the group expanded their community service and activism to include a host of social programs dealing with health care, food, clothing drives, and education, to name a few. Bolstering their demands for "community control," "self-determination," "liberation," and even "socialist redistribution," their "serve the people" programs generated visibility and intense support for the Young Lords in El Barrio.[42] One example of that support came in the form of the community's response to police harassment of the Young Lords. Speaking about an attempt by the police to intimidate and provoke the Young Lords by surrounding the office one day, Pablo "Yoruba" Guzmán recounted the community's response:

"The people came out into the street and were behind us. They asked what are [the police] here for and we told them what they were here for. Our explanation made a connection with what happened to the Black Panther party a week before and the people said 'Why? You haven't hurt anybody.'"[43]

Within that context of increasing community support, the desire to fulfill the objectives of their program and platform, and the broadening of their focus to address coloniality in Puerto Rico and New York, the Young Lords sought out local institutions they perceived to be advancing dominant interests and failing to serve their community. In doing so, the Young Lords approached the First Spanish Methodist Church (hereafter, FSMC) about using their facilities to run a free breakfast program for poor youth. Initially, the Young Lords appealed to the FSMC as part of a broader effort to connect with partners in their various outreach programs. Since churches were eminently visible institutions and carried (through their history as vehicles of colonial domination)[44] credibility among residents of El Barrio, the Young Lords worked to ensure that different churches were actually serving the community in which they operated.

As part of their research and outreach, the Young Lords discovered that most of the churches in El Barrio had some kind of pragmatic community service program that served residents in ways other than spiritual sustenance. The FSMC, however, was a special and unfortunate case. Located in the middle of El Barrio, the FSMC opened its doors only on Sundays for official church services. Failing to involve itself in the community's efforts to rise above deleterious conditions, the FSMC became an institution of particular interest to the Young Lords.[45] According to Yoruba, "The First Spanish Church was chosen because it was right smack dead in the center of the Barrio. It's a beautiful location right in the middle of the community. It was also chosen because it is the one church in the community that has consistently closed itself up to the community."[46] The FSMC, then, became the symbol of colonial intervention in El Barrio and the locus of conflict for the burgeoning Young Lords.

Beginning their discussions with the FSMC in October 1969, negotiations did not progress in the Young Lords' favor for at least three reasons. First, the church congregation was evangelical and conservative. Espousing leftist beliefs, the Young Lords were patently resistant to organized religion, even if many of its members had religious backgrounds. The ideological tension between what the Young Lords advocated politically (decolonial liberation and socialist redistribution) and what the church espoused politically and spiritually appeared to be an insurmountable hurdle. Second, the pastor of the FSMC, Humerto Carrazara, was an anti-Castro Cuban exile; whereas the Young Lords were generally pro-Castro and, more prominently, pro-Che Guevara, the images and words of whom they regularly circulated in the community. Third, the vast majority of the leadership and membership of the FSMC did not reside in the community and, therefore, did not see a pressing need to expend church resources (space, funds, etc.) to support programs for El Barrio. As a spokesperson for the FSMC explained in summary, "The First Spanish Church is a conservative church, as are most of our Evangelical Spanish churches. The tactics of the Young Lords and their ideology have been offensive to the people of the local congregation."[47]

Failing in their initial negotiations with the FSMC, the Young Lords made the decision to appeal directly to the membership of the congregation. On December 7, 1969, after having sat in on services and distributed flyers outside for the previous six Sundays, at least fourteen members of the Young Lords attended the Sunday worship again. At the end of the sermon, a period for free testimonial opened up and Felipe Luciano attempted to address the eighty-member congregation. The trouble began when Luciano arose and shouted, "There is something wrong here. This is not a community." Upon rising and, according to *New York Times* reporter Michael Kaufman, "interrupting the service," Luciano and other Young Lords were confronted by police officers who had been standing by in anticipation.[48] In the clash that followed, five Young Lords and three police officers were injured (Luciano the worst with a broken arm), and fourteen Young Lords were arrested. After the incident, about 150 people in the community took part in a march that ended at the FSMC. Reported Kaufman, "At the church, the marchers stopped for a short rally at which they berated the police as 'cowards' and repeated their demand."[49]

In the weeks that followed, the Young Lords continued trying, progressively with greater vigor (sometimes by leafleting), to negotiate with the FSMC leadership and persuade parishioners (see Figure 5.1). Each Sunday, the Young Lords returned to the church services and requested from the parishioners an agreement to use the space for a free breakfast program, a day care center, a makeshift medical clinic (for tuberculosis and lead poisoning testing), and a "liberation school," which was designed to address the colonial imaginary of the Puerto Rican people.[50] On December 21, for example, about 150 Young Lords and supporters attended Sunday worship. A brief discussion among the Lay Board (the governing body of the FSMC), a representative of the church youths, and some Young Lords followed the service, after which Luciano delivered another plea for use of the space. By that time, however, most of the church members had departed.[51]

The following Sunday brought a substantial change in the scene, according to Kaufman of the *New York Times*:

> As the sound of the final organ chord died down, Juan Gonzalez, a spokesman for the group, rose and attempted to address the congregation. For the last 12 weeks, many of the 80 parishioners and 150 supporters of the Lords have come to regard such speeches as part of the service. . . . This time, however, most of the parishioners filed out of the church . . . as Mr. Gonzalez sought again to persuade them to

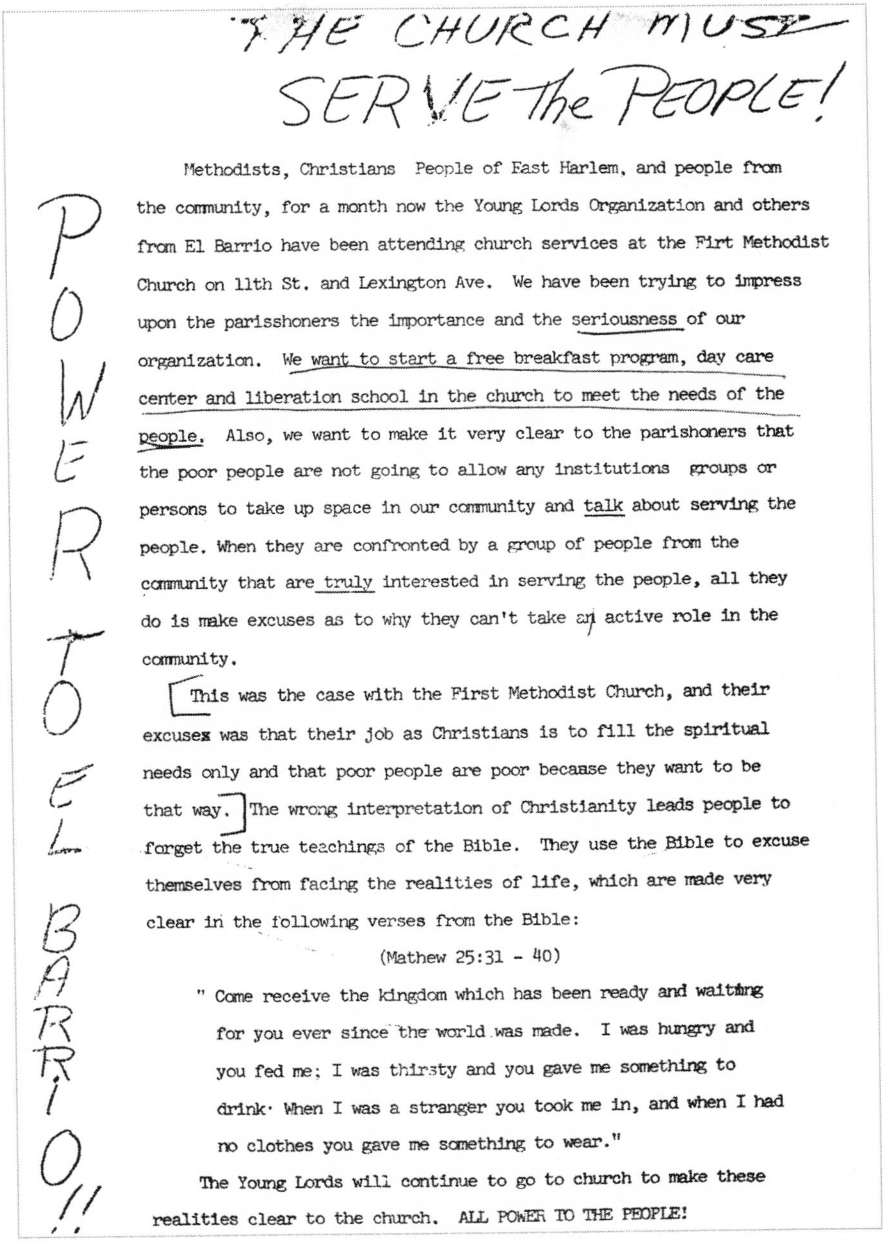

THE CHURCH MUST SERVE the PEOPLE!

P
O
W
E
R

T
O

E
L

B
A
R
R
I
O
!!

Methodists, Christians People of East Harlem, and people from the community, for a month now the Young Lords Organization and others from El Barrio have been attending church services at the Firt Methodist Church on 11th St. and Lexington Ave. We have been trying to impress upon the parisshoners the importance and the seriousness of our organization. We want to start a free breakfast program, day care center and liberation school in the church to meet the needs of the people. Also, we want to make it very clear to the parishoners that the poor people are not going to allow any institutions groups or persons to take up space in our community and talk about serving the people. When they are confronted by a group of people from the community that are truly interested in serving the people, all they do is make excuses as to why they can't take an active role in the community.

This was the case with the First Methodist Church, and their excuses was that their job as Christians is to fill the spiritual needs only and that poor people are poor because they want to be that way. The wrong interpretation of Christianity leads people to forget the true teachings of the Bible. They use the Bible to excuse themselves from facing the realities of life, which are made very clear in the following verses from the Bible:

(Mathew 25:31 - 40)

" Come receive the kingdom which has been ready and waiting
for you ever since the world was made. I was hungry and
you fed me; I was thirsty and you gave me something to
drink· When I was a stranger you took me in, and when I had
no clothes you gave me something to wear."

The Young Lords will continue to go to church to make these realities clear to the church. ALL POWER TO THE PEOPLE!

Figure 5.1　Mimeographed leaflet distributed to the community and appealing directly to parishioners, among others. (New York University Tamiment Library and Robert F. Wagner Labor Archives, National Lawyers Guild, TAM 191, box 92, NYC Young Lords Party, folder 2.)

accept the breakfast program. As they left, crosspieces were quickly nailed onto the church's two doors, which were also chained from the inside.[52]

Choosing to "take" the church rather than continue futile negotiations, the Young Lords announced a "liberated zone" "in the midst of occupied territory."[53] Promptly renaming the First Spanish Methodist Church "the People's Church," the Young Lords began almost immediately to serve the community. According to another *New York Times* report, "Puerto Rican militants provided free meals, medical care, and history classes for neighborhood youngsters yesterday in an East Harlem church that they seized on Sunday."[54]

Outside the church, Luciano later recalled, "The community reacted very favorably. Leaflets, rallies, and marches through the streets proved effective in terms of getting the people out."[55] One mimeographed flyer read:

> The struggle around the First Spanish Methodist Church that the Young Lords have been waging for the past two months has resulted in the transformation of that church into the new People's Church. The Young Lords Organization, members of the community of "El Barrio" and their supporters liberated the church for the use of it by the people. . . . The Young Lords program calls for the immediate opening of the church to the people. The children of our community will have a free breakfast program and a Liberation School. No longer will they go to school hungry. No longer will the oppressor keep from them their true culture and the history of repression in America.[56]

In all, the Young Lords made the People's Church a sanctuary warranted in the name of "the people"—a place for learning, livelihood, and liberation triumphing over an unresponsive and oppressive institution with strong ties to the modern Western project of coloniality.[57] As the Young Lords stated in the group's first published report of this activism, "All institutions that are in this community will serve the people of the community. Either First Methodist opens up to the people of the community or it will not open at all" (see Figure 5.2).[58]

Lasting eleven days, the People's Church was home to all of the programs the Young Lords sought to implement. Furthermore, the church became a political, social, and artistic refuge for "the people" of El Barrio and the residence of some three hundred people. They hosted a children's theatrical event (which was, essentially, a play about the church offensive), numerous speeches, poetry readings (including the first reading of Pedro Pietri's famous poem, "Puerto Rican Obituary"), musical events, and more. Then, at 6:30 A.M. on January 7, 1970, 105 Young Lords and supporters submitted to arrest, bringing a peaceful end to the church offensive.[59] While undeniably short-lived, the holding of the People's Church set the practical and discursive terrain for a

We are not only being persecuted because we feed and educate but because we scream out without fear "Free Puerto Rico Now!"

No solamente nos persiguen porque educamos y alimentámos si no que nos persiguen porque gritamos sin miedo "Viva Puerto Rico Libre Ahora!"

On Sunday, December 7, the Young Lords Organization entered the First Spanish Methodist Church on 111th St. and Lexington in the heart of El Barrio. We had been attending church services for the past two months to request space to institute a free breakfast program for the children of East Harlem and a free day care center for the mothers of the community. During those two months we talked to parishoners and passed out leaflets to make them understand the seriousness of our programs and the need for them in our community.

In addition to the parishoners the Young Lords have had to deal with a "gusano" pastor of this church who is a Cuban exile and therefore as reactionary as hell, Carazana, obviously paranoid after the heavy shit that Che and the people in Cuba put down during one of the greatest revolutions in history, hasn't learned that the will of the people cannot be suppressed with fascist tactics, which are what Carazana has used from the start. Since the Lords have been attending services the pigs have occupied the church. Any attempts or requests to speak to those who would be involved in making a decision on the matter have been answered by calling in the pigs.

Carazana doesn't understand that he cannot run an institution in the Puerto Rican community and not serve the needs of that community. He cannot open that institution for three hours on Sunday and a few hours on Friday and Saturday nights and believe he is serving the needs of the people of El Barrio.

So last Sunday the YLO continued our struggle for a People's Church. We were very tired of listening to Carzana pay lip service to Christian ideals while his actions proved that it was all hypocrisy. Christian ideals do not jibe with a refusal to feed the hungry. Felipe Luciano, Chairman of NY YLO, stood up and asked to speak to the congregation so that he could break down to the people how that hypocrisy was manifesting itself. A pig standing in the back moved up to Felipe, followed by 25 other pigs. The people on the altar (choir, pastor, etc.) began shoving Lords around. The congregation continued to sing "Christian" songs in order to drown out the truth of what Felipe was saying. The pastor stood on the pulpit smiling while our Chairman was clubbed repeatedly on the head by the pigs, who then attacked the other Lords.

El Domingo, 7 de Diciembre, la Organizacion de los Young Lords entraron en la Primera Iglesia Metodista, situada en la calle III y Lexington en el centro del Barrio. Hemos estado llendo a los servicios por dos meses para pedir espacio para desarrollar un programa de desayuno gratis y un centro de cuidar para niños de la communidad.

Durante estos dos meses le hablamos a la gente de la iglesia y pasamos hojas explicando la seriedad y importancia de estos programas en nuestra comunidad. Ademas, los feligreses y Los Young Lords han tenido que luchar con el pastor "gusano" de esta iglesia quien es un Cubano exilado y reaccionario como un diablo. Carazana, el pastor, desde luego con temor despues de lo que Che y el Pueblo de Cuba lograron con la revolucion mas grande en la historia, no ha comprendido que el poder de la gente nunca sera suprimido con tacticas fascistas. Carazana ha usado tacticas fascistas desde principio. Desde que los servicios comenzaron a ir a los servicios los cerdos han ocupado la iglesia. Cada peticion para hablar con los que tienen poder para hacer decisiones fue contestada con una llamada a los puercos.

Carazana no comprende que el no puede dirigir una institucion por tres horas los domingos y una cuantas horas los viernes y sabados por la noche, y creer que el esta sirviendo las necesidades de la gente en el Barrio.

Estabamos cansado de escuchar a Carazana hablando sobre los ideales cristianos mientras que sus acciones indicanaba que era un hipocrita. Los ideales cristianos no estan en acuerdo con no servir a los niños pobres y hambrientos del Barrio. Felipe Luciano, presidente de los Young Lords, se paro y pidio que lo dejaran hablar a la congregacion para explicar la hipocresia que era evidente. Felipe se arrimo a el altar (el pastor, el coro, etc.) comenzaron a empujar a los Young Lords. La congregacion continuo cantando canciones "cristanas" para ahogar la verdad de lo que Felipe decia. El pastor se paro del pulpito sonriendo mientras que nuestro presidente fue atacado continuamente por los puercos.

ATTENTION ━ ATENCIÓN

THE CHURCH AT 111th & LEXINGTON, NEW YORK, IS NOW A PEOPLE'S CHURCH, SERVING THE NEEDS OF THE PEOPLE OF EL BARRIO. SINCE YLO TOOK OVER THE CHURCH ON DECEMBER 28, OVER 125 HUNGRY CHILDREN HAVE BEEN FED THERE EVERY MORNING, CLOSE TO 100 CHILDREN ARE ATTENDING A LIBERATION SCHOOL THAT TEACHES THEM THEIR TRUE HISTORY, AND PEOPLE IN THE COMMUNITY ARE GETTING FREE MEDICAL CARE.

ON JANUARY 2, THE PIGS CELEBRATED THE NEW YEAR BY SERVING AN INJUNCTION AGAINST YLO. AS WE GO TO PRESS, THEY ARE PREPARING TO VAMP DOWN ON THE PEOPLE'S CHURCH.

THE YLO HAS PROMISED THAT THE CHURCH WILL SERVE THE NEEDS OF THE PEOPLE OF EL BARRIO OR CLOSE. THE ACTIVITIES HAPPENING THERE NOW ARE JUST A FIRST STEP IN FULFILLING THAT PROMISE. A PIECE OF PAPER WILL NOT STOP WHAT YLO AND THE PEOPLE HAVE BEGUN.

A SPECIAL EDITION OF THE YLO NEWSPAPER WILL BE OUT SOON, TELLING THE WHOLE STORY OF THE STRUGGLE OF THE PEOPLE'S CHURCH IN EL BARRIO. WATCH FOR IT.

The Young Lords came to the church completely unarmed. No Lord possessed any type of weapon—not even a nail file. Sisters and brothers were clubbed and dragged out into waiting pig cars. Lords defended themselves as best they could against the blackjacks and clubs of the pigs. Blood was splattered all over the floor of the church—which isn't too cool a thing for a place which is heralded as a "sanctuary." Rather than let someone speak for five or ten minutes, the Christians of the parish preferred to spill blood.

When it was all over ten Lords were busted as well as three community people. At their arraignment we saw that our Chairman had a cracked head, a broken right arm, and a broken left hand. Four others also had bandages on their heads and all complained of body injuries. The YLO understands the nature of the racist pigs and the necessity for intensifying the struggle.

The charges were disruption of church services, felonious assault, and riot 1. The highest bail was set at $1,000 and that was against Mirta Gonzalez, Lt. of Information, and Daoud Velasquez, Capt. of Information. Their assault charge weighed heavy in that decision. We were able to raise the necessary bail and everyone was out in 24 hours.

This does not mean that the church action will be ended. It has just begun. The Lords will be at the First Methodist Church. We will bring with us as many people as we can. First Methodist will become a People's Church.

All institutions that are in this community will serve the people of the community. Either First Methodist opens up to the people of the community, or it will not open at all.

Iris, Ministry of Information, NY YLO
ALL POWER TO "EL BARRIO"
DROP CHARGES AGAINST THE TEN LORDS
HANDS OFF THE LORDS
FREE PUERTO RICO NOW

Tambien atacarón a los otros Lords. Los Young Lords entraron a la iglesia completamente desarmados. Ninguno tenia armas—ni tan siquiera una lima de uñas. Hermanas y hermanos fueron atacados y arrastrados hacia los carros se los puercos, los Lords se defendieron contra las macanas de los puercos. Sangre corria por la iglesia que no es una cosa muy chevre siendo un sitio que se supone ser un santuario. En vez de permitir que una persona hable se por cinco o diez minutos los "cristanos" de la iglesia preferie ron derramar sangre de puertorriquenos!

Cuando todo hubo terminado diez de los Young Lords fueron arrestado en compenda de tres miembros de la comunidad. Cuando aparecieron en corte vimos que nuestro presidente tenia la cabeza rota, su brazo derecho partido y su mano izquierda. Cuatro hermanos tenian sus cabezas vendadas y sus cuerpos heridos. Los Young Lords entienden la policia racista y la necesidad de intensificar la lucha.

Las acusaciones fueron? interrumpcion de servicio en la iglesia, accione timiento y agresion, desorden, etc. La fianza mas grande fue de 1,000 dolares y fue contra Mirta Gonzalez, Teniente de Informacion, y Daoud Velasquez, Capitan de Informacion.

Pudimos levantar el dinero suficiente para sacar a los hermanos en 24 horas. Esto no quiere decir que la accion de la iglesia ha terminado. Apenas ha empezado. El proximo domingo, los Lords estaran en la Primera Iglesia Metodista. Llevaremos toda la gente que podamos. La primera Iglesia Metodista sera la Iglesia de La Gente.

Todas las instituciones que estan en esta comunidad serviran a la gente de la comunidad. Si no habren las puertas de la Primera Iglesia Metodista a la gente de la comunidad, esas puertas no abriran jamas!

Iris, Ministerio de Informacion, NY YLO
TODO EL PODER AL BARRIO
VIVA PUERTO RICO LIBRE
ELIMINACION TOTAL DE LOS PUERCOS
QUE NOS BRUTALIZAN CON SU REPRESION FACISTA
VENCEREMOS!

Figure 5.2   The Young Lords' first published report on the church offensive, published in *Y.L.O.* 1, no. 5 (January 1970) in Chicago. (Microfiche, Collections of the Center for Puerto Rican Studies, City University of New York—Hunter College, New York.)

prolonged rearticulation of "the people" that lasted at least until the Young Lords' transformation into the Puerto Rican Revolutionary Workers Organization in 1972.[60]

There are probably obvious ways, given the above narrative, that "the people" was a key ideograph at play in the Young Lords' rhetoric. For example, their choice to rename a seized church "the People's Church" is just the first of many hints that "the people" was central to this action and the Young Lords' rhetoric generally. This should not be surprising given the long tradition of privileging "the people" in U.S. political discourse. According to Daniel T. Rodgers, "Post-Revolutionary America belonged to the people; the terms entered the constitutional lexicon at independence. Through the carefully balanced machinery of their constitutions the people ruled."[61] More important, Rodgers continues, "No political term with as powerful a history as the People disappears; their moment past, such words remain lodged in the patterns of speech, open (with luck) for new tasks and occasions."[62] As I mentioned earlier, Kenneth Burke knew this well when he addressed the American Writers' Congress and argued, unsuccessfully, that "the people" ought to be privileged over "the worker."[63] McGee also understood the power of "the people" in liberal democratic politics—both as product and structure of political myths and as a homogenizing force in U.S. rhetorical culture.[64] Just as these and many other scholars have recognized the power of "the people," the Young Lords, versed in the discourse of U.S. and Latin American democratic traditions, seized on "the people" as a key ideograph in their public discourse. The church offensive is just one example of such rhetoric in action—an example that was sustained through future reiterations of the memory of the church offensive, a later retaking of the FSMC, and continued articulations of "the people" in their activism in subsequent years.[65]

Through verbal discourse, leafleting, artistic performances, and modeling civic and political practices, the Young Lords crafted "the people" in various ways and in a manner that shaped a sustained public image of "the people" in action. The means by which the Young Lords did this was complex and not temporally bound in the immediate context of the church offensive; that is, the Young Lords spoke, wrote, performed, and imaged "the people" into existence in the immediate context of the church offensive and through further advocacy afterward. Much like Maurice Charland's "peuple québécios," the Young Lords' "people" were a "representational effect" of the narratives and other discourses that "create the illusion of merely revealing a unified and unproblematic subjectivity."[66] In the church offensive, the Young Lords crafted "the people" as (a) subverted by the FSMC and dominating institutions; (b) collective rather than individualist; (c) oppressed in everyday life and in their normal/normalized position; (d) oppositional and engaged in liberation, especially through education; and (e) powerful, even omnipotent, at the center of the organization's liberation politics. By constructing the ideograph of "the people" in this way, the Young Lords advanced a decolonial challenge to the modern social imaginary dominant at the time.

To begin, "the people," in the Young Lords' articulation, had been let down, even robbed, by various institutions. Whether in politics, education, the church, or some other institution, the needs of "the people" had not been met. Regarding organized religion generally and the FSMC in particular, Yoruba argued:

> The other issue that has been brought up is that *organized religion has got to respond to the needs of the people.* Now the Board of Directors and members of that church say that we imposed ourselves on them by speaking up and asking for space during their service. We say that *they have imposed themselves* on the community by putting their church in the middle of the community and *then not opening their doors to the people.* That's the true imposition that they fail to see.[67]

In this way, "the people" were constructed as having their will subverted when their attempts to voice their pluriversal lived experiences were silenced. Furthermore, the church had excluded "the people," shut them out in their own community, thus warranting liberatory action on the Young Lords' part. In a related rhetorical move, "the people" were duped and held down by the church. According to Yoruba, "They teach only the parts of the bible that will mollify the people, keep them down, you know, turn the other cheek, be cool, be humble, slow up, wait."[68] In drawing attention to the ways in which the FSMC—understood both as a colonizing power in its own right and as a synecdoche for broader coloniality—occupied both the space of "the people" and their minds, the Young Lords initiated a decolonial rhetoric aimed at delinking "the people" from the modern colonial social imaginary.

Such a rhetorical delinking from coloniality occurred visually as well as verbally. McGee once playfully asserted, "No one has ever seen an 'equality' strutting up the driveway."[69] While I will not challenge the specific example, we can *sight* ideographs.[70] With regard to "the people," Lucaites makes a provocative argument about how the ideograph is figured in documentary photojournalism beginning in the 1930s. According to Lucaites, documentary photography ushered in a technology that disrupted the myth of a unified "people" and highlighted individuality in an apparently fragmented U.S. American public. Starting in the 1930s, photography functioned to imbue "the American people" with a certain character that reduced the sense of collectivity into the individual, thus accenting the liberal dimension of liberal democracy.[71]

Countering the hegemonic formulation of this specific liberal, individualist ideology, the Young Lords visualized "the people" in a manner that privileged collectivism. In a sense, rather than "concretize 'the people' in its individual particularity,"[72] the Young Lords focused attention on the interconnectedness of a heterogeneous people. For example, in the Newsreel film *El Pueblo se Levanta* (which documented the Young Lords' church offensive and other early activism), viewers can find numerous scenes where they cannot tell who any of the specific persons pictured are; rather, viewers are shown "the people" as a collectivity taking over the church—not quite "the people" strutting up the driveway, but close. In the church offensive, then, "the people" asserted their liberation by taking "community control" of the FSMC.[73] Such performances of collective peoplehood were captured on moving images, reported by mainstream news organizations, and filmed by activist still photographers linked up to the Young Lords. Furthermore, such captured images of "the people" performed were circulated beyond the church offensive context. In its circulation, the image of "the people" in action links up with similar images of protest commonplace at the time. In this way, such imaging of "the people" was specific to the Young Lords' decolonizing politics and generalizable to (a) wider populist struggles and constructions of peoplehood and (b) broader Third World decolonial politics.

In rearticulating "the people" through a collectivist and coalitional lens, the Young Lords normalized "the people" as a regular part of everyday life in El Barrio. Furthermore, the Young Lords constructed "the people" in opposition to a ruling class and hierarchies in the church that oppress them in various ways. "The people," in this manner, were "normal" despite, or in the process of, being oppressed. At one point, Yoruba demanded, "The hierarchy of the church has got to come down from up there in the sky and see what's happening with the people."[74] In this sense, "the people" were on the ground figuratively and literally. On the one hand, they were real, historically situated people with practical problems that the church would not address; and on the other hand, they were the materialist counterparts to the church's metaphysical idealism— the products of intersubjective social relations rooted in a lived history of coloniality.

Even something as simple as the Young Lords and supporters gathered in the FSMC for a musical performance became a key figuring of "the people" because of the representational force of this collectivity in the subdued space of the church. Importantly, the representative form of such figurations of "the people" keys us to a particular performance of peopleness and its heterogeneous content.[75] When we look at the images and read or hear the words that capture particular performances, "the people" lack any originality or uniqueness except in their collection en masse, which marks the representative form as remarkable and powerful. Their collective unification in a manner that asserted agency (however normal their acts may seem) marked a performative commitment to the *vita activa* and a resistance to docility and the colonized imaginary.[76] So while they are figured as normal, action and the exercise of a particular type of power is normalized as well. And this is what makes the Young Lords' "people" particularly unique and resistive: rather than reducing collectivity onto the individual, the Young Lords reversed the equation by locating the people in a sense of collectivity or groupness that imagined a democratic and decolonial moment of liberation rooted in the necessity of cultural heterogeneity (the Young Lords were a multiethnic, multiracial group, after all) and its attendant universalization of plurality (pluriversality, in Mignolo's terms).[77]

Within this decolonial moment challenging the modern social imaginary, "the people" were visually and verbally positioned oppositionally to institutions—in this case, the church but also to broader oppressive institutions. In addition to images, words, and activism showing "the people" taking over the institution that had excluded them, the Young Lords articulated and performed a "people" making alternative use of the church's space for a concert, performances, meals, and a liberation school to free them from the restrictive confines of the church's and society's colonial imaginaries.[78] Such oppositional positioning and deterritorialization also placed "the people" within liberation by visually and performatively marking their movement from an excluded position into new spaces and realms, delineating a "liberated zone."[79] They are witnessed in this context as enacting decolonial power and are constructed beyond this context as doing the same.

In a mimeographed issue of *Palante* that appeared after the church offensive, Yoruba featured the Young Lords' rearticulation of "the people's" struggle in the following way: "To fight this oppression, the YOUNG LORDS ORGANIZATION knows it is necessary to unite all The People against the Ruling Class. To do this, we must educate them to the lies we are faced with every day. Once people understand how they are being oppressed, then they can move against those who have their foot on our backs."[80] This passage is important for two reasons. First, it establishes the opposition between "the people" and the "ruling class" (note the capitalization he uses), which delineates the broad scope of their revised "people" in opposition to a modern, universalized "people." Second, it defines a crucial goal of the Young Lords as being the education of "the people" so that they could "move" (in literal and figurative ways) against their oppressors, empowered by new modes of thinking that functioned outside, yet still in contact with, the modern/colonial social imaginary.

In one photograph published in the *New York Times*, we are further clued into the Young Lords' important goal of educating "the people."[81] The image's composition was keyed to the familiar educational setting but was also set aside as unique and revolutionary in this context because audience members (i.e., those viewing the image) knew it was occurring in a nontraditional setting with nontraditional goals ("liberation school"). Combined with the verbal messages about "the people" being denied a history and being repressed by the church, the act of teaching and learning, and the image of both, provided rhetorical and practical resources to rethink the social imaginary outside of coloniality. In this manner, "the people" were normal, oppressed, and preparing to move the social imaginary in significant ways.[82]

In attempting such social movement in the context of continued oppression, "the people" were active and exercised a certain type of power. In a speech delivered at the FSMC, Luciano reasoned as follows:

> Legally, the church is tax exempt. Any tax exempt institution is run by the people. The people should be allowed to use the space. They have no right to close the doors to any group of people, whether they be anti-poverty, revolutionary, or whatever the case may be, they have no right to close their doors.[83]

This "tax exempt" justification for taking over the church was one that the Young Lords deployed often.[84] More important, and similar to the jaibería sensibility I discussed in Chapter 4, "the people" were authorized to act by the same system that oppressed them. In a Burkean sense, the scene-agency relationship became complicated insofar as one of the institutional settings on which "the people" acted became the very agency through which action was made possible.[85] Put differently, the Young Lords again demonstrated their ability to think and act from the interstices or borders between modern/colonial worlds. They engaged in "an other thinking" that could "think from both traditions" at the same time[86] and precipitated a moment "in which the imaginary of the modern world system cracks."[87] Such "other thinking" propelled a liberation rhetoric that was further doubled—one that affirmed a commitment to "the people" while rearticulating its meaning, history, and function.

Unsurprisingly, then, "the people" were elevated in the Young Lords' rhetoric to the highest possible position. Reacting to the tension between their own ideology and the ideology of the church, Luciano said, "It has to be understood that we may not advocate a worship in a God. Our god is our people. That is my god. That is my religion."[88] Displacing what Mignolo calls the modern "theo- and ego-logical hegemony," a "(de-colonizing) geopolitics of knowledge and understanding" emerged in Luciano's rhetoric.[89] More important than any other ideograph, "the people" took a central position as the nodal point of the Young Lords' rhetoric—the point through which they challenged the dominant social imaginary and imagined anew.

As the initial point at which the Young Lords crafted a new vision of "the people," the significance of the rhetoric of the church offensive extended beyond its spatiotemporal context. As José Ramón Sánchez argues, the Young Lords were a media-savvy group and knew that the words they spoke and activities in which they engaged would become otherwise mediated images (film, television, and news photographs) that could circulate within a vernacular (counter)public sphere and to a broader public audience.[90] Circulation, here, does not refer simply to the utterance of words and deployment of performances and images in their initial context. Rather, words, performances, and images of "the people" continued to circulate beyond the actual place and time of the People's Church through flyers, newspapers (e.g., the *New York Times* and *Palante*), television (the church offensive received a lot of news coverage and garnered national attention with appearances by Jane Fonda and Sammy Davis Jr.), and film (*El Pueblo se Levanta*).[91] Such circulation continued past the immediate time of the event to cultivate a memory and imaginary of "the people" that found material instantiation in the media just mentioned, in repeated oral performances of what happened at the People's Church, and in the eventual second takeover of the FSMC after Julio Roldan (a Young Lord) turned up dead in his jail cell from an apparent suicide. Thus, the liberation politics and rearticulation of "the people" advanced by the Lords was re-performed and may even continue to be so today.[92]

Turning attention to the circulation of ideographs brings us back to McGee's demand that we examine these terms in ordinary, everyday, political discourse. Cara Finnegan and Jiyeon Kang posit that "circulation enables us to avoid untenable distinctions between images and texts, focusing not on individual types of discourse, but on their movement in a scene of circulation . . . [that] recognizes the multiplicity of discourse and . . . does not privilege the linguistic and textual over the visual."[93] In bringing such a focus and attitude to bear on "the people" specifically and ideographs generally, attention to circulation encourages critics to examine the ways in which multifarious discourses produce rhetorical scenes and agents (social imaginaries) through the constellation and rearticulation of various ideographs. Add to this a consideration of how embodied practices (the liberation school, poetry performances, theatrical plays, etc.) were also part of the broader discourse, which is both a product and productive of the social imaginary, and we are left with a more nuanced understanding of how ideographs circulate and *do* sociopolitical work. As public-specific understandings, social imaginaries change, fluctuate, and are reinforced with changes in speech, writing, images, performances, et cetera. As new discourse is created or old discourse is reinterpreted and redeployed, social imaginaries are altered.[94]

Decolonizing Rhetoric: Some Concluding Thoughts

The Young Lords Organization's 1969 takeover of the First Spanish Methodist Church in El Barrio was the second public, political "offensive" in which they engaged. Like the garbage offensive, the church offensive was only moderately "successful" when viewed from an instrumentalist framework. Although it was effective for the days in which the Young Lords held control of the FSMC, the revolutionary Latin@s capitulated to pressure from the city and police, surrendering after a week of occupying the space. While meeting material needs and establishing "community control" of local institutions were important to the Young Lords and their supporters, the significance of the church offensive was largely symbolic and operated on the imaginaries of those involved. As Luciano summarized, "It's important that we understand the importance of this institution. This is a symbol. And it must be won over."[95] And won over it was. Even though the Young Lords eventually lost permanent control of the FSMC, "the People's Church" and "the people" remained, through continued circulation, powerful symbols of the group's activism and the possibilities of liberation politics "in the midst of occupied territory." The Young Lords' takeover of the FSMC, then, had constitutive implications insofar as they managed to secure a popular rearticulation of the space as "the People's Church" (a label that continues to be used today) and they modeled practices of liberation and community control in which they engaged until becoming the Puerto Rican Revolutionary Workers Organization.

Such an alternative set of public sensibilities—the different modes and ideals of stranger relationality—was anchored by a rearticulation of "the people" enacting a material rhetorical challenge to the dominant modern social imaginary. This chapter underscores the importance of putting ideographic theory into conversation with notions of social imaginaries because ideographs are, recursively, an important (perhaps *the central*) material rhetorical means by which social imaginaries do their work, as well as a product of revisions to social imaginaries. Understood as the verbal, visual, and embodied symbolic repertoire that is defined by (and defines) the social imaginary, ideographs facilitate ideologically, historically, and doctrinally constrained modes of stranger relationality, thus constituting social imaginaries and sociopolitical subjectivity. A focus on "the people" helps to underscore these connections, especially when examined in the context of the Young Lords' challenge to dominant constructions of a homogenous "people." McGee, for example, posits, " 'We the People of the United States' supposes a cultural and political homogeneity."[96] Such homogeneity, however, hangs its rhetorical hat on the articulation of individuals to a sense of common cause, purpose, and ontology. "The people," in this sense, are individuals positioned as contiguous under the banner "American" and operating in the absence of an "epistemic difference."[97] In this hegemonic formulation, "the people" presumes a certain universality of identity and normative commitments, which is concomitant with a modern colonial imaginary. "The crooked rhetoric that naturalizes 'modernity' as a universal global process and point of arrival," Mignolo argues, "hides its darker side, the constant reproduction of 'coloniality.' "[98] As such, the dominant, Western notion of "the people" is far too limiting and dangerous in its homogenizing drive.

In advancing an alternative conceptualization of "the people" as an ideograph in the church offensive, the Young Lords decolonized the social imaginary and articulated liberation as an alternative to emancipation within the system. "What is at question in this paradigm," writes Quijano, is "the individual and individualist character of the 'subject,' which like every half-truth falsifies the problem by denying intersubjectivity and social totality as the production sites of all knowledge."[99] Rejecting the universal individual as the basis for "the people," the Young Lords sought an "other" way of thinking and being that liberated, in Quijano's formulation, "the production of knowledge, reflection, and communication from the pitfalls of European rationality/modernity."[100] This other way of thinking worked by supplanting homogeneous constructions of "the people" and discursive privileging of individualism with a different "perspective of totality in knowledge [that] includes the acknowledgement of the heterogeneity of all reality."[101] And while I think Maldonado-Torres is right that "coloniality of Being would introduce the question of *being-colonized* or the *damné*, who would appear . . . as an alternative to . . . the modern concept of 'the people,'" the Young Lords demonstrate that the two are not mutually exclusive.[102]

Drawing from embodied, historically and geographically particular experiences, the Young Lords engaged in an "other thinking" that delinked the ideograph "the people" from modern rationality and enunciated a pluriversal alternative to the modern social imaginary. The Young Lords crafted a "people" who had been (and continue to be) excluded from ethico-/theo-political culture; whose lived experience of coloniality has been silenced; whose strength comes from a diversity of experience; who resist racist constructions of docility; who operate on the ground rather than in a specialized or technocratic realm; and who are marked first by their collectivism, from which they garner strength and through which they articulate links of equivalence to other Third World sisters and brothers in struggle. Pluriversality, in this context, denotes the Young Lords' attentiveness to "different colonial histories entangled with imperial modernity."[103] The pluriversality "of each local history and its narrative of decolonization," Mignolo adds, "can connect through . . . common experience and use it as the basis for a new common logic of knowing" bound to "a universal project of delinking from modern rationality and building other possible worlds."[104] Although delinking might often work though new terms and vocabularies, the Young Lords showed that pluriversality does not require such frames of rejection.

In reading the Young Lords' rhetoric of "the people" as a decolonizing rhetoric aimed at delinking from modern/colonial social imaginaries, I have argued that the Young Lords provide "an other thinking," which Mignolo describes as "a way of thinking that is not inspired in its own limitations and is not intended to dominate and to humiliate; a way of thinking that is universally marginal, fragmentary, and unachieved; and, as such, a way of thinking that, because universally marginal and fragmentary, is not ethnocidal."[105] Even if you want to read the Young Lords' popular rhetoric as a form of "subversive complicity," to borrow from Ramón Grosfoguel's lexicon, it would be one of many "forms of resistance that resignify and transform dominant forms of knowledge from the point of view of the non-Eurocentric rationality of subaltern subjectivities thinking from border epistemologies."[106] In my read of their rhetoric, I have tried to demonstrate an other thinking of my own (to "think from both traditions and, at the same time, from neither of them")[107] by joining ideographs and social imaginaries and demonstrating how the Young Lords enunciated a substantive challenge to modern coloniality through a transformation of the meaning and ideology of the dominant political grammar.

Such "other thinking" is already a hallmark of contemporary scholarship in Latin@ studies, but my particular engagement of decoloniality in the Young Lords' rhetoric can push further the theoretical development of Latin@ vernacular discourse. In their essay on ChicanoBrujo performances, for example, Holling and Calafell argue, "A decolonial performance practice performs, embodies, and manifests the ills of colonialism."[108] In their most recent work codifying a metatheory of Latin@ vernacular discourse, Holling and Calafell underscore the ways such discourse "implicates the decolonial; that is, the process of decolonization" through a "conscious awareness" and reflexivity about colonialism's embodied marks.[109] Building from these recognitions, my extension of the scholarship on decoloniality in this chapter offers a layer of specificity, suggesting that a defining characteristic of decoloniality is a critical delinking that offers pluriversal alternatives to modern coloniality. Such alternatives can coalesce in challenges to ideographs like "the people" but must also include broader epistemic shifts privileging geopolitical location and the body politics of knowledge in contradistinction to the dominant social imaginary.[110]

CONCLUSION
Decoloniality in Practice

So, please excuse us if, in presenting what we have learned ourselves or added to our knowledge from the experience of others, we might sound at times a little critical, preachy or even sermonizing. The theme lends itself to committing such errors.

—JESÚS COLÓN, "How to Know the Puerto Ricans,"
in *A Puerto Rican in New York*

This form of love is not the narrative of love as encoded in the West: it is another kind of love, a synchronic process that punctures through traditional, older narratives of love, that ruptures everyday being.

—CHELA SANDOVAL, *Methodology of the Oppressed*

Despite all the social advancements of the last forty-plus years since the New York Young Lords burst onto the scene and began educating countless people in El Barrio and beyond about "our long history of fighting against cultural, as well as economic genocide by the spaniards and now the yanquis," so much work remains to be done.[1] I pen this conclusion at a time in academia when, for example, a formal Latin@ studies professional association is only beginning (again/still) to get off the ground and the nearly quarter-century-old Puerto Rican Studies Association just emerged from financial hardships. I am a professor in a state with a Latin@ population that nearly doubled between the 2000 and 2010 census[2] and at a university with only a handful of faculty who self-identify as doing Latin@ studies (a case that is not truly unique, as there are so few of us with doctorates in academia to begin with). I claim a home within a discipline (communication studies) that, despite having several thousand attendees at our annual convention, includes (to my knowledge) not one Puerto Rican rhetorician with a doctorate beside myself. Yet I am still "the lucky one"—the only person in my family to have graduated college, the only one to escape breaking his body with unrelenting physical labor. How "lucky" I am to be able to count on one hand the number of Puerto Rican colleagues and professors with whom I have worked directly over the years. The more things change, the more they seem to stay the same.

Doom and gloom aside, Puerto Ricans *have* seen "progress"—that classic trope of modernity—over the years. When the Young Lords began to emerge, there were few historical resources on Puerto Rico and Puerto Ricans; but as the 1970s continued, and ethnic studies programs emerged and thrived (today, of course, being rolled back nationwide due to the pitfalls of neoliberal globalization and a surge in anti-Latin@ xenophobia), good scholarship emerged. Beginning in the late 1960s and continuing through the 1970s and beyond, Puerto Rican arts and literature began to flourish in New York City. Piri Thomas, Pedro Pietri, Miguel Piñero, Miguel Algarín, Edwin Torres, Jesús Papoleto Meléndez, Esmeralda Santiago, and many others helped to define a literary Nuyorican movement that continues today, especially in venues like the Nuyorican Poets Café and La Casa Azul in New York City. Subsequent generations of Puerto Ricans have improved our economic standing and educational levels, even as we lag behind national averages and among some Latin@s. There continues to be a need for more work, more improvement, more scholarship; and it is my belief that, toward those ends, we all can learn much from the experiences and activism of the Young Lords.

In her 2012 work of young adult fiction entitled *The Revolution of Evelyn Serrano*, Sonia Manzano—best known for her decades-long role as Maria on the hit children's public television program, *Sesame Street*—weaves together her own memories, fictionalized accounts, and news reports to craft a smart and moving story of a young woman coming into her own in the space-time of the Young Lords' emergence. Focused on some of the same early events that I have written about in prior chapters, Manzano's attentiveness to the feelings of uplift, change, and uncertainty surrounding the garbage and church offensives is remarkable and gives presence to memories of struggle in personal and political revolution. She begins her fifteenth chapter with an apt question: "Who can tell what is the very beginning of a storm? Not a weather storm but a storm of ideas that grows like a flame. . . . I wondered, *What was the very beginning of the Young Lords' storm?* Was it the garbage on fire? Or was it when they opened a storefront office in the neighborhood? Was their office the first flutter of things to come?"[3] Perhaps it was one of those things; or perhaps it goes back further to the banding together of different Nuyorican groups in 1969, or the formation of the Sociedad de Albizu Campos, or the opening of the innovative State University of New York at Old Westbury, or the second great migration of Puerto Ricans from the island to the metropole after World War II, or the Nationalist Party's struggles on the island and mainland, or struggles against U.S. colonization in 1898, or El Grito de Lares in 1868, or Taíno revolts against Spanish colonization at the dawn of the long sixteenth century.

Whatever the origins of the Young Lords' storm, it is undeniable that it hit with a force that was, largely, unprecedented and yet to be repeated; and perhaps that will remain so, especially if the United States has entered a moment in time when revolutions are structurally difficult and increasingly unlikely. And that may be okay. We need not lament a failed revolution, and we ought not, as I have argued several times over the course of this book, measure "success" and "failure" merely in terms of whether the Young Lords accomplished their explicitly stated instrumental goals. Perhaps revolution is the wrong metaphor for us in the present historical conjuncture, though. As it is often conceptualized in the West, Walter Mignolo argues, "'revolution' is engrained in a linear concept of history and of time, and in an epistemology based on a logic in which dichotomies are always in contrary or contradictory relations; they are never complementary."[4] Elaborating on an Andean/Aymaran notion of *Pacha Kuti*, "an imaginary of cyclical repetitions and regular transformations of the natural/social world," Mignolo pushes us to "see the limits of 'final judgment' and 'revolution'"[5] on the contexts of Spanish and U.S. American conquest as well as the politics of the Young Lords.

Exploring the emergence, ideology, and early activism of the New York Young Lords, what are some of the lessons we can learn? In asking this question, I am interested in what there is to learn *about* the Young Lords that has been ignored or understudied in existent literature; but also I am interested equally in what can be learned *from* the Young Lords—from their creative tactics, complicitous critiques, radical imaginaries, and challenges to the Manichean world propped up by colonialism and extended coloniality. To both of these ends, I have embarked in an enactment of *historia*, over the prior chapters, in an effort to recover and craft a usable history (a critical-interpretive story of change over time) of the New York Young Lords' activism that can teach us lessons about decolonial praxis that retain relevance today. In what remains of this book, I want to return to their activism—framed partially around the question of community control with which I began—in order to review the significance of their deeds, tease out some clear lessons about how to theorize and otherwise engage de/coloniality, and identify areas in which we can (and perhaps ought to) move forward.

Rhetoric, Coloniality, and the Geopolitics of "Community Control"

In the turbulence of the 1960s and 1970s, organizations and activists around the country pushed for greater democratization of national, regional, and local institutions and land. From SDS's participatory democracy, to the emergence of the La Raza Unida Party and the Peace and Freedom Party, to the American Indian Movement's takeover of Alcatraz, young and Third World people across the United States and worldwide pushed back against inept models of governance and crafted their own alternatives. These demands for community control represented more than the emergence of a new localism; rather, they were informed by philosophies of liberation, self-determination, and nationalism. For example, in Philadelphia, argues Matthew Countryman, "The demand for community control was rooted in *both* Malcolm X's vision of black self-determination at the community level *and* Bayard Rustin's argument that only a fundamental reorganization of government priorities and spending could address the issue of persistent black poverty."[6] Forceful and nuanced arguments for community control permeated rhetorics of the Global South, yet this significant term has gone virtually unexamined, especially in my home discipline.[7]

Too often, resistance is theorized from an abstracted geopolitical stance such that modes of resistance are justified in a manner that draws from abstract universals rooted in modern/Western political thought. One of the points of decolonial scholarship generally and this book in particular is to counterbalance such abstractions by demanding a greater degree of spatial specificity. Across the prior chapters, I have gestured toward the importance of thinking *from* particular geo-political locations, especially when theorizing resistance that emerges from the underside and exteriority of modernity. Featuring the geopolitics and body-politics of power, knowledge, and being helps us understand better the ways in which engaged modes of resistance from the margins can challenge the particular rhetorical situations they engage but also broader structures of modernity/coloniality. By focusing on the New York Young Lords' rhetoric of "community control," which was a key trope in their 1960s–1970s activism, I argue that their rhetoric figures a geopolitics of knowledge and being that challenges Western/imperial designs in New York City and beyond.

As I discussed in Chapter 1, the Young Lords emerged from a complex historical and social context that ought to be traced back to Spanish colonization, in part, because the Young Lords themselves crafted it in such a manner. Through manifold practices of, what Maylei Blackwell calls, "retrofitted memory,"[8] the Young Lords used various combinations of recovery, correction, reclamation, and connection to craft a usable genealogy of thought and action that anchored their ideology and activism in resistance to the long sixteenth century. As I mentioned in the Introduction, such genealogies are crucial for activating challenges to the coloniality of knowledge/power/being. Significantly, Mignolo argues, "decolonial thinking needs to build its own genealogy of thought; otherwise it would fall prey to genealogies of thought already established and would, in the process, disregard and devalue all other possibilities."[9] Crafting a revised historical terrain and drawing from the multiple influences in their immediate context (e.g., Black Power advocates and others from the Global South), the Young Lords emerged and evolved into a robust organization with a nuanced, ecumenical ideology.

Guided by their "13-Point Program and Platform," one of the Young Lords' principle demands was "community control of our institutions and land." In their platform, they explained: "We want control of our communities by our people and programs to guarantee that all institutions serve the needs of our people. People's control of police, health services, churches, schools, housing, transportation and welfare are needed. We want an end to attacks on our land by urban renewal, highway destruction, universities and corporations. LAND BELONGS TO ALL THE PEOPLE!" Beyond a key slogan, the Young Lords operationalized this democratic demand in a few key ways and protests. They linked their garbage offensive and church offensive to community control, started door-to-door lead poisoning and tuberculosis testing programs, took over Lincoln Hospital in the Bronx and helped institute a community-worker board, worked with schools and students to give the people more input over education, and much more. Given its central placement within their "Program and Platform," and the numerous examples of their activism linked to the term, there can be little doubt that "community control" was crucial to the Young Lords' liberation politics and practices of critical regionalism.

While it is unclear exactly where the term "community control" originates, there are three sources that were probably important to the Young Lords. First, the group modeled some of their ideas after those of the Black Panthers, who made a strong call for community control (linked to the Declaration of Independence) in the tenth and final point of their platform. The Panthers' idea of community control, argues Countryman, was undoubtedly linked to Malcolm X's articulation of "a black nationalist political strategy that called for black activists to take control over political, economic, and social institutions in the black community";[10] and this formulation from Malcolm X would have made it to the Young Lords through the Panthers and through their own readings of Malcolm X's speeches and writings. Second, the Young Lords were influenced strongly by the writings of Frantz Fanon. While Fanon did not write specifically about "community control," his work did influence the group's thoughts about how external control (by a racist, capitalist state, for example) has an epistemic and ontological impact on the people—an exigence to be addressed, in part, by community control and further challenges to the colonial mentality. Finally, the Young Lords were surely influenced by New York City's community control movement, which was a multiracial movement for greater community control of school programs (e.g., local school boards) in Harlem and the Lower East Side and throughout the city. Given that, as James Jennings argues, "This episode in the struggles of Puerto Ricans in the city was . . . an optimistic one"[11] and, as Adina Back notes, "decentralization and community control . . . came to represent New York's civil rights movement,"[12] the Young Lords would have looked to those successes and sought to integrate some of the ideas and demands into their own programs. Jose Yglesias, writing for the *New York Times*, evidences this connection when he opined about the Young Lords, "Their programmatic point on community control certainly extends the meaning that phrase has had in local New York City politics."[13]

Other scholars have read the Young Lords' focus on "community control" as an expression of democratic politics—and it was. Johanna Fernandez, for example, argues, "For a brief moment in the late sixties and early seventies, they pursued the goals of 'community control,' motivated by the idea that by taking possession of major local institutions . . . local communities could begin to exercise genuine direct democracy."[14] Agustín Laó ups the ante on this line of argument, positing that "community control becomes a radical democratic demand for self-management" rooted in the "critique of liberal versions of community empowerment."[15] Both Fernandez and Lao are right, but I think there is more to the Young Lords' calls for community control—or, at least, I think any kind of democratic impulse gleaned must be read through an initial decolonial impulse critical of democracy's articulation to political and economic (neo)liberalism (a point to which I will return shortly). Given the roots of this idea in black nationalism and decoloniality (in Malcolm X and Frantz Fanon), the Young Lords' rhetoric of "community control" can be read as an attempt to offer an alternative spatial logic that both challenged external control (whether on the island or in El Barrio) and encouraged alternatives that would think and act *from* lived and imagined Third World communities.

In challenging external control, the Young Lords rooted their analysis in long-standing Puerto Rican responses, grounded somewhat in nationalist sensibilities, to colonial administration of the island and state regulation of docile bodies in the mainland. Pablo Guzmán argued, for example, that "for centuries we have been taught that we are a small, quiet, insignificant, shuffling people who cannot even govern ourselves and who are very happy having outside governments control our lives. We are taught that revolution is the work of maniacs and fanatics and has nothing to do with nice, docile spics."[16] For Guzmán, colonial control regulated the bodies of Puerto Ricans directly and psychically. Taking a more explicitly Fanonian position, Juan Gonzalez claimed that "absolute control by a system or society works on the mentality of people" to keep them subservient and turn them against one another.[17] When coupled with their broader program and rhetorics of revolutionary nationalism, as I discussed in Chapter 2, this critique of a racist, classist, imperialist system evidences a sensibility attuned to the geo-politics of power, knowledge, and being authorized by modernity/coloniality. Such a politics universalizes Western knowledge and being by advancing, as I examined in the Introduction, an *aspatial* paradigm that denies its locatedness as well as its connections to located bodies. In *willing* such epistemic transparency and universality, the colonial matrix of power skates by; but the rhetoric of "community control" is an antidote. Functioning in part as a nominalist rhetoric, the Young Lords challenged the transparency and privilege of the West and located its deleterious effects in their spaces and on their bodies.

In the garbage offensive, their first major direct action as an organization in New York, the Young Lords' rhetoric is exemplary of such spatial and embodied challenges. Beginning with the crucial move of listening to the people of El Barrio—perhaps the central practice, or at least the first step, of an ethics of decolonial love—the Young Lords grounded their activism in a liberation politics that sought "to expand the horizon of interlocutors beyond colonial and imperial differences."[18] Through a rhetoric of presence, the Young Lords, then, both in the immediate scene and after the protests were over, tropicalized the space of El Barrio, which accented it as colonized. Such a move is itself a decolonial act insofar as it erodes the transparency of modern/colonial zero-point epistemologies by grounding criticism and activism in real and figural locations. Beyond such a nominalist position, though, the Young Lords crafted an affirmative program to reclaim colonized spaces and bodies. Through their acts of cleaning the streets and enlisting the people in struggle, the Young Lords affirmed decolonial subjectivities and agencies that further marked the spaces and bodies of El Barrio as politicized and active.

Garbage was not the only focus, however, of the spatial and embodied critique central to their rhetoric of community control. Addressing the importance of community control at a local high school, for example, the Young Lords took the strong stance that their dispute was not simply about the school; rather, it was "a matter of whether or not we have the right to control our own lives." Operating, again, within a Fanonian and revolutionary nationalist position of self-determination and liberatory empowerment, the Young Lords charted a path for action:

> To all our brothers and sisters in school—if your school is messed up, if the administration and the teachers don't care and don't teach—don't let them force you to drop out. Throw them out. The schools belong to us, not to them. Take all that anger and put it to work for our people. Make revolution inside the schools. If the schools don't function for us, they shouldn't function at all![19]

Drawing from felt, lived anger and from an analysis of the colonized mentality and its relationship to education, the Young Lords' community control rhetoric functioned as an agency that enabled certain kinds of discursive and political opportunities. The call for a school revolt is just one example, but the overall tenor of this rhetoric infused multiple campaigns, protests, speeches, poems, and the very ideology of the organization.

As I discussed in the last chapter, on the church offensive, the rhetoric of community control was further enhanced and extended through additional terminological innovation. Reworking the ideograph of "the people," the Young Lords inventively challenged the modern social imaginary and activated multiple decolonial sensibilities in El Barrio. Although one might assume fairly that relying on such a dominant trope of modern politics could reinforce its epistemic grip, I argued that the Young Lords' rearticulation of "the people" functioned as, what Chela Sandoval calls, an "ideologization of ideology"[20] that transformed the *meaning* of the term while supporting the vocabulary itself. Much like World War II–era black radicals' reworking of vice president Henry Wallace's "people's century" as "peoples' century" to emphasize what Nikhil Pal Singh calls "pluralizing the traditional referent of nationalism,"[21] the Young Lords' verbal, visual, and embodied recrafting of "the people" underscored pluralism, heterogeneity, and a subaltern enactment of power. Furthermore, such a rearticulation of "the people" demonstrated crucial sensibilities of border thinking that underscore the importance of imagining modes of resistance beyond the either/or imposed by modernity/coloniality.

At the end of the day, "community control" was something tied to a number of other tropes, figures, ideographs, and performances that were central to the Young Lords' activism and productive of a political sensibility that operated, almost from the first instance, to denaturalize the place of El Barrio and reaccent it as a decolonial space. It points to some of the ways in which delinking necessitates forms of praxis that enact critical regionalism as a corrective to the presumed geopolitical transparency of modernity/coloniality. While, under coloniality, regional specificity gets lost in grand universalizing gestures, decolonial critical regionalism acts to wrench lose modernity/coloniality's epistemic power. In the Young Lords' rhetoric of "community control," one witnesses an alternative regional accent that is rooted in the explicitness of spatial, geographic, and embodied specificity—a Third World accent that underscores and undergirds a unique politics of liberation delinked from modernity/coloniality.

Democracy with Difference; or, Delinking Democracy

In pointing to the uniqueness of liberation politics within the context of the Young Lords, I want to return to something familiar to most readers in order to demonstrate (in a somewhat speculative and by no means complete manner) one way to prioritize decoloniality. In quotations above from Fernandez and Laó, both scholars mentioned the democratizing praxis and potentiality of the Young Lords—something that Laó goes so far as to call "radical democratic" (as do I in other writings). When I began this project on the Young Lords, as I recounted in the Introduction, I was animated (much as Laó seemed to once be) by the energizing debates surrounding poststructuralist, post-Marxist theorists Ernesto Laclau and Chantal Mouffe. In the moments when I was not preoccupied with disciplinary argumentation, my dissertation was focused on making the case that the Young Lords engaged in radical democratic politics. My first journal article made the same mistake;

and in doing so, I missed the boat through my overreliance on postmodern social movement studies, radical democratic theory, attentiveness to citizenship, and so forth. Enamored by the dominant conversations in the discipline at the time, I fear that in prior work *I have done an injustice* by forcing the Young Lords' activism surrounding the garbage offensive into the modernist vocabulary of citizenship and liberal democracy (as "radical" as it might have been). Worse than an injustice, I fear my framing of their activism in terms of Laclau and Mouffe's radical democracy enacted a kind of symbolic violence by unreflexively reinscribing epistemic coloniality onto their activism.

That said, I think there is something to this idea from Fernandez and Laó that the Young Lords engaged in a form of democratics. But what *is* democracy? Popularly, it is often conceived in proceduralist terms, reduced to a set of institutional structures and concomitant practices of citizenship such as voting, representative governance, and the rule of law.[22] Such a formulation is a product of the long-term articulation (in Stuart Hall's sense of "linking") of the liberal tradition and the democratic tradition; or, more precisely, it is the product of a hegemonic process by which the field of democracy has been articulated *through* the liberal tradition functioning as a nodal point of politics and "the political."[23] Conversely, the question of the *is*-ness of democracy may be misguided because it presumes a stability and fixity that reifies democracy and seems unproductive both theoretically and politically.

As an alternative, Laclau and Mouffe (both together and separately) posit that democracy can be deepened and extended by cultivating a critical openness rooted in a radicalization of the constitutive tensions between liberal and democratic traditions. Mouffe suggests that the "aim is not to create a completely different kind of society, but to use the symbolic resources of the liberal democratic tradition to struggle against relations of subordination."[24] Highlighting openness and challenging its *is*-ness, Laclau cites a "democracy to come" (*democratie à venir*) that "does not involve any teleological assertion . . . but simply the continual commitment to keep open the relation to the other, an opening which is always *à venir*, for the other to which one opens oneself is never already given in any aprioristic calculation."[25]

As neatly as these conceptualizations fit into the critical rhetoric and other post-(fill-in-the-blank) projects, however, there is a fundamental problem: Laclau and Mouffe presume a politics of recognition taking place within and to Western political regimes. In so doing, argue Janet Conway and Jakeet Singh, they are silent about the "profound colonial underside" of modern liberal democracy. "The role of colonialism in co-producing the European contexts and subjects who become the unmarked, and thus universal, subjects of radical democracy is not recognized and so cannot be problematized."[26] As a consequence, critique rooted in radical democratic theory risks reinforcing normative expectations rooted in modernity/coloniality and effacing alternative forms of knowledge and being. Given this critique, I want to approach the question of democracy's becoming Otherwise. What happens when we actually recognize the underside of modernity? What about when we approach democracy from outside of Western traditions or, better yet, from the *exteriority* of modernity/coloniality? What happens when we commit to pluriversality, to "a world in which many worlds can fit"?[27]

The need to ask such questions is made all the more urgent in our present historical moment in the United States. While democratic and liberal traditions have long competed for favorable political position, the emergence of neoliberalism in the 1970s and its strengthened station over the last decade raises critical questions about democracy's present and future. Within this context, neoliberalism enunciates a troubling set of conditions vis-à-vis race and public (mis)understandings of racism. The world in general and liberal political theory in particular has, according to Charles W. Mills, "been shaped for the past five hundred years by the realities of European domination and the gradual consolidation of global white supremacy."[28] But even more so than the classical liberalism before it, racial neoliberalism threatens democracy by driving race and racism underground, inhibiting the scope of public discourse, and securitizing sameness. This homogenizing drive of racial neoliberalism must be countered with radical democratic heterogeneities and a concomitant challenge to racialized democracy—a task for which decolonial theory and praxis may be uniquely suited.

As numerous scholars have demonstrated in recent years, our collective historical moment in the United States is marked by a neoliberal articulation of race.[29] Race and racism have become, in the dominant imaginary, depoliticized in the sense that any public recognitions of race or racism that would prioritize political or social challenges to white supremacy have been driven underground. In David Theo Goldberg's assessment, antiracist politics have been replaced by antiracialism. While the former, antiracism, "requires historical memory, recalling the conditions of racial degradation and relating contemporary to historical and local to global conditions . . . , antiracialism suggests forgetting, getting over, moving on, wiping away the terms of reference."[30] In our brave neoliberal world, I have argued elsewhere, "burying race and rebuffing racisms (except by those who invoke race, of course) become the *modus operandi* of contemporary public discourse."[31] Although racism obviously continues, utterance of "race" itself becomes the political target—a color-blind, postrace world willed into existence to justify white supremacy. The post-Obama emergence of the Tea Party is an exemplary case because it is in their rhetoric (both spoken and visual) that an explicit commitment to the structural irrelevance of race coupled with a vehemently racist discourse that uses neoliberal policy language as an alibi to depoliticize their racism comes to the fore. This complex move—to naturalize the threat of race, depoliticize racism, and chill public discussion of race at nearly any level—is a disaster for democracy.

In some ways, however, racial neoliberalism may not be a unique threat to democracy. After all, argues Joel Olson, "American democracy is a white democracy, a polity ruled in the interests of a white citizenry and characterized by simultaneous relations of equality and privilege: equality among whites, who are privileged in relation to those who are not white."[32] Mills notes, similarly, that the social contract undergirding modern conceptions of democracy is, inherently, a *racial* contract that "prescribes for its signatories an inverted epistemology, an epistemology of ignorance," which mythologizes the relationship between race and politics to create a "racial fantasyland," a Gibsonian "consensual hallucination" that dehistoricizes and naturalizes white supremacy and denies full personhood to those who are subaltern.[33] In this way, the liberal tradition through which U.S. American–style representative liberal democracy has been articulated (a strong suture, Mouffe shows in her *Democratic Paradox* and elsewhere) is fundamentally a white democracy that works through the exclusion of nonwhites and depoliticizes or mythologizes that foundational act of exclusion.

Contemporary racial neoliberalism makes matters worse in two ways. First, neoliberal racelessness (the antiracial attempt to move beyond race by gutting collective memory, driving race underground, and denying racist inequity) reinforces an "epistemology of ignorance," normalizes whiteness, and, in Goldberg's words, conjures "people of color as a problem in virtue of their being of color."[34] Racelessness, then, is marked by a drive toward universalizing homogeneity, which, argues Goldberg again, "can only be purchased with the coin of severe repression, of purging difference and denying its influence if not its miscegenating seed." Homogeneity, he continues, "is a recipe for constitutive conflict and repetitively destructive, debilitating politics."[35] The Tea Party, anti-immigration stalwarts, and others who hide behind antiracialism contribute uniquely to our demise because they radicalize racelessness, first in civil society, then in the state,[36] and cultivate a form of securitization that militantly patrols the literal and figurative borders of the racial state. Second, in order to protect raceless homogeneity, racism is reborn under the banner of the *threat*, which has significant consequences in the neoliberal fantasy and imagining the U.S. body politic. After all, Goldberg notes, "the threat is conjured to the very being of the patria, circulated broadly across the population easily turning the differentiation into enmity, the differentiated into enemies."[37] Such a winner-take-all, "post-political" moralism, which has been the guiding force of the Tea Party and beholden Republicans, creates a neoliberal infinite loop wherein raceless homogeneity authorizes securitized constructions of threat that can maintain a homogenous body politic and allow the purifying loop to continue.

Theoretical and practical applications of democracy present additional unique challenges in our modern/colonial context, as I already mentioned with respect to Laclau and Mouffe. More fundamentally, argues Freya Schiwy (drawing from Álvaro García Linera, Bolivia's vice president and a political theorist), "the struggle over the meaning of democracy and state takes place within a discursive field shaped by the legacies of colonialism—ongoing racial discrimination along with economic exploitation and the corresponding dismissal of indigenous and working-class political thought."[38] Modernity/coloniality, then, raises significant questions about the relationship between democracy and epistemic power. "Behind every word, every discourse," writes Linera, "there is a wordless war over establishing the dominant forms of meaning in the world."[39] This is why it is critically important to turn to local knowledge as a corrective—one that has potential to assist us in delinking democracy from modernity/coloniality and positively expressing "*non-indifference* toward the Other."[40]

So what could be our way out? How do we challenge the homogenizing force of racial neoliberalism that is already rooted in white democracy, the racial contract, and modernity/coloniality? While I can be thankful that the Tea Party has diminished in strength, the ideological infrastructure remains, underwrites anti-immigration xenophobes and other ultraconservatives, and continues to erode democratic potential. Let me start, preemptively, by saying that the discipline of critical whiteness studies is not enough. Not only does it too often neglect Robyn Wiegmann's apt critique of white particularity, namely, that "rendering whiteness particular" fails to "divest whiteness of its universal epistemological power,"[41] but whiteness studies fails also to provide a clear path to "undoing . . . states of racial being and forms of governmentality in their global profusions."[42] Crucially, in Goldberg's assessment, "the aim is to deroutinize and desystematize interlocking worlds of race historically produced and the racially figured exclusions and derogations they entail."[43] In order to start the process, we must begin engaging race and democracy as mutually constitutive. "One of the advantages of analyzing democracy and race as mutually constitutive is that, in addition to providing a better way to understand how race functions," Olson argues, "it renders democratic ideals *political* again. . . . It provides new ways of imagining what democracy is and could be."[44] The first step in this process might be to recognize and vocalize the mutually constitutive relationship between race and democracy, as well as between racism and modernity. Under neoliberal raceless homogeneity, there is a risk of losing entirely a *public vocabulary* rooted in antiracist commitments, and that is something against which scholars and activists can and must struggle daily.[45]

Furthermore, the solution necessitates delinking (at least partially and/or conceptually) democracy from liberalism. So long as the liberal tradition maintains a stranglehold over democracy, we are doomed to myopic proceduralism—and doubly doomed to a racist liberal democratic proceduralism authorized by the racial contract and reinforced under neoliberalism. Distinguishing my thinking from Laclau and Mouffe's "conservative utopia," which, according to Conway and Singh, "derives its utopian dimension from the radicalisation or complete fulfilment of the present,"[46] I believe we should be prepared to practice some "utopistics," which Immanuel Wallerstein defines as "the sober, rational, and realistic evaluation of human social systems, the constraints on what they can be, and the zones open to human creativity."[47] In doing so, scholars and activists can understand the Young Lords as a critical exemplar for delinking democracy, which means turning toward a differential consciousness (à la Chela Sandoval) to map the connecting strands that can help us "change gears" and envision a revised conception of democracy not dependent on a modern/colonial ethic of nonbeing.[48]

A crucial step in this process, Mignolo has argued, is to reconceive of democracy and other terms (like cosmopolitanism and human rights) as *connectors*—spaces of encounter, "nodes" of interaction, and sites of negotiation that *displace* democracy[49] and invoke a "trans-pluri-versal" alternative, which (according to Maldonado-Torres) "transcends and transgresses the imposition of abstract universals while it opens up the path for dialogue among different epistemes."[50] Let me be clear about this: connectors are *not* the same as empty signifiers. Conceived as empty signifiers, terms are ratified as "abstract universal values" that imply an "openness to accommodate 'different' conceptions of democracy."[51] Such a theoretical move (which *is* the stance of Laclau and Mouffe) ultimately lingers unreflexively under modern/colonial control and relies on claims for recognition, which leaves the dominant underlying rhetoric as well as epistemological and ontological orientations unchecked. Connectors, in contrast, solve this problem by eliminating the includer/included (master/slave) dialectic, in preference for trans-pluri-versality.

Along similar lines, democracy should be understood, per Sheldon Wolin, as "an ephemeral phenomenon rather than a settled system."[52] Democracy is flexible, protean, temporary, emergent, and local. It is, in short, *fugitive*—constantly in flight, marked by multiplicity, unbounded, and contingent. Such a conception of "fugitive democracy" both flourishes when bound to and helps to foster heterogeneity. In Goldberg's assessment, "Fugitive democracies would seek sets of social arrangements hospitable to flight and flux, mobilities and motilities, multiplicities and 'metis-friendly institutions' . . . the complexities of counter-memories vested in cultures of the heterogeneous."[53] Engaging heterogeneities more productively, attention must be shifted away from population and attendant technologies of control that undergird the drive for homogeneity. "The emphasis on heterogeneities," Goldberg writes, "stresses and seeks to sustain more or less unconstrained relationalities, activities, interactions." Specifically, attention shifts to "grids of intelligibility and variably informed interests, prompts, and practices breaking with those imposed" under securitized homogeneity.[54]

Such openness, multiplicity, and constitutive antiracism provides a robust starting point from which to launch fugitive, democratic heterogeneities that can challenge homogenizing racial neoliberalism. Lessons learned from both the form and content of the Young Lords' activism can further fill out the perspective of decolonial democratics I advocate here. As I examined in Chapter 2, for example, the Young Lords advanced a "revolutionary national-ist" agenda, which deployed a decolonial critique that disarticulated and delinked their political program from the modern/colonial system. Rather than centering a modern/colonial construction of the nation, the Young Lords' rhetorical "nationalism" (another connector for them) functioned as a "symbolic agency"—a signifying *means*—through which the group decolo-nized their imaginary, reformulated political subjectivity, and opened the space for democratic possibility. Their revolutionary nationalism was ambig-uous and rhetorically exploited the common label of "nationalism," exempli-fying the border thinking/differential consciousness born of the in-between space that remains in contact with modernity/coloniality but is ever so con-scious of that contact. In being more figurative than foundational, revolution-ary nationalism functioned as a connector—as an open site of negotiation that linked Third World people, an intersectional critique of the racist/sexist/capitalist system, and a liberation ethic that challenged coloniality's Manichean nonbeing.

This is further exemplified in the Young Lords' multiple struggles over gender and equality, both within the organization and beyond. In Chapter 3, I examined the complex ways in which women in the organization directly confronted racism/classism/sexism by generating a critique of their lived experience of machismo. In confronting what the leadership originally ren-dered as "revolutionary machismo" in their founding "Program and Platform," these women engaged in embodied acts of resistance within the confines of the organizational structures and spurred change. In an interview with me, Iris Morales explained their resistance and the resultant changes as "a struggle to democratize the organization"[55] by increasing the quantity and quality of voices in leadership and throughout the Young Lords and by holding all mem-bers accountable to the same rules. The Young Lords extended these challeng-es to machismo into a broader public discourse, advancing an innovative and nuanced critique of the intersectionality of oppression. Far from a liberal democratic rhetoric of recognition and inclusion, the Young Lords' libera-tion rhetoric crafted affiliative linkages and generated nonsexist human fraternity—a deepening of the connections between peoples rather than a legitimation of the status quo and its liberal individualism.

As such, the Young Lords' explicit claims to democracy were tempered. On the one hand, they rejected liberal democratic proceduralism as empiri-cally and inherently oppressive. For the Young Lords, electoral democracy was off the table; and you cannot really blame them. In an article entitled "YLP on Elections," Juan Gonzalez observed that "since the amerikkkan invasion of

Puerto Rico in 1898, the united states has controlled the press, radio, television. They control the schools. . . . More than 25,000 amerikkkan troops occupy our territory. With those forces of repression, it is impossible to talk of free elections."[56] Indeed, under the radically unequal conditions established and maintained by modernity/coloniality, liberal democracy seemed to have failed. On the other hand, the Young Lords clearly linked their politics to the rhetoric of democracy—to what Juan "Fi" Ortiz refers to in their pamphlet on ideology as the practices of "democratic discussion and decision-making" and "self-criticism," which they saw as "the key to Party democracy."[57] Furthermore, the Young Lords' decolonial liberation politics envisioned a trans-pluri-verse that totalized heterogeneity, allowing "each local history and its narrative of decolonization [to] connect through [a] common experience and use it as the basis for a new common logic of knowing."[58] This is precisely the vision of coalitional liberation politics imagined by the Young Lords and essential to a truly radical and decolonial democracy.

Please do not misunderstand me, however, as making the claim that recalibrating our perspectives in the aforementioned ways is enough to dismantle racial/racist democracy. Certainly much more would need to happen in order to delink democracy from homogenizing (neo)liberalism and modernity/coloniality; in other words, these are necessary but not sufficient conditions. That said, in a country, and perhaps even a world, often preoccupied with claims to democracy, it would be in all of our interests to reorient and radicalize our approach to democracy in ways that embrace its fugitive qualities, delink it from liberalism's racial contract, privilege heterogeneity and pluriversality, and seek paths to envision it as one of many "connectors" that can underwrite modes of politics that prioritize the voices and needs of the *damné*. And sometimes we have to accept that "democracy" should not be the goal. We need not always try to fit our analyses and activisms into the rhetoric of "democracy" and its attendant cluster of terms, like "citizenship," "recognition," and others. The Young Lords are instructive in these aims. Featuring their many demands for "community control" spanning a host of contexts (the community in general, hospitals, schools, churches, and more), the Young Lords' inventive rhetorics and activism not only provide historical examples of decoloniality in practice but also serve as a critical touchstone for discursive and political *forms and habits* that are even more important for our futures than specific things that they did and accomplished from 1969 to 1976.

Love and the Ethics of Critical Praxis

Viewing the Young Lords as a touchstone, however, is not a call for mimicry. As important as it is to recover their history and cultivate a public memory that highlights the power and commitment of these radical Nuyoricans who led a movement and helped spark political and cultural imagination, simply transplanting what they did into our present moment would be a mistake. In (still) one of the most influential works on rhetorical criticism, Edwin Black explains the meaning of touchstones, in the context of public address criticism, in a manner that could be helpful for thinking about the Young Lords:

> Obviously, no critic could reasonably demand of a contemporary rhetor that he [or she] speak in exactly the same way as, say, Edmund Burke. Touchstones are not models for copying. . . . [They imply] that the critic, or anyone else who cares to, can, by acquainting himself [or herself] with the discourses of Burke, come to hold certain expectations of what rhetorical discourse ought to do, and he can achieve certain insights into what rhetorical discourse is capable of doing. These expectations and insights do not provide him with explicit, mechanically applicable standards; they provide him with that vague quality, *taste*, without which no set of explicit standards can be judiciously applied.[59]

As I said in the Introduction, context is vitally important—not just for a critical-interpretive praxis seeking to glean insight from situated public discourse but also for those of us seeking to theorize and stake out a terrain for action in the present. In conceiving of the Young Lords as a touchstone, we must be careful not to think of them, as Black puts it, as "models for copying"; rather, we must seek to discern key sensibilities, looking for Black's "vague quality, *taste*," that can be made relevant in our present contexts.

My call, therefore, is not for us all to go out and *be* Young Lords. I cannot imagine that would go over particularly well in Iowa City, Dallas, Riverside, or even New York, Chicago, Orlando, Philadelphia, or any other major site of Puerto Rican migration. We are part of a different time, with different cultural and political currents, different public vocabularies and available modes of stranger relationality, and we are constrained substantially by rhetorics of antiracialism and a racial state that has adjusted to what Roopali Mukherjee and others call the postsoul era.[60] The infrastructure of U.S. counterterrorism and intelligence communities, persistently preoccupied with notions of threat and security, dwarfs the COINTELPRO of our past and makes mass movement challenging, to say the least. Yet all is not lost. "Much has changed in the United States," argue Amy Sonnie and James Tracy in the conclusion to their book on white leftists in the 1970s, "yet it would be a mistake to dismiss the 'organize your own' model as a relic of the past."[61] What additional lessons *can* be learned from the Young Lords that would be relevant today?

First, rhetorics of community control remain powerful and full of potential. The old maxim "all politics is local" continues to hold truth. Even in an era marked by the rise of neoliberal globalization and transnational information flows that make the world a smaller place for some, local grassroots politics remains relevant and vitally important. The Young Lords and others in common cause laid an intellectual and practical infrastructure for instigating change by speaking with diverse and allied voices to demand justice in their communities. Rhetorics of community control are malleable enough to have force within the systemic constraints mentioned above, in part, because they neither have inherent conflict with neoliberal rhetorics of "personal responsibility" nor do they require calling for or operating within a logic of "revolution." Instead, at their heart they retain a decolonial commitment to local knowledge and invite attentiveness to the plurality of interests and perspectives that animate community togetherness—commitments that must be retained, cultivated, and strengthened in order to guard against neoliberal co-optation.

Second, we need more scholarship examining de/coloniality in its specific contexts of emergence and action. The theoretical foundation of decolonial theory is strong, but the best way to refine it is through detailed engagements of decoloniality in practice. José David Saldívar's literary critiques, Freya Schiwy's work on South American media and politics, Mignolo's read of the Zapatistas, Maldonado-Torres's analysis of Fanon (among others), Ramón Grosfoguel's study of Puerto Rico, the growing body of work on decolonial aesthetics/aesthesis—all are exemplary of a species of grounded scholarship that examines de/coloniality in its lived specificity and in a manner that pushes the boundaries of our theoretical perspectives.[62] My critical-interpretive engagement of the Young Lords helps anchor concepts like delinking, border thinking, and liberation in their rhetorical and performative specificity in a particular time and place that happens to be central to decoloniality's genealogy of thought. Not only does my read of the Young Lords help us understand better what delinking might look like in practice, but it also helps to build a sense of what delinking can become as a scholarly perspective, directing us to speak *from* and *with* the Global South as well as to generate spaces for and voices of epistemic disobedience in our disparate scholarly contexts.

Such contexts for decoloniality, however, are varied and hard to come by. Certainly, there are large-scale examples like the Young Lords that are accessible to researchers and activists; but there are also small-scale examples that are probably more numerous and perhaps just as significant. Just as the material presence of trash in the era of the garbage offensive underscored the relevance of repertoires (rather than archives) of embodied knowledge for the Young Lords, so too should we probably emphasize those ephemeral, lost-in-time, fleeting examples of resistance that happen in everyday contexts. For example, on a trip to New York a few years ago, I was visiting my favorite bar in El Barrio—a venue with great sangria that is a key meeting place for Puerto Rican intellectuals, activists, and residents. It was midafternoon and the place was populated with a dozen or so other Puerto Ricans and Latin@s meeting up with friends and doing various kinds of work. Suddenly, a half-dozen white hipsters rolled in with art easels and proceeded back to the dance floor area. No one said a word, but one of the other patrons whistled the distinctive notes of the Puerto Rican coquí, a small frog that makes an unmistakable sound that is a key marker of Puerto Rican life (even for someone like me, who did not grow up on the island). The whistle was a performance key, a sonic accent that delinked the space from the surrounding gentrification and the influx of affluent, white hipsters who are changing the neighborhood. It lasted a second or two, but the coquí whistle was powerful and affective for those of us who were "in" on how it worked. Why bring it up? Because, while decoloniality is most obvious in big examples like the Young Lords, it may be most often present in the countless acts of everyday resistance in spaces of the Global South—a form of fugitivity that draws from embodied knowledge and is never easily pinned down by others. Scholarly methods must further innovate in order to find ways to *hear* these tactical communications, which can also be found in such quotidian and protean examples as community gardens, murals, graffiti, certain types of music that fill the air (salsa, bomba y plena, etc.), and more.

Finally, and related to the last point, the Young Lords teach us that *love* must be central to our activist and scholarly practices. In both arenas, we must strive for a Fanonian vision of love that, in Kelly Oliver's assessment, "is not self-centered but other-centered. Love for and between those othered by dominant culture opens up new possibilities" that transcend and transgress liberal political logics.[63] It is, as Sandoval argues, "a complex kind of love . . . where love is understood as affinity—alliance and affection across lines of difference that intersect both in and out of the body."[64] This is a kind of love that centers voices and needs of others—an emphatic *yes* that, in Maldonado-Torres's read, struggles "against the structures of dehumanization" and positively expresses "*non-indifference* toward the Other."[65] It is also a kind of love that requires self-reflexivity and response-ability; it requires us, as the Young Lords showed, to open up the spaces for many voices and many worlds, while remaining attentive to how we are implicated and implicate ourselves in those worlds and with those voices.

Such self-reflexivity must be carried into our own scholarship. I know that many of us can agree on this point in the abstract: it is a central premise of Latin@ studies, critical and cultural studies, and more. Why, then, when folks historicize globalization, for example, do they so often begin in the eighteenth century and fail to engage the long heritage of modernity rooted in colonial expansion across territories, minds, and bodies for more than five hundred years? Why would I, cognizant (even at the time I wrote my dissertation) of the importance of colonialism to the Young Lords, force on them a thoroughly Eurocentric concept like radical democracy? Drawing from Junot Díaz again, "if a critique . . . doesn't first flow through you, doesn't first implicate you, then you have missed the mark; you have, in fact, almost guaranteed its survival and reproduction."[66] For those of us doing work about/with colonized and otherwise marginalized peoples, it is imperative that we consider seriously the ways in which our own theoretical, critical, and interpretive choices implicate and challenge the structures of domination that interest us so much. But it cannot stop there.

We who are colonized or function in some way otherwise cannot be the only ones leading the charge to delink from modernity/coloniality. An ethic of decolonial love requires those who benefit most from the epistemic violence of the West to renounce their privilege, give the gift of hearing, and engage in forms of praxis that can negotiate more productively the borderlands between inside and outside, in thought and in being. It is crucial that all scholars and activists begin to take decolonial options seriously if we wish to do more than perpetuate "a permanent state of exception"[67] that dehumanizes subalterns and maintains the hubris of a totalizing and exclusionary episteme.

This, undoubtedly, will take time. When I began this project, I never would have imagined the transformative effect it would have on my life. The me-of-2003 had no sense for what "speaking from and with the Global South" might entail; I had no sense for how the critical and theoretical perspectives on which I relied reproduced epistemic violence; and I had no sense for how the people around me were enacting a kind of love that would take me many more years to come to terms with, translate, and appreciate. The second stanza of Sandra María Esteves's "Here" seems prescient in light of my experiences:

I speak the alien tongue
in sweet boriqueño thoughts
know love mixed with pain
have tasted spit on ghetto stairways
. . . here, it must be changed
we must change it[68]

Born into a similar experience, the New York Young Lords seized their moment in their place and, by listening to the needs and voices of the people, crafted decolonial and decolonizing spaces, rhetorics, practices, and identities that transformed a generation of Puerto Ricans in New York City and beyond. Although the time for the Young Lords has probably passed, their memory lives on and can function as a critical touchstone, as what Laó calls (quoting Raymond Williams) "resources of hope," to inform decolonial politics and theory today.[69] As long as modernity/coloniality maintains its epistemic and

ontological privilege—whether in the streets, the ivory tower, or elsewhere—
we must continue to cull such resources, give gifts of love, be receptive to the
generosity of others, and resist the constant erasure of the damned. The time
to seek ways, both old and new, to model an ethic of decolonial love that resists
modernity/coloniality's unrepentant homogenizing force is now.

Notes

INTRODUCTION

1. *Nuyorican* is a common term to denote New York Puerto Rican. Although the term wasn't widely in use until further into the 1970s, the Young Lords embraced a "New York point of view" tied to their Puerto Ricanness.

2. Meg Starr, "'Hit Them Harder': Leadership, Solidarity, and the Puerto Rican Independence Movement," in *The Hidden 1970s: Histories of Radicalism*, ed. Dan Berger (New Brunswick, NJ: Rutgers University Press, 2010), 139.

3. Jack Newfield, "Young Lords Do City's Work in the Barrio," *Village Voice* (December 4, 1969): 1, 35.

4. Quoted in ibid., 35.

5. Newfield and others attribute the Young Lords' success with the lead poisoning testing program with citywide awareness of the problem and with a workable solution. See also Johanna Fernandez, "Between Social Service Reform and Revolutionary Politics: The Young Lords, Late Sixties Radicalism, and Community Organizing in New York City," in *Freedom North: Black Freedom Struggles Outside the South, 1940–1980*, ed. Jeanne F. Theoharis and Komozi Woodward (New York: Palgrave Macmillan, 2003), 255–85.

6. This was originally, and in the context of their lead poisoning activism quoted here, point five of their "Program and Platform." In November 1970, it moved to point six and the wording changed slightly. Young Lords Organization, "13 Point Program and Platform," *Palante* 2, no. 2 (1970): 19.

7. By the last third of the nineteenth century, according to James Dietz, "Puerto Rico was forced to import an increasing proportion of its foodstuffs." James L. Dietz, *Economic History of Puerto Rico: Institutional Change and Capitalist Development* (Princeton, NJ: Princeton University Press, 1986), 27–28.

8. Ibid., 128.

9. Ibid., 129.

10. Aníbal Quijano, "Coloniality and Modernity/Rationality," *Cultural Studies* 21, no. 2–3 (2007): 169.

11. Researchers from the Center for Puerto Rican Studies offer an explanation of the economic conditions of Puerto Ricans on the island and in New York (and the relationship between the two) in History Task Force Centro de Estudios Puertorriqueños, *Labor Migration under Capitalism: The Puerto Rican Experience* (New York: Monthly Review Press, 1979).

12. Derived from the original Latino and often used Latina/o, Latin@ is a contemporary corrective term that denotes gender, transgender, and genderqueer inclusivity within explorations of latinidades.

13. See Antonia Pantoja, "Puerto Ricans in New York: A Historical and Community Development Perspective," *Centro Journal* 2, no. 5 (1989): 21–31; Carlos Rodríguez-Fraticelli and Amílcar Tirado, "Notes towards a History of Puerto Rican Community Organizations in New York City," *Centro Journal* 2, no. 6 (1989): 35–47. "Poverty pimps" were social service providers who took a large cut from state funds and passed little on to the people for whom those funds were intended.

14. Lincoln Hospital in the South Bronx would eventually become a target of the Young Lords' activism.

15. Philippe I. Bourgois, *In Search of Respect: Selling Crack in El Barrio* (New York: Cambridge University Press, 1995); Juan Flores, *Divided Borders: Essays on Puerto Rican Identity* (Houston, TX: Arte Publico Press, 1992).

16. On the colonized mentality, see Frantz Fanon, *The Wretched of the Earth* (New York: Grove Press, 1963); Quijano, "Coloniality and Modernity/Rationality," 168–78.

17. There were other radical Puerto Ricans operating in New York City, like the Movimiento Pro-Independencia (MPI); however, the Young Lords were unique in being distinctively Nuyorican rather than rooted in island politics.

18. Andrés Torres, "Introduction: Political Radicalism in the Diaspora—The Puerto Rican Experience," in *The Puerto Rican Movement: Voices from the Diaspora*, ed. Andrés Torres and José E. Velázquez (Philadelphia: Temple University Press, 1998), 1.

19. Ibid., 3.

20. Marta Moreno, "The Young Lords Party, 1969–1975; 'Publisher's Page,'" *Caribe* 7, no. 4 (1983): 2.

21. Emma Pérez, *The Decolonial Imaginary: Writing Chicanas into History* (Bloomington: Indiana University Press, 1999), xv.

22. Kelvin A. Santiago-Valles, *"Subject People" and Colonial Discourses: Economic Transformation and Social Disorder in Puerto Rico, 1898–1947* (Albany: State University of New York Press, 1994), 11.

23. On the distinction between archive and repertoire, see Diana Taylor, *The Archive and the Repertoire: Performing Cultural Memory in the Americas* (Durham, NC: Duke University Press, 2003). Maylei Blackwell complicates Taylor's distinction and highlights the productive tension between the terms. Maylei Blackwell, *¡Chicana Power! Contested Histories of Feminism in the Chicano Movement* (Austin: University of Texas Press, 2011).

24. Caroline Levander and Walter Mignolo, "Introduction: The Global South and World Dis/Order," *Global South* 5, no. 1 (2011): 1–11. "Global South" is the emerging term for what was formerly (and sometimes still is) referred to as the Third World. More than a geopolitical label in any kind of Western realist epistemology, Global South functions as a locus of enunciation from which people speak. As Levander and Mignolo suggest, "from the perspective of the inhabitants (and we say consciously inhabitants rather than

'citizens,' regional or global), the 'Global South' is the location where new visions of the future are emerging and where the global political and decolonial society is at work" (3).

25. Nelson Maldonado-Torres, "Enrique Dussel's Liberation Thought in the Decolonial Turn," *TRANSMODERNITY: Journal of Peripheral Cultural Production of the Luso-Hispanic World* 1, no. 1 (2011): 4.

26. On differential consciousness, see Chela Sandoval, *Methodology of the Oppressed* (Minneapolis: University of Minnesota Press, 2000).

27. Another reason for this separation is that the New York group has a better documented history from which I have been able to assemble a fuller archive of primary texts. A book (or more) deserves to be written on the original Young Lords Organization in Chicago, but this will not be such a book. The same would go for branches in Philadelphia, Newark, and so on.

28. Sandoval, *Methodology of the Oppressed*, 67–79.

29. Readings for that week included the following: Dwight Conquergood, "Rethinking Ethnography: Towards a Critical Cultural Politics," *Communication Monographs* 58, no. 2 (1991): 179–94; Della Pollock, "Performing Writing," in *The Ends of Performance*, ed. Peggy Phelan and Jill Lane (New York: New York University Press, 1998), 73–103; Beverly Skeggs, ed., *Feminist Cultural Theory: Process and Production* (New York: Manchester University Press, 1995).

30. Roberto Santiago, ed., *Boricuas: Influential Puerto Rican Writings—An Anthology* (New York: One World Press, 1995).

31. Walter D. Mignolo, *The Darker Side of Western Modernity: Global Futures, Decolonial Options* (Durham, NC: Duke University Press, 2011), 80. Obviously, there have been many other challenges to Cartesian mind/body dualism from within the epistemic terrain of the West and beyond. What makes Mignolo's challenge so significant for me is the way in which he highlights the location of his critique, from/within the Global South, as a way to rethink global relations of power and oppression in a manner that is attentive to the needs of the Global South.

32. Ibid.

33. This is my own observation from my interactions with former Young Lords. People would allude, off the record, to others vouching for me; and some would also suggest I should use their names in seeking access to others (e.g., "[X] told me to contact you"). Regarding wariness about people exploiting the memory of the Young Lords, numerous folks disdainfully recounted an attempted commercial film project and referred in more general terms to outsiders trying to profit off them.

34. From this point on, I will refer to the New York Young Lords simply as the "Young Lords" unless there is a need to distinguish between different branches of the organization. This is for the sake of brevity and writing clarity and is not intended as a slight to any other branch of the organization.

35. Nelson Maldonado-Torres, "On the Coloniality of Being: Contributions to the Development of a Concept," *Cultural Studies* 21, no. 2–3 (2007): 243.

36. Walter D. Mignolo, "Delinking: The Rhetoric of Modernity, the Logic of Coloniality and the Grammar of De-Coloniality," *Cultural Studies* 21, no. 2–3 (2007): 452. In making the distinction, Mignolo writes:

Coloniality and de-coloniality introduces a fracture with both, the Eurocentered project of post-modernity and a project of post-coloniality heavily dependent on post-structuralism as far as Michel Foucault, Jacques Lacan and Jacques Derrida have been acknowledged as the grounding of the post-colonial canon: Edward

Said, Gayatri Spivak and Hommi Bhabha. De-coloniality starts from other sources. . . . The de-colonial shift, in other words, is a project of de-linking while post-colonial criticism and theory is a project of scholarly transformation within the academy.

Honoring this distinction, I decline to cite the literature on postcolonial theory. Even if one disagrees with Mignolo's distinction, however, I do not think it is necessary to engage postcolonial studies. The scholarship on decoloniality offers a robust and nuanced theoretical framework that suits my purposes well, which I believe is enough of a reason to narrow my focus.

37. Mignolo, *The Darker Side*, 108–9.

38. Ibid., 129.

39. Bernadette Marie Calafell, *Latina/o Communication Studies: Theorizing Performance* (New York: Peter Lang, 2007), 7.

40. William L. Nothstine, Carole Blair, and Gary Copeland, *Critical Questions: Invention, Creativity, and the Criticism of Discourse and Media* (New York: St. Martin's Press, 1994), 11.

41. Nelson Maldonado-Torres, *Against War: Views from the Underside of Modernity* (Durham, NC: Duke University Press, 2008), 7.

42. Mignolo, *The Darker Side*, 116.

43. On this distinction, see ibid., xiv. Also see Maldonado-Torres's call for a "moratorium on the West" in Nelson Maldonado-Torres, "Postimperial Reflections on Crisis, Knowledge, and Utopia: Transgresstopic Critical Hermeneutics and the 'Death of European Man,'" *Review (Fernand Braudel Center)* 25, no. 3 (2002): 277–315.

44. Enrique Dussel, *Philosophy of Liberation*, trans. Aquilina Martinez and Christine Morkovsky (Maryknoll, NY: Orbis Books, 1985); Enrique Dussel, "World-System and 'Trans'-Modernity," *Nepantla: Views from South* 3, no. 2 (2002): 221–44; Enrique D. Dussel, "From Critical Theory to the Philosophy of Liberation: Some Themes for Dialogue," *TRANSMODERNITY: Journal of Peripheral Cultural Production of the Luso-Hispanic World* 1, no. 2 (2011): 16–43; Nelson Maldonado-Torres, "The Topology of Being and the Geopolitics of Knowledge," *City* 8, no. 1 (2004): 29–56; Maldonado-Torres, *Against War*.

45. Maldonado-Torres makes a similar critique of some of Mignolo's earlier works in Maldonado-Torres, "Postimperial Reflections," 277–315.

46. I am thankful to Isaac West for this observation.

47. See, for example, Freya Schiwy, "Decolonization and the Question of Subjectivity: Gender, Race, and Binary Thinking," *Cultural studies* 21, no. 2–3 (2007): 271–94; Freya Schiwy, "'Todos Somos Presidentes/We Are All Presidents': Democracy, Culture, and Radical Politics," *Cultural Studies* 25, no. 6 (2011): 729–56. Mignolo also offers a closer engagement of the Zapatistas in a chapter that appears in *The Darker Side* and elsewhere, and he has an astute analysis of the emergence of "the communal" in South America. See Walter D. Mignolo, "The Communal and the Decolonial," *Turbulence* 5 (2009): 29–31. I do not mean to suggest that Mignolo and others *ignore* practice. In fact, I think that they all use some powerful examples to make their respective cases. What the literature lacks, generally, is *sustained engagement* of case studies. As I show over the course of this book, a sustained engagement of one case generates insights that are harder to come by through periodic examples.

48. Such negative views of rhetoric go back at least to Plato's *Gorgias*, in which he characterized the practices of the Sophists (the strongest practitioners and professors of the art of rhetoric) as a form of trickery that interfered with the attainment of higher

truths. In more modern times, this perspective is illustrated well by another philosopher, Harry Frankfurt, in his 2005 book *On Bullshit*. I prefer a more productive conception of rhetoric—something closer to John Bender and David Wellbery's argument that rhetoric "is neither a unified doctrine nor a coherent set of discursive practices. Rather, it is a transdisciplinary field of practice and intellectual concern, a field that draws on conceptual resources of a radically heterogeneous nature." John Bender and David E. Wellbery, "Rhetoricality: On the Modernist Return of Rhetoric," in *The Ends of Rhetoric: History, Theory, Practice*, ed. John Bender and David E. Wellbery (Stanford, CA: Stanford University Press, 1990), 25.

49. Molefi Kete Asante, for example, has long challenged the Eurocentric bias of U.S. communication studies and rhetoric in particular. See, for example, *Afrocentricity: The Theory of Social Change* (Buffalo, NY: Amulefi, 1980).

50. For example, see Darrel Allan Wanzer, "Delinking Rhetoric, or Revisiting McGee's Fragmentation Thesis through Decoloniality," *Rhetoric and Public Affairs* 15, no. 4 (2012): 647–57. I choose to advance those disciplinary arguments in forums other than this book.

51. Not all people who would identify as rhetoricians would frame these commitments in the same way, as "radical contextualism." But my point is to account for my own perspectives that shape my approach in this book, not to account for everyone else.

52. Lawrence Grossberg, "Does Cultural Studies Have Futures? Should It? (Or What's the Matter with New York?)," *Cultural Studies* 20, no. 1 (2006): 2.

53. Jennifer Daryl Slack, "The Theory and Method of Articulation in Cultural Studies," in *Stuart Hall: Critical Dialogues in Cultural Studies*, ed. Kuan-Hsing Chen and David Morley (London: Routledge, 1996), 125.

54. I am operating partly within the terrain of McGee's thesis on fragmentation. Michael Calvin McGee, "Text, Context, and the Fragmentation of Contemporary Culture," *Western Journal of Speech Communication* 54 (1990): 274–89. For a critique of McGee's fragmentation thesis, see Wanzer, "Delinking Rhetoric," 647–57. This position also points to the broader materiality of discourse, best crafted by Ronald Walter Greene, which I will address more later. Ronald Walter Greene, "Another Materialist Rhetoric," *Critical Studies in Mass Communication* 15, no. 1 (1998): 21–41.

55. I have written before on the intersectionality of rhetorical forms. Darrel Enck-Wanzer, "Trashing the System: Social Movement, Intersectional Rhetoric, and Collective Agency in the Young Lords Organization's Garbage Offensive," *Quarterly Journal of Speech* 92, no. 2 (2006): 174–201.

56. Grossberg, "Does Cultural Studies Have Futures?" 6.

57. Michelle A. Holling and Bernadette M. Calafell, "Tracing the Emergence of Latin@ Vernaculars in Studies of Latin@ Communication," in *Latina/o Discourse in Vernacular Spaces: Somos de una Voz?* ed. Michelle A. Holling and Bernadette M. Calafell (Lanham, MD: Lexington Books, 2011), 17–29; Kent A. Ono and John M. Sloop, "The Critique of Vernacular Discourse," *Communication Monographs* 62, no. 1 (1995): 19–46.

58. Decolonial scholars are averse to nationalism, a topic I take up more in Chapter 2. For example, see Ramón Grosfoguel, *Colonial Subjects: Puerto Ricans in a Global Perspective* (Berkeley: University of California Press, 2003).

59. Ronald Walter Greene, "The Aesthetic Turn and the Rhetorical Perspective on Argumentation," *Argumentation and Advocacy* 35, no. 1 (1998): 19.

60. Please do not misunderstand my usage of the term "machismo." My reference, here, is to the Young Lords' own formulation of "revolutionary machismo" as a particular performance of mental, physical, and political toughness. As I discuss in Chapter 3, this

original formulation was challenged by women within the organization and rejected after a complex, intersectional analysis. In no case do I render "machismo" in essentialist ways. The organization's critique of the term rejected essentialisms as well, while pointing to the ways in which machismo is a product of racism, sexism, capitalism, and imperialism in the context of coloniality.

61. For example, see María Lugones, "Heterosexualism and the Colonial/Modern Gender System," *Hypatia* 22, no. 1 (2007): 186–219; María Lugones, "Toward a Decolonial Feminism," *Hypatia* 25, no. 4 (2010): 742–759; Sandoval, *Methodology of the Oppressed*; Schiwy, "Decolonization," 271–94.

62. The number of scholars for whom this is a truism is too numerous to count. Some scholarship that has long affected my own perspective includes the following: Kevin DeLuca, *Image Politics: The New Rhetoric of Environmental Activism* (New York: Guilford Press, 1999); Kevin DeLuca, "Articulation Theory: A Discursive Grounding for Rhetorical Practice," *Philosophy and Rhetoric* 32, no. 4 (1999): 334–48; Ernesto Laclau and Chantal Mouffe, *Hegemony and Socialist Strategy: Towards a Radical Democratic Practice* (London: Verso, 2001); Phaedra C. Pezzullo, "Resisting 'National Breast Cancer Awareness Month': The Rhetoric of Counterpublics and Their Cultural Performances," *Quarterly Journal of Speech* 89 (2003): 345–65.

63. Laclau and Mouffe, *Hegemony and Socialist Strategy*, 107, 108, and 109, respectively.

64. On the reality/existence distinction, see DeLuca, "Articulation Theory."

65. Admittedly, the distinction between disengagement and complete disavowal is a blurry one. And that is part of my point. As I mentioned in the body of this chapter earlier, the moment we identify a strict line of demarcation or codify certain concepts mandating an inside/outside distinction, we have given up on a more rhetorical conceptualization of delinking. Yes, delinking will always work to decolonize and challenge the epistemic privilege of the West in its context; but contra Audre Lorde, sometimes that *can* be done utilizing "the master's tools." As Lorde notes, those tools "may allow us temporarily to beat him at his own game"; but where she argues "they will never allow us to bring about genuine change," I would argue that they can open up the space for such change to occur. Audre Lorde, "The Master's Tools Will Never Dismantle the Master's House," in *This Bridge Called My Back: Writings by Radical Women of Color*, ed. Cherríe Moraga and Gloria Anzaldúa (Watertown, MA: Persephone Press, 1981), 99.

66. Samir Amin, *Delinking: Towards a Polycentric World*, trans. Michael Wolfers (London: Zed Books, 1990).

67. Ronald Walter Greene and Kevin Douglas Kuswa, "'From the Arab Spring to Athens, from Occupy Wall Street to Moscow': Regional Accents and the Rhetorical Cartography of Power," *Rhetoric Society Quarterly* 42, no. 3 (2012): 277.

68. Mignolo, "Delinking," 453.

69. Ibid., 462. In his eighth footnote in a more recent essay, Mignolo further clarifies that "Amin has maintained himself in the bubble of the modern episteme and his delinking gave rise to a change in content, not in the terms of the conversation. 'Epistemic de-linking,' in contrast, signals the moment of fracture and breakage, a moment of opening." Walter D. Mignolo, "Epistemic Disobedience and the Decolonial Option: A Manifesto," *TRANSMODERNITY: Journal of Peripheral Cultural Production of the Luso-Hispanic World* 1, no. 2 (2012): 64.

70. Mignolo, "Epistemic Disobedience and the Decolonial Option," 45.

71. Judith Butler's explanation of speech's sedimentation is particularly engaging. Judith Butler, *Excitable Speech: A Politics of the Performative* (New York: Routledge, 1997).

72. Mikhail M. Bakhtin, *The Dialogic Imagination: Four Essays*, ed. Michael Holquist, trans. Caryl Emerson and Michael Holquist (Austin: University of Texas Press, 1981), 293–94.

73. Valentin N. Vološhinov, *Marxism and the Philosophy of Language*, trans. Ladislav Matejka and I. R. Titunik (Cambridge, MA: Harvard University Press, 1986), 23 and 81, respectively.

74. Darrel Enck-Wanzer, "Tropicalizing East Harlem: Rhetorical Agency, Cultural Citizenship, and Nuyorican Cultural Production," *Communication Theory* 21, no. 4 (2011): 346. See also Frances R. Aparicio and Susana Chávez-Silverman, "Introduction," in *Tropicalizations: Transcultural Representations of Latinidad*, ed. Frances R. Aparicio and Susana Chávez-Silverman (Hanover, NH: University Press of New England, 1997), 1–17.

75. Greene and Kuswa, "From the Arab Spring to Athens," 273.

76. Ibid., 280.

77. Aparicio and Chávez-Silverman, "Introduction," 1–17.

78. Arlene M. Dávila, *Barrio Dreams: Puerto Ricans, Latinos, and the Neoliberal City* (Berkeley: University of California Press, 2004).

79. Mignolo, "Epistemic Disobedience and the Decolonial Option," 62–63.

80. Stuart Hall, "On Postmodernism and Articulation," *Journal of Communication Inquiry* 10, no. 2 (1986): 53.

81. Mignolo, "Epistemic Disobedience and the Decolonial Option," 64.

82. As I understand articulation theory within cultural studies, it is a valuable heuristic for engaging critically the circulation of discourses along with the force and flows of cultural formations. While cultural studies pushes us to challenge the ways in which those linkages become naturalized, there is no necessary political commitment attached to such a mode of critique (even if it has long been undergirded by certain Marxist sensibilities). Delinking can operate through a decolonially inflected sense of articulation—one that seeks to both challenge articulations in a manner informed by a critique of coloniality and generate new articulations that are decolonial in tone.

83. Roland Barthes, *Mythologies*, trans. Annette Lavers (New York: Noonday Press, 1972). See, especially, the section entitled "Myth on the Left."

84. Sandoval, *Methodology of the Oppressed*, 109.

85. Ibid.

86. Ibid., 114.

87. José Esteban Muñoz, *Disidentifications: Queers of Color and the Performance of Politics* (Minneapolis: University of Minnesota Press, 1999), 11–12.

88. Indeed, it is hard *not* to see the productive potential of putting Muñoz's "disidentification" and Sandoval's "differential consciousness" into conversation, given that both function through a logic that disavows binary thinking and forced choices.

89. Michael C. McGee, "In Search of 'The People': A Rhetorical Alternative," *Quarterly Journal of Speech* 61 (1975): 242 and 249.

90. Charles Taylor, "Modern Social Imaginaries," *Public Culture* 14 (2002): 91–124; Charles Taylor, *Modern Social Imaginaries* (Durham, NC: Duke University Press, 2004).

91. Maldonado-Torres, *Against War*; Maldonado-Torres, "Enrique Dussel's Liberation Thought," 1–30. See also Fanon, *Wretched*; Frantz Fanon, *Black Skin, White Masks*, trans. Charles Lam Markmann (New York: Grove Press, 1967).

92. Mignolo, *The Darker Side*, 312, emphasis added.

93. Dwight Conquergood, "Performance Studies: Interventions and Radical Research," *Drama Review* 46, no. 2 (2002): 145–16; Wanzer, "Delinking Rhetoric," 647–57.

94. Maldonado-Torres, *Against War*, 234, emphasis added.

95. Lisbeth Lipari, "Rhetoric's Other: Levinas, Listening, and the Ethical Response," *Philosophy and Rhetoric* 45, no. 3 (2012): 227–45; Jeffrey W. Murray, "The Face in Dialogue: Emmanuel Levinas and Rhetorics of Disruption and Supplication," *Southern Communication Journal* 68, no. 3 (2003): 250–66; Kelly Oliver, *Witnessing: Beyond Recognition* (Minneapolis: University of Minnesota Press, 2001).

96. Oliver, *Witnessing*, 2. Oliver does not actually engage questions of de/coloniality, but I think there is a certain compatibility between her perspectives and those of, especially, Maldonado-Torres.

97. Maldonado-Torres, *Against War*, 157 and 158.

98. Oliver, *Witnessing*, 42.

99. Maldonado-Torres, *Against War*, 240–41.

100. Sandoval, *Methodology of the Oppressed*, 140.

101. I will address this more fully in the conclusion. Suffice it to say, I believe my youthful exuberance for "post-_____" theories was mistaken, and I seek to correct some of those mistakes in this book.

102. Junot Díaz and Paula M.L. Moya, "The Search for Decolonial Love, Part I," *Boston Review*, June 26, 2012, available at http://www.bostonreview.net/.

103. Maldonado-Torres, *Against War*, 11–12.

104. Mignolo, *The Darker Side*, 21 and 52.

CHAPTER 1

1. Juan Gonzalez, *Harvest of Empire: A History of Latinos in America* (New York: Viking, 2000).

2. James L. Dietz, *Economic History of Puerto Rico: Institutional Change and Capitalist Development* (Princeton, NJ: Princeton University Press, 1986), 4.

3. Ibid., 240.

4. Reinhart Koselleck, *The Practice of Conceptual History: Timing History, Spacing Concepts*, trans. Todd Samuel Presner (Stanford, CA: Stanford University Press, 2002), 25.

5. Emma Pérez, *The Decolonial Imaginary: Writing Chicanas into History* (Bloomington: Indiana University Press, 1999), xv.

6. David Perez, quoted in Young Lords Party and Michael Abramson, *Palante: Young Lords Party* (New York: McGraw-Hill, 1971), 66.

7. Jack Lait and Lee Mortimer, *New York: Confidential* (New York: Crown, 1948), quoted in Philippe I. Bourgois, *In Search of Respect: Selling Crack in El Barrio* (New York: Cambridge University Press, 1995), 62.

8. Frantz Fanon, *Black Skin, White Masks*, trans. Charles Lam Markmann (New York: Grove Press, 1967), 109.

9. Frantz Fanon, *The Wretched of the Earth*, trans. Constance Farrington (New York: Grove Press, 1963), 233–34.

10. Piri Thomas and Kal Wagenheim, "Foreword," in Kal Wagenheim, *Puerto Rico: A Profile* (New York: Praeger, 1970), ix.

11. Ibid., xi and ix–x.

12. Kal Wagenheim, *Puerto Rico: A Profile* (New York: Praeger, 1970). Wagenheim addresses in his preface the general lack of available scholarship and provides an excellent annotated bibliography of the existent sources at the book's end.

13. Maylei Blackwell, *¡Chicana Power! Contested Histories of Feminism in the Chicano Movement* (Austin: University of Texas Press, 2011), 2.

14. Miguel Melendez, *We Took the Streets: Fighting for Latino Rights with the Young Lords* (New York: St. Martin's Press, 2003).

15. For the interested reader, I would recommend a few key books (some of which I will cite below) that serve as compelling introductions to Puerto Rican history, culture, politics, and so forth. Wagenheim's *Puerto Rico: A Profile* stands the test of time as an exemplary introduction to Puerto Rico, especially from the perspective of someone living in 1970. Dietz's *Economic History of Puerto Rico* offers remarkable detail pertaining to economic and institutional change across the history of Puerto Rico. Duany's *The Puerto Rican Nation on the Move* is one of the most eloquently written engagements of Puerto Rican history, culture, identity, and migration available today. Cabán's *Constructing a Colonial People* and Santiago-Valles's *"Subject People" and Colonial Discourses* are both excellent engagements of U.S. colonialism in Puerto Rico. Dávila's *Sponsored Identities* is a brilliant work of history and anthropology that culls a vast archive to craft a compelling narrative of cultural formation in Puerto Rico. Finally, Wagenheim and Jiménez de Wagenheim's edited collection *The Puerto Ricans* is a virtual treasure trove of primary texts that provides a chronicle of Puerto Rico's five hundred years of history. Pedro A. Cabán, *Constructing a Colonial People: Puerto Rico and the United States, 1898–1932* (Boulder, CO: Westview Press, 1999); Arlene M. Dávila, *Sponsored Identities: Cultural Politics in Puerto Rico* (Philadelphia: Temple University Press, 1997); Dietz, *Economic History*; Jorge Duany, *The Puerto Rican Nation on the Move: Identities on the Island and in the United States* (Chapel Hill: University of North Carolina Press, 2002); Kelvin A. Santiago-Valles, *"Subject People" and Colonial Discourses: Economic Transformation and Social Disorder in Puerto Rico, 1898–1947* (Albany: State University of New York Press, 1994); Wagenheim, *Puerto Rico*; Kal Wagenheim and Olga Jiménez de Wagenheim, *The Puerto Ricans: A Documentary History* (Princeton, NJ: M. Wiener Publishers, 1994).

16. Pablo "Yoruba" Guzmán, "History of Boriken 1," *Palante* 3, no. 2 (1971): 20.

17. Ibid., 20. See also Wagenheim, *Puerto Rico*, 36–41. Note the lowercasing of "christopher columbus." Here and throughout their writings, the Young Lords regularly declined to capitalize proper nouns when they were terms of historical significance regarding colonialism, imperialism, and Eurocentrism. This is purposeful on their part—a tactic designed to deny privilege to those people and places that have been central to the domination of Puerto Ricans and other peoples of the Global South.

18. It is important to note that while many Taínos died from abuse, many more died from disease brought by the Spanish colonizers. For a comprehensive account of the Taínos, see Francisco Moscoso, *Sociedad y Economía de Los Taínos* (Río Piedras, PR: Editorial Edil, 1999). See also Wagenheim and de Wagenheim, *The Puerto Ricans*.

19. Roberto Santiago, "Introduction," in *Boricuas: Influential Puerto Rican Writings—An Anthology*, ed. Roberto Santiago (New York: One World, 1995), xviii.

20. Pablo "Yoruba" Guzmán, "History of Boriken 3," *Palante* 3, no. 4 (1971): 5.

21. Pablo "Yoruba" Guzmán, "History of Boriken 4," *Palante* 3, no. 5 (1971): 11.

22. Guzmán, "History of Boriken 3," 5.

23. Dávila, *Sponsored Identities*, 61.

24. For an excellent engagement of this idea in the context of Puerto Rican television, see Yeidy M. Rivero, *Tuning out Blackness: Race and Nation in the History of Puerto Rican Television* (Durham, NC: Duke University Press, 2005).

25. Duany, *Puerto Rican Nation*, 135–36. See, generally, Duany's discussion of cultural nationalism, 122–36.

26. Dávila, *Sponsored Identities*, 71. One of the key national, folklorized images Dávila points to is that of the jíbaro, which "comprises the most important building block

of nationality." The image is problematic, however, because it is constructed as "white, male, rural based, and devoid of recognizable African and Taíno components" (72). The Young Lords offer a brilliant visual challenge to these problematic constructions, which I explore in Chapter 3.

27. See Benedict R. Anderson, *Imagined Communities: Reflections on the Origin and Spread of Nationalism* (London: Verso, 1991).

28. Antonio Martorell, "Imagining Betances," in *Dr. Ramón E. Betances: Abolitionist, Diplomat, Physician, Writer and Caribbean Hero* (New York: Centro de Estudios Puertorriqueños, 2004), 8.

29. According to Maldonado-Denis, while Betance's temporarily lost out to reform-minded "autonomists," the "anticolonialist spirit" remained. Manuel Maldonado-Denis, *Puerto Rico: A Socio-Historic Interpretation*, trans. Elena Vialo (New York: Vintage Books, 1972), 51. This spirit was markedly important for the Young Lords (see, for example, issues of the Young Lords' paper *Palante* around the anniversaries of El Grito de Lares). On El Grito de Lares, see also Francisco Moscoso, *La Revolución Puertor-riqueña de 1868: El Grito de Lares* (San Juan, Puerto Rico: Instituto de Cultura Puertor-riqueña, 2003); Luis de la Rosa Martínez, *La Periferia del Grito de Lares: Antología de Documentos Históricos (1861–1869)* (Santo Domingo, Dominican Republic: Editora Cor-ripio, 1983); Olga Jiménez de Wagenheim, *Puerto Rico's Revolt for Independence: El Grito de Lares* (Princeton, NJ: M. Wiener Publishers, 1993).

30. Iris Morales, "El Grito de Lares," *Palante* 2, no. 12 (1970): 4.

31. Pablo "Yoruba" Guzmán, "Editorial," *Palante* 2, no. 12 (1970): 19.

32. Cabán, *Constructing a Colonial People*, 7.

33. Dietz, *Economic History*, 76.

34. Cabán, *Constructing a Colonial People*, 7.

35. Ibid., Dietz, *Economic History*, 77.

36. Gonzalez, *Harvest of Empire*, 60.

37. Ibid., 61. Note the spelling of "Porto Rico"—a common Americanization of the name that appeared in early U.S. colonial documents.

38. Efrén Rivera Ramos, *The Legal Construction of Identity: The Judicial and Social Legacy of American Colonialism in Puerto Rico* (Washington, DC: American Psychologi-cal Association, 2001), 22.

39. Gonzalez, *Harvest of Empire*, 62.

40. Vine Deloria Jr., "Identity and Culture," in *From Different Shores: Perspective on Race and Ethnicity in America*, ed. Ronald Takaki (New York: Oxford University Press, 1994), 94.

41. Another excellent resource that provides an overview of this history and the difficult political situation faced by many Puerto Ricans is Raquel Ortiz, Sharon Simon, and Julia Dixon Eddy, *Mi Puerto Rico* (Los Angeles: NLCC Educational Media, 1996).

42. Dietz, *Economic History*, 97–98.

43. For an exemplary analysis of this constitutive and hegemonic process, see Rivera Ramos, *Legal Construction of Identity*, 145–237. See also Cabán, *Constructing a Colonial People*, 198–205.

44. José Manuel Torres Santiago, "100 Years of Don Pedro Albizu Campos," available at http://www.hunter.cuny.edu/blpr/albizu.html.

45. Ibid.

46. Pablo "Yoruba" Guzmán, "History of Boriken 9," *Palante* 3, no. 11 (1971): 2. Muñoz Marin was elected governor in 1948.

47. Ibid.

48. Nikhil Pal Singh, *Black Is a Country: Race and the Unfinished Struggle for Democracy* (Cambridge, MA: Harvard University Press, 2004), 202.

49. Iris Morales, Columbia Oral History Transcript, 49; quoted in Lorrin Thomas, *Puerto Rican Citizen: History and Political Identity in Twentieth-Century New York City* (Chicago: University of Chicago Press, 2010), 239.

50. Clara E. Rodríguez, "Puerto Ricans and the Political Economy of New York," in Takaki, *From Different Shores*, 118.

51. Antonia Pantoja, "Puerto Ricans in New York: A Historical and Community Development Perspective," *Centro Journal* 2, no. 5 (1989): 24 and 25.

52. Virginia E. Sánchez Korrol, *From Colonia to Community: The History of Puerto Ricans in New York City* (Berkeley: University of California Press, 1994), 53.

53. Roberto P. Rodriguez-Morazzani, "Puerto Rican Political Generations in New York: Pioneros, Young Turks and Radicals," *Centro Journal* 4, no. 1 (1991): 101.

54. Ibid.

55. Ibid.

56. Pablo "Yoruba" Guzmán, "History of Boriken 8," *Palante* 3, no. 9 (1971): 4.

57. Rodriguez-Morazzani, "Puerto Rican Political Generations," 102.

58. Ibid., 101.

59. Ibid., 102.

60. Ibid., 101–2. Additionally, Rodriguez-Morazzani suggests that the young turks sought a professionalization of their work, which lead to further restraints on the scope of their activities. In other words, they became more conservative and establishment minded as time went on.

61. Ibid., 103.

62. Carlos Rodríguez-Fraticelli, and Amílcar Tirado, "Notes towards a History of Puerto Rican Community Organizations in New York City," *Centro Journal* 2, no. 6 (1989): 42.

63. Ibid., 43. Also see Pantoja, "Puerto Ricans in New York," 21–31.

64. Joseph Boskin, "The Revolt of the Urban Ghettos, 1964–1967," *Annals of the American Academy of Political and Social Science* 382, no. 1 (1969): 4–5.

65. Ibid., 5.

66. Ibid., 14.

67. Wagenheim, *Puerto Rico*, 196.

68. Young Lords Party and Abramson, *Palante: Young Lords Party*, 74.

69. Ibid.

70. Luis Aponte-Parés, "Lessons from El Barrio—The East Harlem Real Great Society/Urban Planning Studio: A Puerto Rican Chapter in the Fight for Urban Self-Determination," *New Political Science* 20, no. 4 (1998): 401.

71. Boskin, "Revolt of the Urban Ghettos," 2.

72. Singh, *Black Is a Country*, 192.

73. Thomas, *Puerto Rican Citizen*, 227.

74. "Interview with Cha Cha Jimenez, Chairman—Young Lords Organization," *Black Panther* (June 7, 1969): 17.

75. For better or worse, it seems like the Black Panthers get most of the attention when discussions turn to Black Power. As I discuss subsequently, however, there is good reason for this when it comes to the Young Lords—not the least of which being that the original chapter in Chicago was founded partly because of Fred Hampton's influence. Be that as it may, one would do well to remain cognizant of the deeper roots of Black Power that echo throughout the Panthers and others. Robin D. G. Kelly, for example, does an

exemplary job tracing the origins, actions, and ideology of the Revolutionary Action Movement (RAM), who "sought to understand the African-American condition through an analysis of global capitalism, imperialism, and Third World liberation well before the riots of the mid-1960s" (62). RAM's twelve-point program, revolutionary nationalist structure and ideology, appropriation of Maoist thought, and so on, undoubtedly made an impression on the Panthers. In fact, argues Kelley, "It was in the context of the urban rebellions that several streams of black radicalism, including RAM, converged and gave birth to the Black Panther Party for Self-Defense in Oakland, California" (93). Robin D. G. Kelley, *Freedom Dreams: The Black Radical Imagination* (Boston: Beacon Press, 2003).

76. Pablo Guzmán, *Pablo "Yoruba" Guzmán on the Young Lords Legacy: A Personal Account*, ed. Joseph Luppens (New York: Institute for Puerto Rican Policy, 1995), 53.

77. Pablo Guzmán, "Ain't No Party like the One We Got: The Young Lords Party and *Palante*," in *Voices from the Underground: Insider Histories from the Vietnam Era Underground Press*, ed. Ken Wachsberger (Ann Arbor, MI: Azenphony, 1991), 294.

78. Denise Oliver-Velez, interview by the author, May 24, 2004. Oliver is an interesting case for a variety of reasons. Born in Brooklyn in a multiracial family, her mother was white and her father was one of the first black actors to integrate Broadway. Like up to 30 percent of the Young Lords (estimates vary), Oliver was not a Puerto Rican; but she shared similar radical beliefs and was operating within some of the same traditions of resistance as Young Lords like Guzmán, Mickey Melendez, Felipe Luciano, and Juan Gonzalez.

79. On connections between African Americans and Puerto Ricans, see Juan Flores, *Divided Borders: Essays on Puerto Rican Identity* (Houston, TX: Arte Publico Press, 1992), 157–98; Nicholas de Genova and Ana Y. Ramos-Zayas, *Latino Crossings: Mexicans, Puerto Ricans, and the Politics of Race and Citizenship* (New York: Routledge, 2003); Ramón Grosfoguel and Chloé S. Georas, "The Racialization of Latino Caribbean Migrants in the New York Metropolitan Area," *CENTRO: Journal of the Center for Puerto Rican Studies* 8, no. 1–2 (1996): 191–201; Agustín Laó-Montes, "Niuyol: Urban Regime, Latino Social Movements, Ideologies of Latinidad," in *Mambo Montage: The Latinization of New York*, ed. Agustín Laó-Montes and Arlene M. Dávila (New York: Columbia University Press, 2001), 119–58.

80. Rodriguez-Morazzani, "Puerto Rican Political Generations," 110.

81. Roberto P. Rodriguez-Morazzani, "Political Cultures of the Puerto Rican Left in the United States," in *The Puerto Rican Movement: Voices from the Diaspora*, ed. Andrés Torres and José E. Velázquez (Philadelphia: Temple University Press, 1998), 37.

82. Pablo "Yoruba" Guzman, "Malcolm Spoke for Puerto Ricans," *Palante* 2, no. 1 (1970): 3.

83. Singh, *Black Is a Country*, 189.

84. Manuel Maldonado-Denis, "The Puerto Ricans: Protest or Submission?" *Annals of the American Academy of Political and Social Science* 382, no. 1 (1969): 28.

85. Fanon, *Wretched*, 129.

86. Singh, *Black Is a Country*, 189.

87. Carlos Rovira, interview by the author, May 22, 2004.

88. Guzmán, "Ain't No Party," 294.

89. Luis Garden Acosta, interview by the author, March 14, 2006.

90. It is important to note, here, that I cannot document every significant pre–Young Lords organization because every member took his or her own unique path. The organizations I talk about here seem to have the clearest direct connections to the formation of the Young Lords in New York.

91. Young Lords Party and Abramson, *Palante: Young Lords Party*, 8.

92. While Guzmán does not name Illich in any of his biographies, according to others I interviewed, his encounter with Illich was formative. For more on Illich, see Chase Madar, "The People's Priest," *American Conservative*, February 1, 2010, available at http://www.amconmag.com/articles/the-peoples-priest/.

93. Aponte-Parés, "Lessons from El Barrio," 405–6.

94. RGS/UPS Proposal, submitted to the Ford and Astor Foundations, quoted in Aponte-Parés, "Lessons from El Barrio," 409.

95. The Young Lords recognized this antecedent to their own activism, but the RGS name is left out. In a footnote, Aponte-Parés takes issue with Guzmán's recollection of RGS's involvement, pointing to Willie Vásquez's argument "that when Guzmán, Luciano and others came to East Harlem, they had lost connection to *el Barrio*, and that, in fact, had not Mauricio Gastón, Papo Giordani and Harry Quintana urged them to get in contact with the Chicago Lords, etc., these 'young Puerto Rican students would have never made the connections.'" Aponte-Parés, "Lessons from El Barrio," 411–12.

96. According to multiple former Young Lords interviewed, many Puerto Ricans left the Denver conference when Chicanos insisted that the convention floor was for Latin@s only. Puerto Ricans who had gone to the conference with African American allies saw little point in such essentialist identity politics. The Young Lords would come to have a mixed, though generally supportive, relationship with various Chicano movement organizations. The Young Lords would only ever work closely, however, with the Brown Berets.

97. The historiography of this origin tale is messy, to say the least. Official Young Lords documents indicate that Martinez met Cha Cha for the first time at the SDS convention in May. Carlito Rovira, who was organized with Martinez, contends that it was the Chicano conference in Denver in March. I'm inclined to believe the latter since he was part of the Lower East Side group and because Iris Morales tells a similar story of meeting Cha Cha in Denver; but the fact ultimately may not matter in terms of the Young Lords' emergence in New York. For the official Young Lords story, see Young Lords Party and Abramson, *Palante: Young Lords Party*. According to Guzmán, Jiménez never granted Martinez a charter to organize Young Lords in New York. See Guzmán, "Ain't No Party," 296.

98. Guzmán, "Ain't No Party," 297.

99. Anonymous, interview by the author, March 11, 2006.

100. "Interview with Cha Cha," 6. As I mentioned earlier, however, this history is contested. Members of RGS claim that they were the first to inform SAC members about the Young Lords. Regardless of whether that was the case, the Young Lords themselves make the *Black Panther* interview central to their origin narrative.

101. José Jiménez and Ángel G. Flores-Rodréguez, "The Young Lords, Puerto Rican Liberation, and the Black Freedom Struggle: Interview with José 'Cha Cha' Jiménez," *OAH Magazine of History* 26, no. 1 (2012): 61–64.

102. Iris Morales, "¡PALANTE, SIEMPRE PALANTE! The Young Lords," in Torres and Velázquez, *Puerto Rican Movement*, 212. It is worth noting that in Morales's and other New York Young Lords' telling of Jiménez's story, they often attribute the conversion to Fred Hampton. While Jiménez certainly developed a friendship and coalition with Hampton, Jiménez's personal narratives indicate that his conversion happened prior to that friendship.

103. See Aponte-Parés, "Lessons from El Barrio."

104. Pablo Guzmán, "La Vida Pura: A Lord of the Barrio," *Village Voice* (March 21, 1995): 25.

105. Diego Pabón remained connected to the Young Lords, but it appears that this was only through coalitional work. The Puerto Rican Revolutionary Workers Organization (the Young Lords' third phase of development) mentions Pabón in their founding documents. Puerto Rican Revolutionary Workers Organization, *Resolutions and Speeches; 1st Congress; Puerto Rican Revolutionary Workers Organization (Young Lords Party)* (New York, November 1972), 4. There is also evidence that he eventually became a Puerto Rican Student Union leader and spoke at a large student conference (which the Young Lords also attended and helped organize) in September 1970. Basilio Serrano, "'¡Rifle, Cañon, y Escopeta!' A Chronicle of the Puerto Rican Student Union," in Torres and Velázquez, *Puerto Rican Movement*, 133.

106. Guzmán, "Ain't No Party," 296.

107. Agustín Laó, "Resources of Hope: Imagining the Young Lords and the Politics of Memory," *CENTRO: Journal of the Center for Puerto Rican Studies* 7, no. 1 (1995): 36.

108. Melendez, *We Took the Streets*, 93. This kind of quasi-intellectualism bears some similarity to that of the SDS, which makes sense because of both the YLO's temporal and spatial proximity to SDS and Juan Gonzalez's involvement with SDS at Columbia after Mark Rudd ascended to national leadership. For another account of such intellectualism, see Todd Gitlin, *The Sixties: Years of Hope, Days of Rage* (New York: Bantam Books, 1993).

109. Young Lords Party and Abramson, *Palante: Young Lords Party*, 74.

110. Young Lords Party and Abramson, *Palante: Young Lords Party*, 10.

111. Morales, "¡PALANTE, SIEMPRE PALANTE!" 213–14.

112. Jack Newfield, "Young Lords Do City's Work in the Barrio," *Village Voice* (December 4, 1969): 1+.

113. Young Lords Party and Abramson, *Palante: Young Lords Party*, 138.

114. There are obvious resemblances between these Rules of Discipline and similar documents from RAM and Mao Zedong. See Kelley, *Freedom Dreams*, 86–87.

115. The newspaper began in Chicago as a monthly, where only five issues were produced. The first featuring the New York chapter was the undated volume 1, number 4, in 1969, when it was simply called *Y.L.O.* In January 1970, the national YLO office published volume 1, number 5. After that point, all publishing was done out of New York—beginning with volume 2, number 1, in January or February (there is no clear date), which was a mimeographed paper renamed *Palante*. The paper was rebooted as a biweekly and produced on tabloid-sized newsprint with volume 2, number 2, dated Friday, May 8.

116. Yoruba and Graciela Mm Smith, "Interview with Yoruba, Minister of Information, Young Lords Organization, Regarding Confrontations at the First Spanish Methodist Church in El Barrio (Spanish Harlem); December 19, 1969," in *Young Lords Organization*, ed. National Council of the Churches of Christ in the United States of America (New York: NCC Communication Center, December 19, 1970), 27.

117. José Ramón Sánchez, *Boricua Power: A Political History of Puerto Ricans in the United States* (New York: New York University Press, 2007), 206–7.

118. Ibid., 205.

119. Guzmán, "Ain't No Party," 304.

120. Many who have written and talked about their time in the Young Lords have reflected on this split. The official party explanation can be found in their book, *Palante: Young Lords Party*. Guzmán offers some more detailed explanations in Guzmán, "Ain't No Party," 296 and 304.

121. Juan Gonzalez, "Untitled Speech Given in Hawaii on November 16, 1971," in *Juan Gonzalez Papers* (New York: Center for Puerto Rican Studies, CUNY Hunter College, 1971), 6.

122. The uprising at Attica was rooted in prisoners' demands for humane treatment. After negotiations led by a panel of community activists and government officials were cut short, the standoff was ended by military-style assault on the prison in which numerous prisoners and guards were slaughtered.

123. Gonzalez, "Untitled Speech," 8.

124. The health-care programs and activism of the Young Lords deserve more attention than I give them in this book. Truthfully, an entire book could be written on this topic alone. The Lincoln Hospital offensive was spurred in large part by the neglectful death of a Puerto Rican patient undergoing an abortion procedure at the hospital. The incident is discussed in the context of the Young Lords' feminism in Jennifer A. Nelson, " 'Abortions under Community Control': Feminism, Nationalism, and the Politics of Reproduction among New York City's Young Lords," *Journal of Women's History* 13, no. 1 (2001): 157–80.

125. While I was conducting interviews for this project, many former Young Lords confided in me that, in retrospect, it may very well have been a suicide. At the time, however, they were shocked and sincerely believed no Young Lord would ever kill him- or herself.

126. Young Lords Party and Abramson, *Palante: Young Lords Party*, 13.

127. The *New York Times* reported that only 3,000 people attended. The 10,000-person figure is from multiple Young Lords' reports. Perhaps the truth lies somewhere in between; but that should not distract from the enormous symbolic significance of thousands of Puerto Ricans marching from El Barrio to the United Nations.

128. Guzmán, "La Vida Pura: A Lord of the Barrio," 25–26.

129. Morales, "¡PALANTE, SIEMPRE PALANTE!" 221–23.

130. Ibid., 222.

131. Ibid. The move to the island was a disaster for a few key reasons. First, it put the Young Lords on the radar of those (like the Central Intelligence Agency) who had an interest in people or organizations providing material support for Puerto Rican independence. Second, the move to the island was a drain on the Young Lords' resources, which could have better contributed to existent programs stateside. Third, the Young Lords did not have a strong grasp on or experience with Puerto Rican politics, which meant (a) they could not be effective organizers and (b) they were treated as outsiders by folks who had long been active in the independence movement on the island.

132. Max Elbaum, *Revolution in the Air: Sixties Radicals Turn to Lenin, Mao and Che* (London: Verso, 2002), 104.

133. Laó, "Resources of Hope," 44.

134. The U.S. government investigated the PRRWO under counterterrorism laws. A congressional study documents the PRRWO's actions infiltrating unions and operating principally "underground," which is consistent with what is known about their office and branch closures. See Subcommittee to Investigate the Administration of the Internal Security Act and Other Internal Security Laws, *The Puerto Rican Revolutionary Workers Organization: A Staff Study* (Washington, DC: U.S. Government Printing Office, March 1976). While *Palante* kept printing through at least April 1973, it increasingly covered general news stories and decreasingly covered the Young Lords over the course of 1972.

135. Elbaum, *Revolution in the Air*, 185.

136. Ibid., 187.

137. Ibid., 199.

138. Ibid., 199–200.

139. David C. Brotherton and Luis Barrios, *The Almighty Latin King and Queen Nation: Street Politics and the Transformation of a New York City Gang* (New York: Columbia

University Press, 2004); Sonia Manzano, *The Revolution of Evelyn Serrano* (New York: Scholastic Press, 2012).

    140. Laó, "Resources of Hope," 45.

CHAPTER 2

    1. See, for example, Christina Duffy Burnett and Burke Marshall, eds., *Foreign in a Domestic Sense: Puerto Rico, American Expansion, and the Constitution* (Durham, NC: Duke University Press, 2001); Pedro A. Cabán, *Constructing a Colonial People: Puerto Rico and the United States, 1898–1932* (Boulder, CO: Westview Press, 1999); Nathaniel I. Córdova, "The Constitutive Force of the *Catecismo Del Pueblo* in Puerto Rico's Popular Democratic Party Campaign of 1938–1940," *Quarterly Journal of Speech* 90, no. 2 (2004): 212–33; Nathaniel I. Córdova, "The Incomplete Subject of Colonial Memory: Puerto Rico and the Post/Colonial Biopolitics of Congressional Recollection," *Communication Review* 11, no. 1 (2008): 42–75; Arlene M. Dávila, *Sponsored Identities: Cultural Politics in Puerto Rico* (Philadelphia: Temple University Press, 1997); Jorge Duany, *The Puerto Rican Nation on the Move: Identities on the Island and in the United States* (Chapel Hill: University of North Carolina Press, 2002); Luis Angel Ferrao, *Pedro Albizu Campos y el Nacionalismo Puertorriqueño* (San Juan, PR: Editorial Cultural, 1990); Ramón Grosfoguel, Frances Negrón-Muntaner, and Chloé S. Georas, "Beyond Nationalist and Colonialist Discourses: The *Jaiba* Politics of the Puerto Rican Ethno-Nation," in *Puerto Rican Jam: Rethinking Colonialism and Nationalism*, ed. Frances Negrón-Muntaner and Ramón Grosfoguel (Minneapolis: University of Minnesota Press, 1997), 1–36; Ramón Grosfoguel, "The Divorce of Nationalist Discourses from the Puerto Rican People," in *Latino/a Thought: Culture, Politics, and Society*, ed. Francisco H. Vázquez (Lanham, MD: Rowman and Littlefield, 2009), 417–37; Lillian Guerra, *Popular Expression and National Identity in Puerto Rico: The Struggle for Self, Community, and Nation* (Gainesville: University Press of Florida, 1998); Alfredo Lopez, *The Puerto Rican Papers; Notes on the Re-Emergence of a Nation* (Indianapolis, IN: Bobbs-Merrill, 1973); Manuel Maldonado-Denis, "The Puerto Ricans: Protest or Submission?" *Annals of the American Academy of Political and Social Science* 382, no. 1 (1969): 26–31; Manuel Maldonado-Denis, *Puerto Rico: A Socio-Historic Interpretation*, trans. Elena Vialo (New York: Vintage Books, 1972); Edwin Meléndez and Edgardo Meléndez, eds., *Colonial Dilemma: Critical Perspectives on Contemporary Puerto Rico* (Boston: South End Press, 1993); Frances Negrón-Muntaner and Ramón Grosfoguel, eds., *Puerto Rican Jam: Rethinking Colonialism and Nationalism* (Minneapolis: University of Minnesota Press, 1997); Frances Negrón-Muntaner, ed., *None of the Above: Puerto Ricans in the Global Era* (New York: Palgrave Macmillan, 2007); Carlos Pabón, *Nación Postmortem: Ensayos Sobre los Tiempos de Insoportable Ambigüedad*, Colección en Fuga. Ensayos (San Juan, PR: Ediciones Callejón, 2002); Ana Y. Ramos-Zayas, *National Performances: The Politics of Class, Race, and Space in Puerto Rican Chicago* (Chicago: University of Chicago Press, 2003); Efrén Rivera Ramos, *The Legal Construction of Identity: The Judicial and Social Legacy of American Colonialism in Puerto Rico* (Washington, DC: American Psychological Association, 2001); Yeidy M. Rivero, *Tuning out Blackness: Race and Nation in the History of Puerto Rican Television* (Durham, NC: Duke University Press, 2005); Kelvin A. Santiago-Valles, "*Subject People*" *and Colonial Discourses: Economic Transformation and Social Disorder in Puerto Rico, 1898–1947* (Albany: State University of New York Press, 1994); Juan Angel Silén, *We, the Puerto Rican People; A Story of Oppression and Resistance* (New York: Monthly Review Press, 1971); Antonio M. Stevens Arroyo, *The Political Philosophy of*

Pedro Albizu Campos: Its Theory and Practice (New York: New York University Ibero-American Language and Area Center, 1974).

2. Andrés Torres and José E. Velázquez, eds., *The Puerto Rican Movement: Voices from the Diaspora* (Philadelphia: Temple University Press, 1998); Carmen Teresa Whalen and Víctor Vázquez-Hernández, eds., *The Puerto Rican Diaspora: Historical Perspectives* (Philadelphia: Temple University Press, 2005).

3. Lorrin Thomas, *Puerto Rican Citizen: History and Political Identity in Twentieth-Century New York City* (Chicago: University of Chicago Press, 2010), 202.

4. I share this skepticism with Thomas. See, for example, Thomas, *Puerto Rican Citizen*, 227. For examples of overstating the influence of the Panthers, see Jeffery O. G. Ogbar, *Black Power: Radical Politics and African American Identity* (Baltimore, MD: Johns Hopkins University Press, 2005); Laura Pulido, *Black, Brown, Yellow, and Left: Radical Activism in Los Angeles* (Berkeley: University of California Press, 2006).

5. Thomas, *Puerto Rican Citizen*, 202–3.

6. Jeffrey O. G. Ogbar, "Puerto Rico en Mi Corazón: The Young Lords, Black Power and Puerto Rican Nationalism in the U.S., 1966–1972," *Centro Journal* 18, no. 1 (2006): 150.

7. Thomas, *Puerto Rican Citizen*, 222.

8. Ibid., 228.

9. Ogbar, "Puerto Rico," 152.

10. I want to be clear about my agreements and disagreements here. Thomas's work is exemplary, especially on matters of the historical record. My disagreement with her lies on interpretive grounds, namely, that I think *coloniality* is a better interpretive frame than *recognition* for narrativizing and conceptualizing the significance of the Young Lords—especially when you acknowledge the uniqueness of "revolutionary nationalism." Her argument is not solely about the Young Lords or nationalism either, and it may be that "recognition" is the best option for thinking broadly about that generation of Nuyorican activists. I have the luxury of focusing on one organization, so I can deploy a more tailored theoretical apparatus. I will address the question of recognition more in the next chapter. As the coming pages will illustrate, however, my differences with Ogbar are more pronounced. Where Thomas documents well the intellectual and rhetorical influences, contexts, and actual discourse of the Young Lords and other Nuyoricans, Ogbar engages too little primary textual evidence. While his argument might hold for the Chicago branch (which is his main source of primary textual evidence), it does not for New York. Furthermore, too interested in his formulation of "radical ethnic nationalism," Ogbar imposes a theoretical apparatus that simply does not fit the Young Lords, especially given the uniqueness of their articulation of "*revolutionary* nationalism."

11. On symbolic agency, see Karlyn Kohrs Campbell, "The Rhetoric of Radical Black Nationalism: A Case Study in Self-Conscious Criticism," *Central States Speech Journal* 22, no. 3 (1971): 151–60. Campbell has also elaborated her thoughts on agency in an often-cited, more recent essay. See Karlyn Kohrs Campbell, "Agency: Promiscuous and Protean," *Communication and Critical/Cultural Studies* 2, no. 1 (2005): 1–19.

12. Decolonial scholars are averse to nationalism. For example, see Ramón Grosfoguel, *Colonial Subjects: Puerto Ricans in a Global Perspective* (Berkeley: University of California Press, 2003). Mignolo seems to be coming around to the productive potential of nationalist claims. In one brief passage, he writes, "Post-nationalism in the West means the end of nationalism, while in the non-European world it means the beginning of a new era in which the concept of nationalism serves to reclaim identities as the basis of state sovereignty." Walter D. Mignolo, *The Darker Side of Western Modernity: Global Futures, Decolonial Options* (Durham, NC: Duke University Press, 2011), 5.

13. Janet Conway and Jakeet Singh, "Radical Democracy in Global Perspective: Notes from the Pluriverse," *Third World Quarterly* 32, no. 4 (2011): 689–706. Mignolo makes a similar argument earlier than Conway and Singh, but their argument is a stronger and more thorough indictment than Mignolo's. See Walter D. Mignolo, "The Zapatista's Theoretical Revolution: Its Historical, Ethical, and Political Consequences," *Review* 25, no. 3 (2002): 245–75.

14. On the "colonial difference," see Nelson Maldonado-Torres, "Postimperial Reflections on Crisis, Knowledge, and Utopia: Transgresstopic Critical Hermeneutics and the 'Death of European Man,'" *Review (Fernand Braudel Center)* 25, no. 3 (2002): 277–315; Walter D. Mignolo, *Local Histories/Global Designs: Coloniality, Subaltern Knowledges, and Border Thinking* (Princeton, NJ: Princeton University Press, 2000), 49–90. In the wake of Maldonado-Torres's critique of Mignolo's earlier formulation of colonial difference, Mignolo backed off of some of his more problematic claims. As such, Maldonado-Torres's revision of the concept is probably more germane.

15. Ogbar, "Puerto Rico," 150–52.

16. Ibid., 152. See also Jyoti Puri, *Encountering Nationalism* (Malden, MA: Blackwell, 2004).

17. Ogbar, "Puerto Rico," 152.

18. Ibid., 157.

19. Also see Ogbar, *Black Power.*

20. Felipe Luciano, *Pa'lante No. 1*, Pacifica Radio Archive BB3583, WBAI broadcast, March 27, 1970.

21. Agustín Laó-Montes, "Mambo Montage: The Latinization of New York City," in *Mambo Montage: The Latinization of New York*, ed. Agustín Laó-Montes and Arlene M. Dávila (New York: Columbia University Press, 2001), 9.

22. Ramos-Zayas, *National Performances*, 19–20.

23. Thomas, *Puerto Rican Citizen*, 227.

24. Ramón A. Gutiérrez, "Internal Colonialism: An American Theory of Race," *Du Bois Review* 1, no. 2 (2004): 282.

25. Ibid., 282.

26. J. Herman Blake, "Black Nationalism," *Annals of the American Academy of Political and Social Science* 382, no. 1 (1969): 23.

27. Harold Cruse, "Revolutionary Nationalism and the Afro-American," in *Rebellion or Revolution?* (Minneapolis: University of Minnesota Press, 2009), 74–75. Cruse's essay originally appeared in *Studies on the Left* 2, no. 3 (1962).

28. Huey P. Newton, "Message at Boston College" (November 18, 1970), E.

29. Blake, "Black Nationalism," 24.

30. William J. Wilson, "Revolutionary Nationalism 'versus' Cultural Nationalism Dimensions of the Black Power Movement," *Sociological Focus* 3, no. 3 (1970): 47.

31. James A. Tyner, "Defend the Ghetto: Space and the Urban Politics of the Black Panther Party," *Annals of the Association of American Geographers* 96, no. 1 (2006): 113.

32. The Black Panthers in New York would, locally, revive a focus on revolutionary nationalism in 1971. After the split in leadership between the Huey Newton–David Hilliard faction (nationally) on the one hand and the Eldridge Cleaver faction (in New York) on the other, the New York chapter began publishing its own newspaper, *Right On!*, in April 1971. Several months later, over the course of three issues in September and October, the New York Panthers published a three-part series titled "On Revolutionary Nationalism." The essays drew from Malcolm X (he "was the theoretician, the architect, the activist of revolutionary nationalism in black america," they claimed), Frantz Fanon, and

various examples of revolutionary nationalist struggles to advance a series of claims about the importance of revolutionary nationalism in the black liberation struggle. Revolutionary nationalism, in their assessment, "gives oppressed people new values and redefines the people's conceptions of life. When organizing in the ghettos, the revolutionary nationalist must understand that Black people have a strong feeling of nationalism. Nationalism must be defined as the feeling among Blacks that whatever affects one Black person ultimately affects all Black people" (*Right On!* 2, no. 4 [1971]: 13). This formulation echoes the Young Lords' historically earlier articulation of revolutionary nationalism, which I address below; but as this quotation illustrates, the Panthers had to engage in more definitional work to craft a sense of nationalism and its importance. The Young Lords, in contrast, had the advantage of a prima facie acceptance (or, at least, recognition) of nationalism among their Puerto Rican audience; and as a result, they did not have to engage in the same kind of persuasive definitional work.

33. Nikhil Pal Singh, *Black Is a Country: Race and the Unfinished Struggle for Democracy* (Cambridge, MA: Harvard University Press, 2004), 198. See also Nikhil Pal Singh, "The Black Panthers and the 'Undeveloped Country' of the Left," in *The Black Panther Party Reconsidered*, ed. Charles E. Jones (Baltimore, MD: Black Classic Press, 1998), 57–105.

34. Thomas, *Puerto Rican Citizen*, 227.

35. Maldonado-Denis, "The Puerto Ricans," 27.

36. Proposal submitted by RGS/UPS to the Ford and Astor Foundations, 1969, p. 4. Quoted in Luis Aponte-Parés, "Lessons from El Barrio—The East Harlem Real Great Society/Urban Planning Studio: A Puerto Rican Chapter in the Fight for Urban Self-Determination," *New Political Science* 20, no. 4 (1998): 409.

37. Thomas, *Puerto Rican Citizen*, 237.

38. Ramos-Zayas, *National Performances*, 19–20.

39. Ibid., 30.

40. Juan Flores, *From Bomba to Hip-Hop: Puerto Rican Culture and Latino Identity* (New York: Columbia University Press, 2000), 38.

41. Aníbal Quijano, "Coloniality and Modernity/Rationality," *Cultural Studies* 21, no. 2–3 (2007): 169. See also Nelson Maldonado-Torres, "On the Coloniality of Being: Contributions to the Development of a Concept," *Cultural Studies* 21, no. 2–3 (2007): 240–70; Mignolo, *Local Histories*; Walter D. Mignolo, "Delinking: The Rhetoric of Modernity, the Logic of Coloniality and the Grammar of De-Coloniality," *Cultural Studies* 21, no. 2–3 (2007): 449–514.

42. Grosfoguel, *Colonial Subjects*, 9.

43. Campbell, "Rhetoric of Black Nationalism," 155.

44. Mignolo, "Delinking," 492.

45. See Kevin DeLuca, "Articulation Theory: A Discursive Grounding for Rhetorical Practice," *Philosophy and Rhetoric* 32, no. 4 (1999): 334–48; Ernesto Laclau and Chantal Mouffe, *Hegemony and Socialist Strategy: Towards a Radical Democratic Practice* (London: Verso, 2001).

46. Mariana Ortega and Linda Martín Alcoff, "Introduction: The Race of Nationalism," in *Constructing the Nation: A Race and Nationalism Reader*, ed. Mariana Ortega and Linda Martín Alcoff (Albany: State University of New York Press, 2009), 4.

47. On the "rhetorical situation" and exigency, see Barbara A. Biesecker, "Rethinking the Rhetorical Situation from within the Thematic of *Différence*," *Philosophy and Rhetoric* 22 (1989): 110–30; Lloyd F. Bitzer, "The Rhetorical Situation," *Philosophy and Rhetoric* 1, no. 1 (1968): 1–14; Richard E. Vatz, "The Myth of the Rhetorical Situation," in *Contemporary*

Rhetorical Theory: A Reader, ed. John Louis Lucaites, Celeste Michelle Condit, and Sally Caudill (New York: Guilford Press, 1999), 226–31.

48. Felipe Luciano, "On Revolutionary Nationalism," *Palante* 2, no. 2 (1970): 10–11.

49. Gloria Gonzalez, "Protracted War in Puerto Rico," in *The Ideology of the Young Lords Party* (New York, February 1972), 17.

50. Denise Oliver, "Colonized Mentality and Non-Conscious Ideology," in *The Ideology of the Young Lords Party,* 26–27.

51. There is a, perhaps obvious, Foucauldian dimension to the power relations that the Young Lords engaged (or in my description of it). Michel Foucault, "The Subject and Power," in *Power: Essential Works of Foucault, 1954–1984,* ed. James D Faubion and Paul Rabinow (New York: New Press, 2000), 326–48.

52. Quijano, "Coloniality and Modernity/Rationality," 169.

53. Oliver, "Colonized Mentality," 27, emphasis added.

54. Luciano, "On Revolutionary Nationalism," 10–11.

55. Felipe Luciano, "Felipe on Political and Armed Struggle," *Palante* 2, no. 8 (1970): 11.

56. Ibid., 11.

57. Luciano, "On Revolutionary Nationalism," 10–11.

58. Max Elbaum, *Revolution in the Air: Sixties Radicals Turn to Lenin, Mao and Che* (London: Verso, 2002).

59. Miriam Jimenez Román, "Un Hombre (Negro) del Pueblo: José Celso Barbosa and the Puerto Rican 'Race' toward Whiteness," *Centro Journal* 8, no. 1–2 (1996): 9.

60. Iris Morales, "¡PALANTE, SIEMPRE PALANTE! The Young Lords," in Torres and Velázquez, *The Puerto Rican Movement,* 219.

61. Oliver, "Colonized Mentality," 28.

62. Iris Morales Luciano, "Puerto Rican Racism," *Palante* 2, no. 7 (1970): 6.

63. Ibid., 7.

64. Ibid.

65. Ibid.

66. Oliver, "Colonized Mentality," 28.

67. Ibid., 29.

68. Freya Schiwy, "Decolonization and the Question of Subjectivity: Gender, Race, and Binary Thinking," *Cultural Studies* 21, no. 2–3 (2007): 274.

69. On the politics of sexuality in Puerto Rican contexts, see Eileen J. Suárez Findlay, *Imposing Decency: The Politics of Sexuality and Race in Puerto Rico, 1870–1920* (Durham, NC: Duke University Press, 1999). On infantilization, see Santiago-Valles, *Subject People.*

70. Oliver, "Colonized Mentality," 31.

71. Ibid., 32.

72. Luciano, "On Revolutionary Nationalism," 10–11.

73. Ibid.

74. Kenneth Burke, "Literature as Equipment for Living," in *The Philosophy of Literary Form* (Berkeley: University of California Press, 1973), 293–304.

75. Pablo "Yoruba" Guzmán quoted in Young Lords Party and Michael Abramson, *Palante: Young Lords Party* (New York: McGraw-Hill, 1971), 83.

76. Chela Sandoval, *Methodology of the Oppressed* (Minneapolis: University of Minnesota Press, 2000).

77. Grosfoguel, *Colonial Subjects,* 9.

78. Denise Oliver, "Yanquis Own Puerto Rico," *Palante* 2, no. 17 (1970): 7.

79. Luciano, "On Revolutionary Nationalism," 10–11.

80. Luciano, "Political and Armed Struggle," 11.

81. Mignolo, *Local Histories*, 49–90.

82. Campbell, "Rhetoric of Black Nationalism," 155.

83. Juan Gonzalez, "The Vote or the Gun," *Palante* 2, no. 3 (1970): 10–11.

84. Most scholars would probably point to Deleuze as the origin, or at least inspiration, for their use of this phrase. Gilles Deleuze, *Difference and Repetition*, trans. Paul Patton (New York: Columbia University Press, 1994). I, however, am more inclined to think about repetition and difference within the black imaginary of the time. See, for example, Nealon's engagement of Amiri Baraka, which turns to DuBois, Gates, Baraka, and others, in addition to Deleuze. Jeffrey T. Nealon, "Refraining, Becoming-Black: Repetition and Difference in Amiri Baraka's Blues People," *symplokē* 6, no. 1–2 (1998): 83–95.

85. Sandoval, *Methodology of the Oppressed*, 44.

86. Ibid., 60.

87. José Esteban Muñoz, *Disidentifications: Queers of Color and the Performance of Politics* (Minneapolis: University of Minnesota Press, 1999).

88. Felipe Luciano quoted in Young Lords Party and Abramson, *Palante: Young Lords Party*, 31. I mention their general take on compatibility in Chapter 1.

89. Guzmán quoted in ibid., 80.

90. Benedict R. Anderson, *Imagined Communities: Reflections on the Origin and Spread of Nationalism* (London: Verso, 1991).

91. The earliest printed usage of "amerikkka" by the Young Lords appears in the first fully typeset and properly printed edition (on tabloid-sized news stock) of their newspaper, *Palante*, in New York City on May 8, 1970 (volume 2, issue 2). The term is used in Luciano's "On Revolutionary Nationalism" and in the "13 Point Program and Platform," which is dated October 1969. Whether "amerikkka" was originally in the Program and Platform in October 1969 is hard to tell because there are no known surviving copies prior to the aforementioned edition of *Palante*. It is also hard to determine precisely where and from whom the term originated. By January 1970, for example, the Black Panthers used the term extensively in an essay published in their newspaper, *The Black Panther*. See Landon Williams, "The Black Panther: Mirror of the People," in *The Black Panthers Speak*, ed. Philip S. Foner (Cambridge, MA: De Capo Press, 2002), 8–14. But it is otherwise hard to determine an origin more precise than somewhere in the Third World Left, sometime between mid-1969 and early 1970. By mid-1970, the term was in widespread use throughout the white and Third World Left across the United States.

92. Guzmán quoted in Young Lords Party and Abramson, *Palante: Young Lords Party*, 80.

93. Luciano, "On Revolutionary Nationalism," 10–11.

94. Guzmán quoted in Young Lords Party and Abramson, *Palante: Young Lords Party*, 83.

95. See Frantz Fanon, *The Wretched of the Earth*, trans. Constance Farrington (New York: Grove Press, 1963).

96. Ibid., 311.

97. Schiwy, "Decolonization," 275.

98. Oliver, "Colonized Mentality," 32.

99. Mignolo, "Delinking," 492. Mignolo's terminological inversion is from "a *politics based on identity*" to "an *identity based on politics*."

100. Juan "Fi" Ortiz, "The Party and the Individual," in *The Ideology of the Young Lords Party*, 37.

101. Ibid., 38.

102. Ibid.
103. Ibid., 39.
104. Oliver, "Colonized Mentality," 28.
105. Ibid., 32.
106. Luciano, "On Revolutionary Nationalism," 10–11.
107. Mignolo, "Delinking," 494.
108. Ibid., 497.
109. Ibid., 493.
110. Grosfoguel, *Colonial Subjects*, 62.

CHAPTER 3

1. Maylei Blackwell, *¡Chicana Power! Contested Histories of Feminism in the Chicano Movement* (Austin: University of Texas Press, 2011); Elaine Brown, *A Taste of Power: A Black Woman's Story* (New York: Pantheon, 1992); Alma M. García, *Chicana Feminist Thought: The Basic Historical Writings* (New York: Routledge, 1997); Karl Knapper and Angela Brown, "Women and the Black Panther Party," *Socialist Review* 26, no. 1–2 (1996): 33–67; Jennifer A. Nelson, "'Abortions under Community Control': Feminism, Nationalism, and the Politics of Reproduction among New York City's Young Lords," *Journal of Women's History* 13, no. 1 (2001): 157–80.

2. Gays and lesbians were at an even greater disadvantage largely because their voices threatened stable notions of masculinity and femininity.

3. Nelson, "'Abortions under Community Control,'" 161. The reasons were varied and included specific issues (e.g., health, housing, and police brutality) and the desire to be in a progressive, grassroots political organization.

4. Ibid.

5. Ibid. Nelson's account is the best, but it leaves out crucial details that I discuss later.

6. Marianne Hirsch and Valerie Smith, "Feminism and Cultural Memory: An Introduction," *Signs* 28 (2002): 6.

7. Kristen Hoerl, "Selective Amnesia and Racial Transcendence in News Coverage of President Obama's Inauguration," *Quarterly Journal of Speech* 98, no. 2 (2012): 181.

8. I use the term "protofeminist" here and "feminist" elsewhere very reluctantly. From an analytical perspective, we can look back at what the Young Lords did as being consistent with some kind of feminism. At the time, however, some women were reluctant to use the label and identify with feminism as such because (a) they felt it enforced division between the sexes and (b) feminism as a political project had been dominated by liberal white women. On the suspicion of white feminisms, see bell hooks, *Feminist Theory: From Margin to Center* (Boston: South End Press, 1984). Chicana feminists made similar critiques. For examples, see García, *Chicana Feminist Thought*. And for broader U.S. Third World feminist critiques of hegemonic Western feminism, see Chela Sandoval, "U.S. Third World Feminism: The Theory and Method of Oppositional Consciousness in the Postmodern World," *Genders* 10 (1991): 1–24; Chela Sandoval, *Methodology of the Oppressed* (Minneapolis: University of Minnesota Press, 2000).

9. Blackwell, *Chicana Power*, 10. On archive and repertoire, see Diana Taylor, *The Archive and the Repertoire: Performing Cultural Memory in the Americas* (Durham, NC: Duke University Press, 2003).

10. According to the Latina Feminist Group, "*Testimonio* is often seen as a form of expression that comes out of intense repression or struggle, where the person bearing

witness tells the story to someone else, who then transcribes, edits, translates, and publishes the text elsewhere." See Latina Feminist Group, "Introduction: *Papelitos Guardados: Theorizing Latinidades* through *Testimonio*," in *Telling to Live: Latina Feminist Testimonios*, ed. Latina Feminist Group (Durham, NC: Duke University Press, 2001), 13.

11. Aimee Carrillo Rowe, *Power Lines: On the Subject of Feminist Alliances* (Durham, NC: Duke University Press, 2008).

12. Linda Alcoff, "The Problem of Speaking for Others," *Cultural Critique*, no. 20 (1991): 5–32.

13. Whenever I align "macho" with an ontological position, I am still meaning to use it as a term referencing performance. Macho, masculinity, femininity—all possible gendered subject positions are always performed.

14. Denise Oliver-Velez, interview by author, New York, May 24, 2004.

15. Ibid.

16. Iris Morales, interview by author, New York, May 26, 2004.

17. María Lugones, "Heterosexualism and the Colonial/Modern Gender System," *Hypatia* 22, no. 1 (2007): 186–219; María Lugones, "Toward a Decolonial Feminism," *Hypatia* 25, no. 4 (2010): 742–59; Freya Schiwy, "Decolonization and the Question of Subjectivity: Gender, Race, and Binary Thinking," *Cultural Studies* 21, no. 2–3 (2007): 271–94.

18. Oliver-Velez, interview by author, May 24, 2004.

19. Olguie Robles, interview by author, New York, May 24, 2004.

20. Morales, interview by author, May 26, 2004.

21. Oliver-Velez, interview by author, May 24, 2004.

22. Robles, interview by author, May 24, 2004.

23. Kelly Oliver, "Beyond Recognition: Witnessing Ethics," *Philosophy Today* 44, no. 1 (2000): 41.

24. Oliver-Velez, interview by author, May 24, 2004. By "Third World women," Oliver references the broad spectrum of women of color whose oppressions are rooted in some important ways in relationships of coloniality.

25. On transhistorical narratives and their centrality to constituting subjects, see Maurice Charland, "Constitutive Rhetoric: The Case of the Peuple Québécois," *Quarterly Journal of Speech* 73, no. 2 (1987): 133–50.

26. Denise Oliver-Velez, interview by author, New York, October 20, 2004.

27. Oliver-Velez, interview by author, May 24, 2004.

28. Discipline was handed down by the central committee and included reading and copying (by hand) Marxist texts. While this may not seem like a harsh form of discipline, it was added to an already full daily schedule, which meant that it traded off with time that had been reserved for sleep and family.

29. Oliver-Velez, interview by author, May 24, 2004.

30. Ibid. It is important to note the deep distrust of the dominant (white) feminist politics of the time, something that continued beyond that moment. For a productive engagement of some of those tensions, see hooks, *Feminist Theory*, 1–15.

31. Oliver-Velez, interview by author, May 24, 2004.

32. Oliver-Velez, interview by author, October 20, 2004.

33. Ibid.

34. Ibid.

35. Oliver-Velez, interview by author, May 24, 2004.

36. Oliver-Velez, interview by author, October 20, 2004.

37. Ibid.

38. Basically, several members of the Central Committee had been out partying and, allegedly, womanizing.

39. Oliver-Velez, interview by author, October 20, 2004.

40. Ibid.

41. The two existent accounts are offered by historian Jennifer Nelson and founding Young Lord Mickey Melendez. Nelson's account is good but light on details regarding the transition explained here. Melendez's account is more seriously flawed. In his entire book, one paragraph is devoted to the struggle for gender equity within the organization; and his account only details an agreement of principles made by the Central Committee some time before the climactic events I am describing here. See Nelson, "'Abortions under Community Control,'" 157–80; Miguel Melendez, *We Took the Streets: Fighting for Latino Rights with the Young Lords* (New York: St. Martin's Press, 2003).

42. Oliver-Velez, interview by author, October 20, 2004.

43. Morales, interview by author, New York, 26 May 2004.

44. Oliver-Velez, interview by author, May 24, 2004.

45. Mickey Melendez, interview by author, New York, May 25, 2004.

46. Robles, interview by author, May 24, 2004.

47. Jorge Matos, formerly a research librarian from the Center for Puerto Rican Studies, deserves thanks for this insight.

48. The Puerto Rican Left appropriated this image in the 1950s and 1960s in a manner that gave the races more agency and called into question the "harmonious mixing" espoused by the government.

49. For years, I had read this figure as male—as had each person to whom I ever showed the image. Friend and colleague Marianne Bueno questioned this interpretation when discussing a draft of this chapter. From those discussions, I came to read the figure as androgynous; but I have decided not to make too much of this point in terms of a gender performativity because I do not have other evidence to support the argument. On close inspection, especially when compared with Figure 3.1 and Figure 3.3, I think the ambiguity of the illustrated figure's sex is hard to deny; so it seems worth entertaining the question of representation in the chapter text.

50. For a recent scholarly engagement of the symbolic force of the jíbaro, see Nathaniel I. Córdova, "The Constitutive Force of the *Catecismo del Pueblo* in Puerto Rico's Popular Democratic Party Campaign of 1938–1940," *Quarterly Journal of Speech* 90, no. 2 (2004): 212–33.

51. Nelson Maldonado-Torres, *Against War: Views from the Underside of Modernity* (Durham, NC: Duke University Press, 2008), 133.

52. Lolita Lebrón solidified the phrase's place in history when she became one of the most iconic figures of Nationalist Party politics that day. This interpretation of the link between the image and the phrase is supported further by the text inside the issue, which I will discuss shortly.

53. In some early Chicano filmic representations, women are objectified through a visual linkage to Aztlán. See Rosa Linda Fregoso, *The Bronze Screen: Chicana and Chicano Film Culture* (Minneapolis: University of Minnesota Press, 1993). As I discussed in Chapter 2, for the Young Lords, Puerto Rico did not serve a similar symbolic or libidinal function as Aztlán did for Chicanos. For island-linked nationalists, it may have functioned similarly; but for the Young Lords of 1970, it did not.

54. Although one could posit the genocide of Taínos as an irony in my read, at this point in history the Young Lords had done substantial work to elevate the status of Taínos in the cultural imaginary.

55. Central Committee, "Young Lords Party Position Paper on Women," *Palante* 2, no. 12 (1970): 11–14. Hereafter, all references will be in text.

56. Nelson's work is an exemplary analysis of the Young Lords' reproductive politics in its historical context. Nelson, "'Abortions under Community Control,'" 157–80.

57. It is worth noting that the version published in *Palante* contains a major typesetting error that makes this final section of the PPW somewhat nonsensical because things appear out of order. A republished version in my *The Young Lords: A Reader* has been corrected.

58. Such an either/or mentality was partially endemic of various cultural nationalisms, including MEChA's at this time. See Blackwell, *Chicana Power*; Carlos Muñoz, *Youth, Identity, Power: The Chicano Movement* (London: Verso, 2007); Emma Pérez, *The Decolonial Imaginary: Writing Chicanas into History* (Bloomington: Indiana University Press, 1999).

59. See Muñoz, *Youth, Identity, Power*. Blackwell documents well the emergence of women's voices, particularly Hijas de Cuauhtémoc, within the Chicano movement. See Blackwell, *Chicana Power*.

60. For other examples, see Max Elbaum, *Revolution in the Air: Sixties Radicals Turn to Lenin, Mao and Che* (London: Verso, 2002).

61. Maldonado-Torres, *Against War*, 243.

62. Walter D. Mignolo, *The Darker Side of Western Modernity: Global Futures, Decolonial Options* (Durham, NC: Duke University Press, 2011), 80.

63. Lugones, "Heterosexualism," 188. See also Lugones, "Toward a Decolonial Feminism."

64. Kelly Oliver, *Witnessing: Beyond Recognition* (Minneapolis: University of Minnesota Press, 2001), 18–19.

65. Young Lords Party and Michael Abramson, *Palante: Young Lords Party* (New York: McGraw-Hill, 1971), 53, emphasis in original.

66. Ibid., 54.

67. Ibid., emphasis added.

68. Mignolo, *The Darker Side*, 23–24.

69. Ibid., 122–23.

70. Ibid., 123.

71. Young Lords Party and Abramson, *Palante: Young Lords Party*, 56.

72. Maldonado-Torres, *Against War*, 244.

73. Ibid., 151.

74. Judith Butler, *Gender Trouble: Feminism and the Subversion of Identity* (New York: Routledge, 1990), 14.

75. Young Lords Party and Abramson, *Palante: Young Lords Party*, 46.

76. Ibid.

77. Similar critiques of dominant second-wave feminism are not uncommon. For example, see hooks, *Feminist Theory*; Sandoval, "U.S. Third World Feminism," 1–24.

78. On intersectionality, see Kimberle Crenshaw, "Demarginalizing the Intersection of Race and Sex: A Black Feminist Critique of Antidiscrimination Doctrine, Feminist Theory, and Antiracist Politics," *University of Chicago Legal Forum* 1989 (1989): 139–67; Kimberle Crenshaw, "Mapping the Margins: Intersectionality, Identity Politics, and Violence against Women of Color," *Stanford Law Review* 43 (1991): 1241–99.

79. Young Lords Party and Abramson, *Palante: Young Lords Party*, 46.

80. Ibid.

81. Ibid., 47, emphasis added.

82. Evidence of uptake for this sensibility is mixed. On the one hand, as I demonstrate subsequently, there was enough uptake to create a safe and productive space for LGBTQ activists like Sylvia Rivera. On the other hand, as with sexism directed toward women, some men had a hard time adapting. Little else was written on these issues after the *Palante* book was published, in part because of a shift in organizational focus to class issues with the transformation from the Young Lords to the Puerto Rican Revolutionary Workers Organization in 1972.

83. Frantz Fanon, *Black Skin, White Masks*, trans. Charles Lam Markmann (New York: Grove Press, 1967), 8.

84. This, too, was a move at odds with mainstream feminism, which was receiving a lot of criticism from lesbian communities for ignoring their personal and political needs.

85. Sylvia Rivera and Leslie Feinberg, "An Interview with Sylvia Rivera," July 2, 1998, available at http://www.signalfire.org/articles.php?detail=1&detailID=25.

86. Lorrin Thomas, *Puerto Rican Citizen: History and Political Identity in Twentieth-Century New York City* (Chicago: University of Chicago Press, 2010), 202–3.

87. Walter D. Mignolo, "The Geopolitics of Knowledge and the Colonial Difference," *South Atlantic Quarterly* 101, no. 1 (2002): 66.

88. Maldonado-Torres, *Against War*, 149.

89. On monotopic and pluritopic hermeneutics, see Nelson Maldonado-Torres, "Postimperial Reflections on Crisis, Knowledge, and Utopia: Transgresstopic Critical Hermeneutics and the 'Death of European Man,'" *Review (Fernand Braudel Center)* 25, no. 3 (2002): 277–315.

90. Maldonado-Torres, *Against War*, 230.

CHAPTER 4

1. Gonzalez, quoted in Miguel Melendez, *We Took the Streets: Fighting for Latino Rights with the Young Lords* (New York: St. Martin's Press, 2003), 94.

2. Pablo "Yoruba" Guzmán, "One Year of Struggle," *Palante* (1970): 12–13.

3. Darrel Enck-Wanzer, "Trashing the System: Social Movement, Intersectional Rhetoric, and Collective Agency in the Young Lords Organization's Garbage Offensive," *Quarterly Journal of Speech* 92, no. 2 (2006): 174–201. This argument about intersectional rhetoric was central to my early work about the Young Lords and social movement. I take it as a starting assumption in this chapter and focus attention on the practices of delinking in this instance of struggle.

4. Quoted in Cheryl Geisler, "How Ought We to Understand the Concept of Rhetorical Agency," *Rhetoric Society Quarterly* 34, no. 3 (2004): 13.

5. I am thinking of different social movement organizations that do not operate principally through speech or writing. This might include different feminist, LGBTQ, or environmental movement organizations.

6. Joseph P. Fried, "East Harlem Youths Explain Garbage-Dumping Demonstration," *New York Times*, August 19, 1969, 86.

7. Pablo Guzmán, "La Vida Pura: A Lord of the Barrio," in *The Puerto Rican Movement: Voices from the Diaspora*, ed. Andrés Torres and José E. Velázquez (Philadelphia: Temple University Press, 1998), 155.

8. This means of going out into the community taps into a tradition of "community organizing" at least as old as Saul Alinsky's work in the 1930s. Although not published until after the "garbage offensive," see Saul David Alinsky, *Rules for Radicals: A Practical Primer for Realistic Radicals* (New York: Random House, 1971). This tactic was certainly

similar to those used by SNCC in the South and SDS in New York and New Jersey in the 1960s (Juan Gonzalez, as mentioned previously, had been active in SDS leadership at Columbia before helping form the Lords).

9. Quoted in Melendez, *We Took the Streets*, 95.

10. Ibid., 96.

11. Felipe Luciano, *Pa'lante No. 1*, Pacifica Radio Archive BB3583, WBAI broadcast, March 27, 1970. The Pacifica Radio Archive has catalogued this source as "*Pa'lante*," which is the grammatically correct spelling of the term (because it is a contraction); however, the Young Lords always omitted the apostrophe for the radio program, newspaper, etc. In the text, I use the spelling the Young Lords used, but I cite it as the archive does.

12. Please see my discussion of garbage and the RGS in Chapter 1. Although the Young Lords never acknowledge explicitly learning the tactic from others, there is evidence that the RGS engaged in garbage protests earlier than the Young Lords. This is also discussed in Luis Aponte-Parés, "Lessons from El Barrio—The East Harlem Real Great Society/Urban Planning Studio: A Puerto Rican Chapter in the Fight for Urban Self-Determination," *New Political Science* 20, no. 4 (1998): 399–420.

13. Nelson Maldonado-Torres, *Against War: Views from the Underside of Modernity* (Durham, NC: Duke University Press, 2008), 246.

14. Ibid.

15. Lisbeth Lipari, "Rhetoric's Other: Levinas, Listening, and the Ethical Response," *Philosophy and Rhetoric* 45, no. 3 (2012): 228.

16. Maldonado-Torres, drawing from Chela Sandoval and Fanon, argues, "Decolonial love is positive, and not, like traditional conceptions of critique, only negative." Maldonado-Torres, *Against War*, 157.

17. Frantz Fanon, *Black Skin, White Masks*, trans. Charles Lam Markmann (New York: Grove Press, 1967), 8.

18. Maldonado-Torres, *Against War*, 158.

19. Kelly Oliver, *Witnessing: Beyond Recognition* (Minneapolis: University of Minnesota Press, 2001), 18.

20. Ibid., 20.

21. Ibid., 217.

22. Luciano, *Pa'lante No. 1*.

23. Diana Taylor, *The Archive and the Repertoire: Performing Cultural Memory in the Americas* (Durham, NC: Duke University Press, 2003).

24. The closest they come is in volume one, issue four, where there are several small news pieces about the garbage offensive. Even here, however, the narrative remains fragmented, disjointed, and (by nature of there being several pieces) repetitive. A slightly more refined narrative is recounted by Luciano on their radio program. See Luciano, *Pa'lante No. 1*.

25. Dwight Conquergood, "Performance Studies: Interventions and Radical Research," *Drama Review* 46, no. 2 (2002): 146.

26. See Michael Calvin McGee, "Text, Context, and the Fragmentation of Contemporary Culture," *Western Journal of Speech Communication* 54 (1990): 274–89. Also see Kevin DeLuca, *Image Politics: The New Rhetoric of Environmental Activism* (New York: Guilford Press, 1999), 147–55.

27. "El Barrio and the YLO Say No More Garbage in Our Community," *Y.L.O.* 1, no. 4 (1969): 19.

28. Quoted in Matthew Gandy, *Concrete and Clay: Reworking Nature in New York City* (Cambridge, MA: MIT Press, 2002), 165–66.

29. Guzmán, "One Year," 12.

30. Taylor, *Archive and the Repertoire*, 5. For an account of the narrative and an attendant critique of docility, see Juan Flores, *Divided Borders: Essays on Puerto Rican Identity* (Houston, TX: Arte Publico Press, 1992), 13–60.

31. Guzmán, quoted in Young Lords Party and Michael Abramson, *Palante: Young Lords Party* (New York: McGraw-Hill, 1971), 75.

32. DeLuca uses "mind bomb" to reference the explosive psychological effect image events (staged activist moments that garner media attention and function constitutively even when they fail instrumentally) have on collective consciousness. DeLuca, *Image Politics*, 1–22.

33. Guzmán, "One Year," 12.

34. Melendez, *We Took the Streets*, 105.

35. Luciano, *Pa'lante No. 1*.

36. Ministry of Information, "Pigs Oink in Fear as YLO and the People March thru the Streets," *Palante* 1, no. 4 (1969): 17.

37. Luciano, *Pa'lante No. 1*.

38. Quoted in "El Barrio and the YLO Say No More Garbage," 19.

39. Guzmán, "One Year," 12.

40. Talk about the Young Lords as constructing a space is meant to draw attention to two things: first, the Young Lords redefined the barrioscape to make it an acceptable location for contestation and dissent; second, and more important, the Young Lords helped to constitute a "people" who could, contrary to popular and academic characterizations, *be political* (an agentic change). As such, my position is fairly in line with Michel de Certeau's explanation of space as "practiced place." See Michel de Certeau, *The Practice of Everyday Life* (Berkeley: University of California Press, 1984), 117.

41. Johanna Fernandez, "Between Social Service Reform and Revolutionary Politics: The Young Lords, Late Sixties Radicalism, and Community Organizing in New York City," in *Freedom North: Black Freedom Struggles outside the South, 1940–1980*, ed. Jeanne F. Theoharis and Komozi Woodward (New York: Palgrave Macmillan, 2003), 255–85.

42. Luciano, *Pa'lante No. 1*.

43. Carl Davidson, "Young Lords Organize in New York," *Guardian* (October 18, 1969): 6.

44. Melendez, *We Took the Streets*, 109. I am not oversimplifying Melendez's account here. This is as far as his read of the purpose and significance of the garbage offensive goes.

45. Agustín Laó, "Resources of Hope: Imagining the Young Lords and the Politics of Memory," *CENTRO: Journal of the Center for Puerto Rican Studies* 7, no. 1 (1995): 37.

46. Ibid.

47. Guzmán, "One Year," 12, emphasis added.

48. A survey of the primary literature on Black Power, the Black Panther Party, Students for a Democratic Society, and others makes this evident. See Max Elbaum, *Revolution in the Air: Sixties Radicals Turn to Lenin, Mao and Che* (London: Verso, 2002). By "devil figure," I allude to Richard Weaver's notion of an ultimate term that carries a negative force. A "devil term" is the dialectical counterpart to a "god term," which Weaver defines as "that expression about which all other expressions are ranked as subordinate and serving dominations and powers." Richard M. Weaver, *The Ethics of Rhetoric* (Davis, CA: Hermagoras Press, 1985), 212.

49. Herbert Marcuse, *One-Dimensional Man* (Boston: Beacon Press, 1964).

50. Iris Morales, "¡PALANTE, SIEMPRE PALANTE! The Young Lords," in Torres and Velázquez, *Puerto Rican Movement*, 213.

51. "Presence" is usually talked about in terms of verbal discourse drawing attention to something. In the case of the Young Lords, however, images and embodied acts also function symbolically to create presence. For more on presence, see Chaïm Perelman and Lucie Olbrechts-Tyteca, *The New Rhetoric: A Treatise on Argumentation* (Notre Dame, IN: University of Notre Dame Press, 1971), 119–20. In many ways, *The New Rhetoric* largely is about the relationship between presence and argumentation. I am also particularly indebted to Phaedra Pezzulo's work on presence in the context of environmental justice.

52. Phaedra C. Pezzullo, *Toxic Tourism: Rhetorics of Pollution, Travel, and Environmental Justice* (Tuscaloosa: University of Alabama Press, 2009), 9.

53. This, in part, is what led Edwin Black to critique neo-Aristotelian critics; and it is certainly part of Maurice Charland's motivation behind his work on the Québécois. See Edwin Black, *Rhetorical Criticism: A Study in Method* (Madison: University of Wisconsin Press, 1965); Maurice Charland, "Constitutive Rhetoric: The Case of the Peuple Québécois," *Quarterly Journal of Speech* 73, no. 2 (1987): 133–50.

54. Charland, "Constitutive Rhetoric," 133–50. See also Barbara A. Biesecker, "Rethinking the Rhetorical Situation from within the Thematic of *Différence*," *Philosophy and Rhetoric* 22 (1989): 110–30; Ronald Walter Greene, "The Aesthetic Turn and the Rhetorical Perspective on Argumentation," *Argumentation and Advocacy* 35, no. 1 (1998): 19–29; Michael C. McGee, "In Search of 'the People': A Rhetorical Alternative," *Quarterly Journal of Speech* 61 (1975): 235–49; Michael Calvin McGee, "The 'Ideograph': A Link between Rhetoric and Ideology," *Quarterly Journal of Speech* 66 (1980): 1–16; Michael Calvin McGee, "On Feminized Liberty," in *Van Zelst Lecture* (Evanston, IL: Northwestern University School of Speech, May, 1985), 1–31.

55. José Esteban Muñoz, "Feeling Brown: Ethnicity and Affect in Ricardo Bracho's *The Sweetest Hangover (and Other STDs)*," *Theatre Journal* 52, no. 1 (2000): 72.

56. Ramón Grosfoguel, Frances Negrón-Muntaner, and Chloé S. Georas, "Beyond Nationalist and Colonialist Discourses: The *Jaiba* Politics of the Puerto Rican Ethno-Nation," in *Puerto Rican Jam: Rethinking Colonialism and Nationalism*, ed. Frances Negrón-Muntaner and Ramón Grosfoguel (Minneapolis: University of Minnesota Press, 1997), 30–31.

57. Ibid., 31.

58. Luciano, *Pa'lante No. 1*.

59. For an analysis of Puerto Ricans' modern colonial status see Ramón Grosfoguel, *Colonial Subjects: Puerto Ricans in a Global Perspective* (Berkeley: University of California Press, 2003), 4–5.

60. Kenneth Burke, "Definition of Man," in *Language as Symbolic Action: Essays on Life, Literature, and Method* (Berkeley: University of California Press, 1966), 3–24.

61. Taylor, *Archive and Repertoire*, 29.

62. Lisa A. Flores, "Creating Discursive Space through a Rhetoric of Difference: Chicana Feminists Craft a Homeland," *Quarterly Journal of Speech* 82, no. 2 (1996): 153, emphasis added.

63. Raka Shome, "Space Matters: The Power and Practice of Space," *Communication Theory* 13, no. 1 (2003): 42.

64. Walter D. Mignolo, "Delinking: The Rhetoric of Modernity, the Logic of Coloniality and the Grammar of De-coloniality," *Cultural Studies* 21, no. 2–3 (2007): 494.

65. Darrel Enck-Wanzer, "Tropicalizing East Harlem: Rhetorical Agency, Cultural Citizenship, and Nuyorican Cultural Production," *Communication Theory* 21, no. 4 (2011): 352.

66. Ibid. The quotation is from Frances R. Aparicio and Susana Chávez-Silverman, "Introduction," in *Tropicalizations: Transcultural Representations of Latinidad*, ed. Frances R. Aparicio and Susana Chávez-Silverman (Hanover, NH: University Press of New England, 1997), 12.

67. Lisa A. Flores and Mark Lawrence McPhail, "From Black and White to *Living Color*: A Dialogic Exposition into the Social (Re)construction of Race, Gender, and Crime," *Critical Studies in Mass Communication* 14, no. 1 (1997): 116–17.

68. By interpellation, I refer to the process of subjectivization whereby one accepts a hail (an invitation) to identify with and/or embody a particular subject position. For example, see Louis Althusser, "Ideology and Ideological State Apparatuses (Notes towards an Investigation)," in *Mapping Ideology*, ed. Slavoj Žižek (London: Verso, 1994), 100–140.

69. Walter D. Mignolo, *The Darker Side of Western Modernity: Global Futures, Decolonial Options* (Durham, NC: Duke University Press, 2011), 80.

70. Nominalism—the critical praxis of naming and challenging or elucidating definitions—is laid out by Raymie McKerrow in his work on critical rhetoric and received uptake by others. See, for example, Raymie E. McKerrow, "Critical Rhetoric: Theory and Praxis," *Communication Monographs* 56, no. 2 (1989): 91–111; Raymie E. McKerrow, "Critical Rhetoric in a Postmodern World," *Quarterly Journal of Speech* 77, no. 1 (1991): 75–78; Thomas K. Nakayama and Robert L. Krizek, "Whiteness: A Strategic Rhetoric," *Quarterly Journal of Speech* 81, no. 3 (1995): 291–309. For a particularly astute critique of such critical praxis in the context of critical whiteness studies, see Robyn Wiegman, "Whiteness Studies and the Paradox of Particularity," *Boundary 2* 26, no. 3 (1999): 115–50.

71. Ronald Walter Greene and Kevin Douglas Kuswa, "'From the Arab Spring to Athens, from Occupy Wall Street to Moscow': Regional Accents and the Rhetorical Cartography of Power," *Rhetoric Society Quarterly* 42, no. 3 (2012): 273.

CHAPTER 5

1. Johanna Fernandez, "Between Social Service Reform and Revolutionary Politics: The Young Lords, Late Sixties Radicalism, and Community Organizing in New York City," in *Freedom North: Black Freedom Struggles outside the South, 1940–1980*, ed. Jeanne F. Theoharis and Komozi Woodward (New York: Palgrave Macmillan, 2003), 255–85; Jack Newfield, "Young Lords Do City's Work in the Barrio," *Village Voice* (December 4, 1969): 1+.

2. Quoted in Robert L. Wilson, *The First Spanish Methodist Church and the Young Lords* (New York: United Methodist Church, 1970), 15.

3. Quotations are from Michael C. McGee, "In Search of 'the People': A Rhetorical Alternative," *Quarterly Journal of Speech* 61 (1975): 242 and 249, emphasis in original. See also Maurice Charland, "Constitutive Rhetoric: The Case of the Peuple Québécois," *Quarterly Journal of Speech* 73, no. 2 (1987): 133–50; Fernando Pedro Delgado, "Chicano Movement Rhetoric: An Ideographic Interpretation," *Communication Quarterly* 43, no. 4 (1995): 446–54. On the intersections of the verbal, visual, and embodied in Latin@ communication scholarship and marginalized discourse, see Bernadette Marie Calafell, *Latina/o Communication Studies: Theorizing Performance* (New York: Peter Lang, 2007), 1–9; Bernadette Marie Calafell, "Rhetorics of Possibility: Challenging Textual Bias through the Theory of the Flesh," in *Rhetorica in Motion: Feminist Rhetorical Methods and Methodologies*, ed. Eileen E. Schell and K. J. Rawson (Pittsburgh: University of Pittsburgh Press, 2010), 104–17; Dwight Conquergood, "Performance Studies: Interventions and Radical Research," *Drama Review* 46, no. 2 (2002): 145–56.

4. Charles Taylor, "Modern Social Imaginaries," *Public Culture* 14 (2002): 106. See also Dilip Parameshwar Gaonkar, "Toward New Imaginaries: An Introduction," *Public Culture* 14, no. 1 (2002): 1–19; Charles Taylor, *Modern Social Imaginaries* (Durham, NC: Duke University Press, 2004).

5. Michael Calvin McGee, "The 'Ideograph': A Link between Rhetoric and Ideology," *Quarterly Journal of Speech* 66 (1980): 7.

6. Taylor, "Modern Social Imaginaries," 106.

7. Kevin DeLuca, "Articulation Theory: A Discursive Grounding for Rhetorical Practice," *Philosophy and Rhetoric* 32, no. 4 (1999): 334–48; Joshua Gunn and Shaun Treat, "Zombie Trouble: A Propaedeutic on Ideological Subjectification and the Unconscious," *Quarterly Journal of Speech* 91, no. 2 (2005): 144–74. While DeLuca advances an argument against focusing on ideology, Gunn and Treat argue in support of a more (psychoanalytically) robust formulation of ideology and seek to explain why rhetorical scholars have turned away from ideological critique. I take no position here on the merits of either normative position.

8. Walter D. Mignolo, "Coloniality at Large: The Western Hemisphere in the Colonial Horizon of Modernity," *CR: The New Centennial Review* 1, no. 2 (2001): 26.

9. Walter D. Mignolo, "On Subalterns and Other Agencies," *Postcolonial Studies* 8, no. 4 (2005): 384.

10. Nelson Maldonado-Torres, "On the Coloniality of Being: Contributions to the Development of a Concept," *Cultural Studies* 21, no. 2–3 (2007): 251.

11. Walter D. Mignolo, "Delinking: The Rhetoric of Modernity, the Logic of Coloniality and the Grammar of De-Coloniality," *Cultural Studies* 21, no. 2–3 (2007): 459, emphasis and capitalization in original.

12. McGee, "'Ideograph,'" 1–16.

13. Celeste Michelle Condit and John Louis Lucaites, *Crafting Equality: America's Anglo-African Word* (Chicago: University of Chicago Press, 1993), xiii.

14. McGee, "'Ideograph,'" 15.

15. Celeste Michelle Condit, "Democracy and Civil Rights: The Universalizing Influence of Public Argumentation," *Communication Monographs* 54, no. 1 (1987): 3.

16. On visual ideographs, see Dana L. Cloud, "'To Veil the Threat of Terror': Afghan Women and the <Clash of Civilizations> in the Imagery of the U.S. War on Terrorism," *Quarterly Journal of Speech* 90, no. 3 (2004): 285–306; Janis L. Edwards and Carol K. Winkler, "Representative Form and the Visual Ideograph: The Iwo Jima in Editorial Cartoons," *Quarterly Journal of Speech* 83 (1997): 289–310; John Louis Lucaites, "Visualizing 'the People': Individualism and Collectivism in *Let Us Now Praise Famous Men*," *Quarterly Journal of Speech* 83 (1997): 269–89; Michael M. Osborn, "The Invention of Rhetorical Criticism in My Work," in *Critical Questions: Invention, Creativity, and the Criticism of Discourse and Media*, ed. William L. Nothstine, Carole Blair, and Gary A. Copeland (Boston: McGraw-Hill, 2003), 92–94; Catherine H. Palczewski, "The Male Madonna and the Feminine Uncle Sam: Visual Argument, Icons, and Ideographs in 1909 Anti-Woman Suffrage Postcards," *Quarterly Journal of Speech* 91 (2005): 365–94. Though not exclusively focused on visual ideographs, DeLuca also makes a significant contribution to this scholarly literature. Kevin DeLuca, *Image Politics: The New Rhetoric of Environmental Activism* (New York: Guilford Press, 1999). Finally, one could also read Hariman and Lucaites's work on iconic photographs as an extension and reworking of the ideograph in the context of visual culture. Robert Hariman and John Louis Lucaites, *No Caption Needed: Iconic Photographs, Public Culture, and Liberal Democracy* (Chicago: University of Chicago Press, 2007). Altogether, ideographic theory has moved beyond McGee's focus on terms

and phrases to address more fully the functionality of ideographs in discourse broadly considered.

17. On stranger relationality, see Danielle S. Allen, *Talking to Strangers: Anxieties of Citizenship since* Brown v. Board of Education (Chicago: University of Chicago Press, 2004); Michael Warner, *Publics and Counterpublics* (New York: Zone Books, 2002).

18. Gaonkar, "Toward New Imaginaries," 5.

19. Ibid., 12.

20. Lefort and Castoriadis are invoked implicitly and explicitly in the contemporary literature on social imaginaries. For an explicit attempt at recovering Lefort and Castoriadis on the subject, see John B. Thompson, "Ideology and the Social Imaginary: An Appraisal of Castoriadis and Lefort," *Theory and Society* 11 (1982): 659–81. For the contemporary discussions, see Benjamin Lee and Edward LiPuma, "Cultures of Circulation: The Imaginations of Modernity," *Public Culture* 14 (2002): 191–213; Taylor, "Modern Social Imaginaries," 91–124; Taylor, *Modern Social Imaginaries*. While invocation of an "imaginary" cannot escape psychoanalytic considerations (e.g., Castoriadis turned to Jacques Lacan), I will not make such a move in this chapter.

21. Gaonkar, "Toward New Imaginaries," 4.

22. Taylor, *Modern Social Imaginaries*, 23.

23. Ibid., 24.

24. Gaonkar, "Toward New Imaginaries," 11.

25. Taylor, *Modern Social Imaginaries*, 25.

26. Michael Calvin McGee, "A Materialist's Conception of Rhetoric," in *Rhetoric, Materiality, and Politics*, ed. Barbara A. Biesecker and John Louis Lucaites (New York: Peter Lang, 2009).

27. Ronald Walter Greene, "Another Materialist Rhetoric," *Critical Studies in Mass Communication* 15, no. 1 (1998): 21–41; Dana L. Cloud, "The Materiality of Discourse as Oxymoron: A Challenge to Critical Rhetoric," *Western Journal of Communication* 58, no. 3 (1994): 141–63.

28. Maldonado-Torres, "Coloniality of Being," 244.

29. Aníbal Quijano, "Coloniality and Modernity/Rationality," *Cultural Studies* 21, no. 2–3 (2007): 169. Flores refers to this as the "lite colonial" in Juan Flores, *From Bomba to Hip-Hop: Puerto Rican Culture and Latino Identity* (New York: Columbia University Press, 2000). See also Maldonado-Torres, "Coloniality of Being"; Walter D. Mignolo, *Local Histories/Global Designs: Coloniality, Subaltern Knowledges, and Border Thinking* (Princeton, NJ: Princeton University Press, 2000); Mignolo, "Delinking."

30. On the zero-point epistemology, see Walter D. Mignolo, *The Darker Side of Western Modernity: Global Futures, Decolonial Options* (Durham, NC: Duke University Press, 2011).

31. Mignolo, *Local Histories*, 38.

32. Michael Calvin McGee, "Power to the (People)," *Critical Studies in Mass Communication* 4, no. 4 (1987): 436 and 434.

33. Mignolo, "Delinking," 456, capitalization in original.

34. Mignolo, *The Darker Side*, 122 and 206.

35. Mignolo, "On Subalterns and Other Agencies," 384.

36. Nelson Maldonado-Torres, "Enrique Dussel's Liberation Thought in the Decolonial Turn," *TRANSMODERNITY: Journal of Peripheral Cultural Production of the Luso-Hispanic World* 1, no. 1 (2011): 18.

37. Maldonado-Torres, "Coloniality of Being," 251.

38. Chela Sandoval, *Methodology of the Oppressed* (Minneapolis: University of Minnesota Press, 2000), 109.

39. Kenneth Burke, "Revolutionary Symbolism in America," in *American Writers' Congress*, ed. Henry Hart (New York: International Publishers, 1935), 87–94.

40. Kent A. Ono and John M. Sloop, "The Critique of Vernacular Discourse," *Communication Monographs* 62, no. 1 (1995): 19–46. The example Ono and Sloop work through is of a Japanese American newspaper published during World War II. Newspapers (like the Young Lords' *Palante*) are particularly well suited for such an analysis. See also Bernadette Marie Calafell and Fernando P. Delgado, "Reading Latina/o Images: Interrogating *Americanos*," *Critical Studies in Media Communication* 21, no. 1 (2004): 1–21; Calafell, *Latina/o Communication Studies*; Fernando P. Delgado, "When the Silenced Speak: The Textualization and Complications of Latina/o Identity," *Western Journal of Communication* 62 (1998): 420–38; Darrel Enck-Wanzer, "Gender Politics, Democratic Demand and Anti-Essentialism in the New York Young Lords," in *Latina/o Discourse in Vernacular Spaces: Somos de un(a) Voz?* ed. Michelle A. Holling and Bernadette Marie Calafell (Lanham, MD: Lexington Books, 2011); Michelle A. Holling, "Retrospective on Latin@ Rhetorical-Performance Scholarship: From 'Chicano Communication' to 'Latina/o Communication?'" *Communication Review* 11, no. 4 (2008): 293–332.

41. Mignolo, *Local Histories*, 67.

42. The Young Lords had numerous programs in place, starting in late 1969, which focused on issues of health, food, clothing, and addiction. These "serve the people" programs were modeled after similar programs the Black Panthers established, but they targeted and were unique to the needs of people in Latin@ communities, particularly East Harlem/El Barrio. See, for example, Darrel Enck-Wanzer, *The Young Lords: A Reader* (New York: New York University Press, 2010), 218–30; Johanna Fernandez, "The Young Lords and the Postwar City: Notes on the Geographical and Structural Reconfigurations of Contemporary Urban Life," in *African American Urban History since World War II*, ed. Kenneth L. Kusmer and Joe W. Trotter (Chicago: University of Chicago Press, 2009), 60–82; Fernandez, "Between Social Service," 255–85; Lorrin Thomas, *Puerto Rican Citizen: History and Political Identity in Twentieth-Century New York City* (Chicago: University of Chicago Press, 2010), 200–244.

43. The Black Panthers had been similarly harassed the previous week. Pablo "Yoruba" Guzmán and Graciela M. Smith, "Interview with Yoruba, Minister of Information, Young Lords Organization, Regarding Confrontations at the First Spanish Methodist Church in El Barrio (Spanish Harlem); December 19, 1969," in *Young Lords Organization*, ed. National Council of the Churches of Christ in the United States of America (New York: NCC Communication Center, December 19, 1970), 28.

44. See, for example, Walter D. Mignolo, "Huntington's Fears: 'Latinidad' in the Horizon of the Modern/Colonial World," in *Latin@s in the World-System: Decolonization Struggles in the 21st Century U.S. Empire*, ed. Ramón Grosfoguel, Nelson Maldonado-Torres, and José David Saldívar (Boulder, CO: Paradigm Publishers, 2005), 57–74.

45. The FSMC also became an institution of interest because one friend of the Young Lords, founding Nuyorican poet Pedro Pietri, had grown up attending the church.

46. Yoruba and Smith, "Interview with Yoruba," 27.

47. Spokesman for the United Methodist Spanish Church in Spanish Harlem, "Unofficial Statement of First Methodist Spanish Church in El Barrio; Re: The Confrontation by the Young Lords," in National Council of the Churches of Christ in the United States of America, *Young Lords Organization*, 41.

48. Michael T. Kaufman, "8 Hurt, 14 Seized in a Church Clash," *New York Times* (December 8, 1969): 53. While Kaufman does not identify the police as already waiting for the Young Lords, numerous interviews by the author confirm this was the case.

49. Ibid.

50. "Liberation school" was an educational program for youths that focused instruction on political, cultural, and social history of Puerto Ricans and other Third World peoples. There was also an emphasis on critical thinking and community political consciousness. It was a core part of the Young Lords' efforts to transcend their colonial imaginary.

51. Felipe Luciano and Graciela M. Smith, "Speech by Felipe Luciano, New York State Chrmn., Young Lords Organization, at the First Spanish Methodist Church in El Barrio (11th St. & Lexington) on Sunday December 21, 1969," in National Council of the Churches of Christ in the United States of America, *Young Lords Organization*, 1.

52. Michael T. Kaufman, "200 Armed Young Lords Seize Church after Taking Body There," *New York Times* (October 19, 1970): 26.

53. Quoted in Wilson, *The First Spanish Methodist Church*, 15.

54. Arnold H. Lubasch, "Young Lords Give Food and Care at Seized Church," *New York Times* (December 30, 1969): 30.

55. Quoted in Miguel Padilla, "How N.Y. Young Lords Developed," *The Militant* (January 30, 1970): 3.

56. Quoted in Wilson, *The First Spanish Methodist Church*, 15.

57. Mignolo makes the connection between organized religion and coloniality in multiple places. See Mignolo, *Local Histories*; Mignolo, "Delinking," 449–514.

58. Iris Luciano, "We Are Not Only Being Persecuted because We Feed and Educate but because We Scream out without Fear; 'Free Puerto Rico Now!'" *Y.L.O.* 1, no. 5 (1970): 20.

59. Michael T. Kaufman, "105 Members of Young Lords Submit to Arrest, Ending 11-Day Occupation of Church," *New York Times* (January 8, 1970): 28.

60. In 1972, the Young Lords transformed into the Puerto Rican Revolutionary Workers Organization, which I discussed in Chapter 1.

61. Daniel T. Rodgers, *Contested Truths: Keywords in American Politics since Independence* (New York: Basic Books, 1987), 80.

62. Ibid., 84.

63. Burke, "Speech," 87–94.

64. McGee, "In Search of the People," 235–49; McGee, "Power to the (People)," 432–37.

65. We could probably turn to numerous other Young Lords examples and arrive at a similar point of analysis about "the people." I root my discussion of ideographs generally and "the people" in particular in a case study of the church offensive because it is the most overt example and was a defining moment in the history of the Young Lords.

66. Charland, "Constitutive Rhetoric," 139.

67. Yoruba and Smith, "Interview with Yoruba," 28, emphasis added.

68. A similar rationale explains why the Young Lords saw a large part of their role in the community as being focused on education (e.g., "We're educating the people to what it is to be born in Kenya, what it is to be Puerto Rican, and also to the contradictions in the society"). See Yoruba and Smith, "Interview with Yoruba," 28.

69. McGee, "'Ideograph,'" 10.

70. See Note 16 on visual ideographs.

71. Lucaites, "Visualizing," 281–84.

72. Ibid., 274.

73. *El Pueblo se Levanta* (New York: Newsreel, 1971).

74. Yoruba and Smith, "Interview with Yoruba," 29.

75. On markers or "keys" of performance, see Richard Bauman, *Verbal Art as Performance* (Rowley, MA: Newbury House Publishers, 1978), 16–24.

76. See Darrel Enck-Wanzer, "Trashing the System: Social Movement, Intersectional Rhetoric, and Collective Agency in the Young Lords Organization's Garbage Offensive," *Quarterly Journal of Speech* 92, no. 2 (2006): 185.

77. Mignolo, "Delinking," 499–500.

78. The film *El Pueblo se Levanta* offers the best documentation of these activities.

79. Quoted in Wilson, *The First Spanish Methodist Church*, 15.

80. Pablo "Yoruba" Guzmán, "The United Front against the People," *Palante* 2, no. 1 (1970): 3, capitalization in original.

81. Photo by Michael Evans in Lubasch, "Young Lords Give Food."

82. This idea of moving the social is consistent with Michael Calvin McGee, "'Social Movement': Phenomenon or Meaning?" *Central States Speech Journal* 31, no. 4 (1980): 233–44.

83. Luciano and Smith, "Speech by Felipe Luciano," 2, emphasis added.

84. Another good example of this deployment is in Jose Yglesias, "Right on with the Young Lords," *New York Times* (June 7, 1970): 215.

85. See, for example, Kenneth Burke, *A Grammar of Motives* (Berkeley: University of California Press, 1969), 3–20.

86. Mignolo, *Local Histories*, 67.

87. Ibid., 23.

88. Luciano and Smith, "Speech by Felipe Luciano," 3.

89. Mignolo, "Delinking," 460.

90. Whether ideographs circulate among a public, counterpublic, or both is not at issue here. Whatever one wants to call the audience of the Young Lords, the fact remains that ideographs were circulating and were addressed. For the distinction between public and counterpublic, see Warner, *Publics and Counterpublics*, 65–124.

91. José Ramón Sánchez, *Boricua Power: A Political History of Puerto Ricans in the United States* (New York: New York University Press, 2007), 171–209. Sánchez demonstrates some of the ways in which the Young Lords were media savvy and got their images to circulate.

92. In what has become a far-too-regular ritual, people continue to gather at the FSMC to commemorate the lives of former Young Lords as they pass away.

93. Cara A. Finnegan and Jiyeon Kang, "'Sighting' the Public: Iconoclasm and Public Sphere Theory," *Quarterly Journal of Speech* 90 (2004): 396.

94. Taylor, *Modern Social Imaginaries*, 109–10.

95. Luciano and Smith, "Speech by Felipe Luciano," 4.

96. McGee, "Power to the (People)," 434.

97. Ibid., 436.

98. Mignolo, "Delinking," 450.

99. Quijano, "Coloniality and Modernity/Rationality," 172.

100. Ibid., 177.

101. Ibid.

102. Nelson Maldonado-Torres, "The Topology of Being and the Geopolitics of Knowledge," *City* 8, no. 1 (2004): 44.

103. Mignolo, "Delinking," 497.

104. Ibid., 497–98.

105. Mignolo, *Local Histories*, 68.

106. Ramón Grosfoguel, "Decolonizing Post-Colonial Studies and Paradigms of Political Economy: Transmodernity, Decolonial Thinking, and Global Coloniality,"

TRANSMODERNITY: Journal of Peripheral Cultural Production of the Luso-Hispanic World 1, no. 1 (2011): 24.

107. Mignolo, *Local Histories*, 67.

108. Michelle A. Holling and Bernadette Marie Calafell, "Identities on Stage and Staging Identities: ChicanoBrujo Performances as Emancipatory Practices," *Text and Performance Quarterly* 27, no. 1 (2007): 78.

109. Michelle A. Holling and Bernadette M. Calafell, "Tracing the Emergence of Latin@ Vernaculars in Studies of Latin@ Communication," in Holling and Calafell, *Latina/o Discourse in Vernacular Spaces*, 22.

110. Although he does not talk about Latin@ vernacular discourse or decoloniality, Fernando Delgado's work on Chicano movement ideographic challenges could be another example of the kind of decolonial work in which the Young Lords and other Latin@ vernacular discourses engage. See Delgado, "Chicano Movement Rhetoric," 446–54.

CONCLUSION

1. Young Lords Party, "13 Point Program and Platform," November 1970.

2. State Data Center of Iowa, "Latinos in Iowa: 2013," Iowa Library Services, State Library (September 2013), available at http://www.iowadatacenter.org/Publications/latinos2013.pdf. Latin@s are the largest minority in Iowa at 5.3 percent of the state population.

3. Sonia Manzano, *The Revolution of Evelyn Serrano* (New York: Scholastic Press, 2012), 101.

4. Walter D. Mignolo, *The Darker Side of Western Modernity: Global Futures, Decolonial Options* (Durham, NC: Duke University Press, 2011), 158.

5. Ibid.

6. Matthew J. Countryman, "'From Protest to Politics': Community Control and Black Independent Politics in Philadelphia, 1965–1984," *Journal of Urban History* 32, no. 6 (2006): 850.

7. There are three mentions, and no elaboration, in the rhetorical studies journals within communication studies, and two of them are from me. See Darrel Enck-Wanzer, "Trashing the System: Social Movement, Intersectional Rhetoric, and Collective Agency in the Young Lords Organization's Garbage Offensive," *Quarterly Journal of Speech* 92, no. 2 (2006): 174–201; Darrel Enck-Wanzer, "Decolonizing Imaginaries: Rethinking 'the People' in the Young Lords' Church Offensive," *Quarterly Journal of Speech* 98, no. 1 (2012): 1–23; Theodore Otto Windt, "The Diatribe: Last Resort for Protest," *Quarterly Journal of Speech* 58, no. 1 (1972): 1–14. Elsewhere, there is scant attention paid to the meaning of community control. Some exceptions include Adina Back, "Exposing the 'Whole Segregation Myth': The Harlem Nine and New York City's School Desegregation Battles," in *Freedom North: Black Freedom Struggles outside the South, 1940–1980*, ed. Jeanne F. Theoharis and Komozi Woodard (New York: Palgrave Macmillan, 2003), 65–91; Jennifer Brier, "Save Our Kids, Keep AIDS Out": Anti-AIDS Activism and the Legacy of Community Control in Queens, New York," *Journal of Social History* 39, no. 4 (2006): 965–87; Countryman, "'From Protest to Politics,'" 813–61; James Jennings, Francisco Chapman, and Luis Fuentes, "Puerto Ricans and the Community Control Movement," in *The Puerto Rican Movement: Voices from the Diaspora*, ed. Andrés Torres and Jose E. Velázquez (Philadelphia: Temple University Press, 1998), 280–95.

8. Maylei Blackwell, *¡Chicana Power! Contested Histories of Feminism in the Chicano Movement* (Austin: University of Texas Press, 2011).

9. Mignolo, *The Darker Side*, 108–9.

10. Countryman, "'From Protest to Politics,'" 816.

11. Jennings, Chapman, and Fuentes, "Puerto Ricans and the Community Control Movement," 281.

12. Back, "Exposing the 'Whole Segregation Myth,'" 66.

13. Jose Yglesias, "Right on with the Young Lords," *New York Times* (June 7, 1970): 32+.

14. Johanna Fernandez, "Between Social Service Reform and Revolutionary Politics: The Young Lords, Late Sixties Radicalism, and Community Organizing in New York City," in Theoharis and Woodward, *Freedom North*, 266.

15. Agustín Laó, "Resources of Hope: Imagining the Young Lords and the Politics of Memory," *CENTRO: Journal of the Center for Puerto Rican Studies* 7, no. 1 (1995): 40 and 45.

16. Guzmán in Young Lords Party and Michael Abramson, *Palante: Young Lords Party* (New York: McGraw-Hill, 1971), 102.

17. Gonzalez in ibid., 64.

18. Nelson Maldonado-Torres, *Against War: Views from the Underside of Modernity* (Durham, NC: Duke University Press, 2008), 234.

19. Richie Pérez, "H.S. Revolt!" *Palante* 2, no. 13 (1970): 8.

20. Chela Sandoval, *Methodology of the Oppressed* (Minneapolis: University of Minnesota Press, 2000), 109.

21. Nikhil Pal Singh, *Black Is a Country: Race and the Unfinished Struggle for Democracy* (Cambridge, MA: Harvard University Press, 2004), 133.

22. Scholars like Habermas exemplify this position. See Jürgen Habermas, *Between Facts and Norms: Contributions to a Discourse Theory of Law and Democracy* (Cambridge, MA: MIT Press, 1996).

23. Ernesto Laclau and Chantal Mouffe, *Hegemony and Socialist Strategy: Towards a Radical Democratic Practice* (London: Verso, 2001); Chantal Mouffe, *The Democratic Paradox* (London: Verso, 2000).

24. Chantal Mouffe, "Radical Democracy or Liberal Democracy?" *Socialist Review* 20, no. 2 (1990): 57–58.

25. Ernesto Laclau, *Emancipation(s)* (London: Verso, 1996), 74.

26. Janet Conway and Jakeet Singh, "Radical Democracy in Global Perspective: Notes from the Pluriverse," *Third World Quarterly* 32, no. 4 (2011): 692.

27. Maldonado-Torres, *Against War*, 230. Maldonado-Torres is quoting the Zapatistas for this notion. Mignolo does the same in Walter D. Mignolo, "The Zapatista's Theoretical Revolution: Its Historical, Ethical, and Political Consequences," *Review* 25, no. 3 (2002): 245–75; Mignolo, *The Darker Side*.

28. Charles W. Mills, *The Racial Contract* (Ithaca, NY: Cornell University Press, 1997), 20.

29. A complete list would simply be too long. For a sampling of recent scholarship, see Eduardo Bonilla-Silva, *Racism without Racists: Color-Blind Racism and the Persistence of Racial Inequality in the United States* (Lanham, MD: Rowman and Littlefield, 2006); Eduardo Bonilla-Silva, "The Invisible Weight of Whiteness: The Racial Grammar of Everyday Life in Contemporary America," *Ethnic and Racial Studies* 35, no. 2 (2012): 173–94; Darrel Enck-Wanzer, "Barack Obama, the Tea Party, and the Threat of Race: On Racial Neoliberalism and Born Again Racism," *Communication, Culture and Critique* 4, no. 1 (2011): 22–29; David Theo Goldberg, *The Threat of Race: Reflections on Racial Neoliberalism* (Malden, MA: Wiley-Blackwell, 2009); David Theo Goldberg, "Call and Response," *Patterns of Prejudice* 44, no. 1 (2010): 89–106; Kristen Hoerl, "Selective Amnesia and Racial Transcendence in News Coverage of President Obama's Inauguration," *Quarterly Journal*

of Speech 98, no. 2 (2012): 178–202; Roopali Mukherjee, *The Racial Order of Things: Cultural Imaginaries of the Post-Soul Era* (Minneapolis: University of Minnesota Press, 2006); Malini Johar Schueller, *Locating Race: Global Sites of Post-Colonial Citizenship* (Albany: State University of New York Press, 2009); Singh, *Black Is a Country*.

30. Goldberg, *Threat of Race*, 21.

31. Enck-Wanzer, "Barack Obama," 25.

32. Joel Olson, *The Abolition of White Democracy* (Minneapolis: University of Minnesota Press, 2004), xv.

33. Mills, *Racial Contract*, 18.

34. David Theo Goldberg, *The Racial State* (Oxford: Blackwell, 2002), 223.

35. Goldberg, *Threat of Race*, 369.

36. Ibid., 59.

37. Ibid., 101. Also see Enck-Wanzer, "Barack Obama," 27.

38. Freya Schiwy, "'Todos Somos Presidentes/We Are All Presidents': Democracy, Culture, and Radical Politics," *Cultural Studies* 25, no. 6 (2011): 731.

39. Quoted in ibid.

40. Maldonado-Torres, *Against War*, 158.

41. Robyn Wiegman, "Whiteness Studies and the Paradox of Particularity," *Boundary 2* 26, no. 3 (1999): 150.

42. Goldberg, *Racial State*, 264.

43. Ibid.

44. Olson, *Abolition*, xvii.

45. For an account of the state of our current vocabulary, see Bonilla-Silva, *Racism without Racists*, 53–73.

46. Conway and Singh, "Radical Democracy," 692.

47. Quoted in Gabriela Nouzeilles and Walter D. Mignolo, "An Other Globalization: Toward a Critical Cosmopolitanism," *Nepantla: Views from South* 4, no. 1 (2003): 2.

48. Sandoval, *Methodology of the Oppressed*, 6.

49. Walter D. Mignolo, "The Many Faces of Cosmo-Polis: Border Thinking and Critical Cosmopolitanism," *Public Culture* 12, no. 3 (2000): 742; Mignolo, "Zapatista's Theoretical Revolution," 257 and 263.

50. Maldonado-Torres, *Against War*, 11–12.

51. Mignolo, "Zapatista's Theoretical Revolution," 257 and 263.

52. Sheldon S. Wolin, *Politics and Vision: Continuity and Innovation in Western Political Thought* (Princeton, NJ: Princeton University Press, 2004), 602.

53. Goldberg, *Racial State*, 276.

54. Goldberg, *Threat of Race*, 368.

55. Iris Morales, interview by author, New York, 26 May 2004.

56. Juan Gonzalez, "YLP on Elections," *Palante* 3, no. 19 (1971): 13.

57. Juan "Fi" Ortiz, "The Party and the Individual," in *The Ideology of the Young Lords Party* (New York, February 1972), 38.

58. Walter D. Mignolo, "Delinking: The Rhetoric of Modernity, the Logic of Coloniality and the Grammar of De-Coloniality," *Cultural Studies* 21, no. 2–3 (2007): 497. Quijano similarly demands "the acknowledgement of the heterogeneity of all reality; of the irreducible, contradictory character of the latter; of the legitimacy, i.e., the desirability, of the diverse character of the components of all reality—and therefore, of the social." Aníbal Quijano, "Coloniality and Modernity/Rationality," *Cultural Studies* 21, no. 2–3 (2007): 177.

59. Edwin Black, *Rhetorical Criticism: A Study in Method* (Madison: University of Wisconsin Press, 1965), 67–68.

60. Mukherjee, *Racial Order*.

61. Amy Sonnie and James Tracy, *Hillbilly Nationalists, Urban Race Rebels, and Black Power: Community Organizing in Radical Times* (New York: Melville House Books, 2011), 172.

62. Ramón Grosfoguel, *Colonial Subjects: Puerto Ricans in a Global Perspective* (Berkeley: University of California Press, 2003); Maldonado-Torres, *Against War*; Mignolo, "Zapatista's Theoretical Revolution," 245–75; José David Saldívar, *Trans-Americanity: Subaltern Modernities, Global Coloniality, and the Cultures of Greater Mexico* (Durham, NC: Duke University Press, 2011); Freya Schiwy, "Decolonization and the Question of Subjectivity: Gender, Race, and Binary Thinking," *Cultural Studies* 21, no. 2–3 (2007): 271–94; Schiwy, "'Todos Somos Presidentes,'" 729–56.

63. Kelly Oliver, *Witnessing: Beyond Recognition* (Minneapolis: University of Minnesota Press, 2001), 42.

64. Sandoval, *Methodology of the Oppressed*, 170.

65. Maldonado-Torres, *Against War*, 157 and 158.

66. Junot Díaz and Paula M. L. Moya, "The Search for Decolonial Love, Part I," *Boston Review*, June 26, 2012, available at http://www.bostonreview.net/.

67. Maldonado-Torres, *Against War*, 218.

68. Sandra María Esteves, "Here," in *Yerba Buena* (Greenfield Center, NY: Greenfield Review Press, 1980), 20.

69. Laó, "Resources of Hope," 45.

Index

Darrel Wanzer-Serrano is Assistant Professor of Communication Studies at the University of Iowa, and editor of *The Young Lords: A Reader*.